Tennessee Central Railway: History Through the Miles

Barton Jennings

Tennessee Central Railway: History Through the Miles
Copyright © 2018 by Barton Jennings

All rights reserved. This book may not be duplicated or transmitted in any way, or stored in an information retrieval system, without the express written consent of the publisher, except in the form of brief excerpts or quotations for the purpose of review. Making copies of this book, or any portion, for any purpose other than your own, is a violation of United States copyright laws.

Publisher's Cataloging-in-Publication Data
Jennings, Barton

Tennessee Central Railway: History Through the Miles
268p.; 21cm.
ISBN: 978-0-9849866-8-2

Library of Congress Control Number: 2018905459

First Edition

Cover photos by Sarah Jennings

Please send comments or corrections to sarah@techscribes.com

TechScribes, Inc.
PO Box 620
Avon, IL 61415
www.techscribes.com

Printed in the United States of America

*for my friends at the
Southern Appalachia Railway Museum
and across Tennessee*

Other books by this author:

Arkansas & Missouri Railroad: History Through the Miles
Alaska Railroad: History Through the Miles
Iowa Interstate Railroad: History Through the Miles
Everett Railroad: History Through the Miles

Contents

Tennessee Central Map 7
Tennessee Central Timetable 8
Preface 9
History of the Tennessee Central Railway 11

Tennessee Central Eastern Division **21**
    Nashville (TN) to Harriman (TN)

    Nashville (TN) to Monterey (TN) 27
        Nashville & Eastern Railroad

    Monterey (TN) to Crab Orchard (TN) 107
        Abandoned

    Crab Orchard (TN) to Rockwood (TN) 119
        Lhoist North America

    Rockwood (TN) to Harriman (TN) 149
        Norfolk Southern Railway

    Old Hickory Branch 165
        Stones River (TN) to DuPont (TN)
            Nashville & Eastern Railroad

    Carthage Branch 177
        Carthage Junction (TN) to South Carthage (TN)
            Nashville & Eastern Railroad

    Crawford Branch 185
        Monterey (TN) to Wilder (TN)
            Nashville & Eastern Railroad

    Isoline Branch 195
        Campbell Junction (TN) to Isoline (TN)
            Abandoned

Tennessee Central Western Division 197
   Nashville (TN) to Hopkinsville (KY)

   Southern Junction (TN) to Vine Hill (TN) 203
      Nashville & Eastern Railroad

   Vine Hill (TN) to Van Blarcom (TN) 207
      Abandoned

   Van Blarcom (TN) to Gravelotte (TN) 211
      Nashville & Western Railroad

   Gravelotte (TN) to Edgoten (TN) 225
      Abandoned

   Edgoten (TN) to Tulane (KY) 247
      Fort Campbell Railroad

   Tulane (KY) to Hopkinsville (KY) 253
      Abandoned

   North Nashville Lead 261
      U.S. Tobacco to Central Junction
         Nashville & Western Railroad

About the Author 267

From *The Official Railway Guide North American Freight Service Edition*, January 1904.

From *The Official Railway Guide North American Freight Service Edition,* January 1904.

Preface

This guide is not designed to be a complete history of the Tennessee Central, but instead it provides a great deal of information for those who like to ask, "Where are we and what once happened here?" Because of this, the guide includes information about current as well as former station locations, historic towns, and major stream crossings along the line.

The historic Tennessee Central Railway essentially ended on January 23, 1969, when the Interstate Commerce Commission agreed to a plan that divided the railroad between the Illinois Central, Louisville & Nashville, and the Southern Railway. With this division, the railroad was broken up into separate parts, many of which didn't survive for long. However, it may have become even more famous as excursion trains returned to parts of the line. On the eastern end, fall excursion trains to Crossville became common throughout the 1970s and 1980s. In the Nashville area, the Tennessee Central Railway Museum has been operating excursion trains over the Nashville & Eastern into the Cumberland Plateau region of central and eastern Tennessee for almost three decades. These trips can go from Nashville to the Mile-Long Yard Sale at Watertown, a winery trip to DelMonaco, or even a trip to the end of the line at Monterey.

This route description was first written in the 1980s and 1990s for several rides over part of the railroad. As the Nashville & Eastern restored the track eastward, and the Tennessee Central Railway Museum extended their trips, it was updated and added to. With the extension of the line to Monterey, a decision was made to update it for the entire railroad. Much of the information comes from internal railroad records, government and public records, railroad workers, and conversations with old and new friends. It is hoped that you enjoy your adventure with the Tennessee Central Railway and that this book will be of assistance in some ways – *Tennessee Central Railway: History Through the Miles.*

History of the Tennessee Central Railway

There are several good histories of the Tennessee Central Railway, but probably the best is *Tennessee Central Railway – History, Locomotives and Cars* by Cliff Downey. Anyone interested in learning more about the history of the railroad should check it out. For those who need information now, here is a short version of an amazing history.

Nashville & Knoxville Railroad (1884 - 1902)
Tennessee Central Railway Company (1901 - 1902)

The history of the Tennessee Central Railway started in 1884 when Alexander Crawford chartered the Nashville & Knoxville Railroad with plans to build a railroad across the Cumberland Mountains and connect two of the major cities in Tennessee. At the time, the eastern and central parts of Tennessee might as well have been across the ocean from each other. A few rugged mountain roads crossed the mountains, but rail service between the two areas was via Cincinnati, Ohio, or Chattanooga, Tennessee. The idea was that a railroad directly connecting the two cities would allow coal and other minerals from east Tennessee to be moved west, and foods and goods could then be moved east. Additionally, early surveys showed there to be coal, iron ore, and other resources in the Cumberland Plateau that the railroad could tap.

Alexander Crawford had started as a farmer in Pennsylvania, but soon got into the lime, flour milling, coal and iron businesses. Creating this freight interested him in the railroad business, and he soon chartered and built the New Castle & Franklin Railroad. His biography also credits him with helping to build the Youngstown & Ashtabula Railroad; the Lawrence Railroad; the St. Louis, Salem & Little Rock; the Newcastle & Beaver Valley; and the Nashville & Knoxville Railroad.

Construction of the Nashville & Knoxville Railroad (N&K) focused on Lebanon east toward Knoxville. The route between Nashville and Lebanon was already served by a railroad – the Lebanon Branch of the Nashville, Chattanooga & St Louis Railway

(NC&StL). This NC&StL route was opened in the mid-1870s and ran just south of the current Nashville & Eastern. After the Tennessee Central built on west to Nashville, business on the Lebanon Branch began to fall, and the last train ran in 1935. Much of the NC&StL property in Lebanon was sold to the Tennessee Central (TC), and parts of the branch became roads.

Alexander Crawford died on April 1, 1890, but the railroad continued to expand. The Nashville & Knoxville was completed between Lebanon and Standing Stone (Monterey), a total of 76 miles, by late 1893. However, without a strong leader, the railroad stalled out, having never turned a profit or even able to pay its bills.

Things soon changed, however, as "Colonel" Jere Baxter, a successful lawyer and entrepreneur, chartered the Tennessee Central Railroad on August 25, 1893, with the purpose of buying several railroads to link Nashville with eastern Tennessee and break the monopoly that the Louisville & Nashville had on the Nashville area. Baxter had earlier invested in the Memphis & Charleston Railway, becoming its president. He also had served as the vice-president of the East Tennessee, Virginia & Georgia Railroad. Both of these railroads soon were merged with other railroads, eventually becoming the Southern Railway.

While Baxter and others were trying to build what would be the east end of the railroad, the Crawford heirs were still working to make the Nashville & Knoxville profitable. They saw a chance to use the Tennessee Central to expand east, but also looked for a way west to Nashville, or to sell the railroad. The Crawfords saw a way to achieve both when in 1901 they reached an agreement with Baxter to lease him the N&K, but only after he built a route from Lebanon west to Nashville. Baxter at first looked to buy the NC&StL Lebanon Branch, but his offers were rejected. So, to build the new line between Nashville and Lebanon, Baxter created the Tennessee Central Railway Company on February 5, 1901, and the Tennessee Construction Company was awarded a contract to oversee the construction of the line on March 8th of that year.

History of the Tennessee Central Railway

Tennessee Central Railroad (1893 - 1897)
Tennessee Central Railway (1897 - 1902)

Jere Baxter's original Tennessee Central Railroad was chartered in 1893 with the idea of building a railroad from the Cincinnati, New Orleans & Texas Pacific (CNO&TP) at Glenmary, Tennessee, west to Standing Stone (Monterey) where it would connect to the existing Nashville & Knoxville, which was then building from Cookeville to Monterey. Soon surveyors changed the route, starting the line at Emory Gap on the CNO&TP. This location also meant that the nearby industrial town of Harriman was within Baxter's reach.

Baxter's timing could not have been worse. The Panic of 1893 ended the ability to find investment money and Baxter, as well as several local governments, were forced to provide the capital to build the line. Meanwhile, Baxter was also busy on the Nashville end. According to the 1922 *Poor's Manual of Railroads*, the Nashville Terminal Company was chartered August 1893. Other documents state that it was created for "constructing, maintaining, operating, or leasing to others railroad terminal facilities for the accommodation of railroad passengers, and for handling and transferring freight." This plan resulted in little initially except forcing the NC&StL and the L&N to create their own Union Station and terminal operating company. Back on the east end of the railroad, the expensive construction into the mountains was using up what little money was available, and the Tennessee Central Railroad was forced into receivership in April 1895. Baxter was now out and new management was running the construction project, with no more success.

Freed of daily responsibilities, Baxter was able to work to raise funds for the railroad and tried to reacquire the Tennessee Central. Baxter's efforts paid off when a bankruptcy court ordered the sale of the Tennessee Central Railroad on January 27, 1897. On June 14, 1897, the Tennessee Central Railway was chartered and bought the Tennessee Central Railroad on June 24, 1897. With this new organization came the opportunity to grow the company, soon focused on the connecting N&K.

One of the first tasks that Baxter accomplished was working out an agreement to acquire the N&K, but there were a number of conditions, including the previously mentioned requirement to control a rail route between Lebanon and Nashville. Baxter also had plans to build on past Nashville, and on August 3, 1897, the charter of the new Tennessee Central was changed to allow it to build from Nashville on to the northwest to Clarksville, Tennessee, and a possible connection with the Illinois Central Railroad. To protect his existing investment, Baxter chartered the Nashville & Clarksville Railroad on April 20, 1901, to build the line on to Clarksville.

By 1902, things were lining up. Baxter had financial backers to consolidate all of the lines between the CNO&TP at Emory Gap and the projected line to Clarksville. Construction was underway between Lebanon and Nashville, and terminal facilities were being planned for Nashville. On the east end, the railroad was being extended from Emory Gap northward to Harriman. It was time to make the change that would create the new Tennessee Central Railroad.

Tennessee Central Railroad Company (1902 - 1922)

The consolidation of all of the railroads required to form the Tennessee Central began with an agreement dated February 1, 1902. The consolidation plan was complicated, with the first step being the as-yet-unbuilt Nashville & Clarksville Railroad renaming itself the Tennessee Central Railroad Company on April 30, 1902. The next day, the new Tennessee Central Railroad acquired the Nashville & Knoxville Railroad, the Tennessee Central Railway (Emory Gap to Monterey), and the Tennessee Central Railway Company (then building a line between Nashville and Lebanon).

Along with this came the lease of the Nashville Terminal Company. According to the 1922 *Poor's Manual of Railroads*, in May 1902 the Tennessee Central Railroad leased the Nashville Terminal Company for ninety-nine years. With the lease came the start of construction, building the terminal facilities along the Cumberland River that the railroad has used since. In April 1911, the lease was extended to 2010, with the lease payments being a

5% payment on the construction bonds of the terminal company, plus all taxes and other charges.

This era was marked by the competition of the Western Division, built by the Tennessee Construction Company between Nashville and Clarksville, and on to the Illinois Central at Hopkinsville, Kentucky. The final spike was driven on October 20, 1903, and full service began in January 1904. The January 1904 issue of *The Official Guide of the Railways and Steam Navigation Lines of the United States, Porto Rico, Canada, Mexico and Cuba* reported on the event by publishing an announcement by the traffic department of the "Tennessee Central R.R. Co. – The Harriman Route."

> *The Tennessee Central Railroad Company is pleased to announce the completion of its line of railroad from Nashville, Tenn., to Hopkinsville, Ky., at which point a connection is made with the Illinois Central Railroad, making a short line between St Louis and Chicago and all Western points, and Nashville, Clarksville, Lebanon, Rockwood, Harriman, Knoxville, and Bristol, Tenn., as well as all points in East Tennessee, the Carolinas and Virginia.*
>
> *At Emory Gap, Tenn., connection is made with the Cincinnati, New Orleans & Texas Pacific Railway, and at Harriman, Tenn., connection is made with the Southern Railway, making the shortest line between Nashville and Washington, D.C., and all Eastern Seaboard Cities, as well as between Nashville and points in Carolinas, Virginia and the Southeast, and affording an excellent service between Clarksville and Hopkinsville and all the points and territories named.*
>
> *From Harriman to Hopkinsville the distance is 252 miles. In addition to this, there are 48 miles of branches, making an aggregate of 300 miles of operated line.*
>
> *Traffic arrangements have been perfected with the Cincinnati, New Orleans & Texas Pacific Railway and Southern Railway on the East, and with the Illinois Central Railroad on the West, putting the Tennessee Central Railroad in a position to handle freight (foreign or domestic) and passengers*

to and from all points in the United States, Mexico and Canada.

The road extends for about seventy miles through the Cumberland Plateau, tapping some of the richest fields of bituminous coal in the Union, and opening up virgin forests of hardwood timber. The remainder of the line serves a fine country, which grows successfully all the products of the temperate zone. The west end of the line, from Nashville to Hopkinsville, is a fine tobacco country. Clarksville is the second tobacco market in the world.

The entire road, from Hopkinsville to Harriman, offers an unusually beautiful scenic route. From Caney Fork River to Harriman the scenery rivals the far famed "Land of the Sky" around Asheville, while the line hugging the Cumberland River all the way from Nashville to Clarksville presents charming views surpassed by those along the Hudson.

The enclosed folder furnishes a map of the line, and gives also an excellent map of the State of Tennessee. Attention is called particularly to the map of the terminals in and about Nashville, offering most excellent opportunities for the location of industrial plants.

Your support of the line is earnestly solicited.

The undersigned invites correspondence in regard to all matters pertaining to the traffic of the road, and assures the public that it will be his pleasure at all times to furnish all information at his command in relation thereto.

E. H. Hinton, Traf. Mgr. – Nashville, Tenn., December 19, 1903

Not long after the completion of the railroad, Jere Baxter died on February 29, 1904. This cost the railroad a leader, another change at the top that became fairly typical for the railroad – as was the constant challenge of making a profit, or at least paying its bills. Because of this, the Standard Trust Company took up a three-year option to buy the railroad, with plans to turn the Eastern Division over to the Southern and the Western Division to the Illinois Central. Almost immediately, on July 1, 1905, the two railroads began operating the Tennessee Central under a lease. These leases ended on June 30, 1908, after three years of heavy investments and equally heavy losses, and the railroad returned to local operations. The completion of the railroad also led the State of Tennessee to conduct a mineral survey along the line. In Volume III, Number 2 of *The Resources of Tennessee*, published by the State Geological Survey in April 1913, a report entitled "Mineral Products Along the Tennessee Central Railroad" expounded on the subject, providing a detailed description of the route. In particular, products such as coal, iron ore, limestone, sand and clay were described for potential investors.

The next few years saw several changes in management and a continued failure to pay even the debt the company owed. Efforts were made to modernize the railroad and cut needless expenses. New locomotives were bought and track was upgraded. However, with the railroad's debt, a bankruptcy judge ordered the sale of the railroad on October 9, 1916, with a minimum bid of $1.35 million. The sale resulted in no takers, and five more sales at even lower prices still resulted in no bidders. The nationalization of America's railroads in 1917 preventing any further attempts to sell the line. The railroad was returned to local control in 1920 and was again offered for sale several times with no bidders. Finally, on January 10, 1922, an offer was received from a group of local businessmen, and the railroad became theirs on January 31, 1922.

Tennessee Central Railway Company (1922 - 1968)

The life of the Tennessee Central Railroad Company ended on February 1, 1922, when the railroad was sold and began operating as the Tennessee Central Railway Company. With the removal of the construction debt, the company was able to pay its bills and put away some profit until the end of World War II. This profitable period of time saw more bridges rebuilt or filled in, heavier rail installed, and a number of other improvements made across the railroad. The railroad promoted its passenger service with the slogan *The Scenic Railway of the South*. The first diesel-electric locomotives also began to arrive on the line in the late 1930s as the railroad modernized.

World War II brought business and profits to the railroad. Fort Campbell (originally known as Camp Campbell when it was established on July 16, 1941) attracted a number of troop trains, and industries all along the railroad grew to handle the war business. The Tennessee Central bought a number of used steam locomotives to handle the business, and other equipment was acquired when available. However, 1943 was the peak year of traffic and the railroad saw a reduction of almost $1 million in passenger and freight revenue when the war ended.

After the war, new investors stepped into the picture. They immediately were faced with a reduction in business, but worked to keep coal moving. In 1952, the railroad took out a Reconstruction Finance Corporation loan for more diesel locomotives and 200 coal hoppers, used to move coal to the new Kingston coal-fired power generating plant operated by the Tennessee Valley Authority (TVA). Further loans were used to buy more locomotives and coal hoppers and the railroad again became profitable during the early 1950s, but the railroad began to lose the coal business and profits ended. To cut losses, regular passenger service ended on July 31, 1955. On the east end of the railroad, coal mines closed, many first getting and then losing contracts to supply the new TVA power plant near Emory Gap. The coal started coming from sources on other railroads, leaving the Tennessee Central with just a switching move to the utility. On the western end of the railroad, the many timber bridges were expensive to maintain and limited the tonnage of freight on a car, giving the Louisville & Nashville an advantage on the Hopkinsville to Nashville route. The construction of new Interstate freeways, Interstate 40 in particular, also moved traffic to trucks.

By the late 1960s, the Tennessee Central was a failed railroad. Equipment and track were failing, the on-line coal business was gone, and bills were piling up (more than $10 million at the time). On September 1, 1968, the railroad was liquidated. It was split between three other railroads, with the Southern taking the eastern line between Harriman and Crossville; the Louisville & Nashville acquiring the line from Crossville to Nashville; and the line northwest of Nashville going to the Illinois Central (IC).

The former Tennessee Central took a significant mileage hit when its belt around the southwest side of Nashville was sold and the land used for Interstate 440, completed in 1987. The IC abandoned or sold off its lines by the mid-1980s. Southern eventually cut their part of the line back to Crab Orchard and then handed it off to the limestone quarry there. Most of the track acquired by the Louisville & Nashville had a more fortunate history.

The later history of each of the routes is covered with the description of each Division. In addition, a great deal of detail about the operations of the Tennessee Central is covered as well to explain the facilities and customers at the various locations along the line.

**Tennessee Central Eastern Division
Nashville (TN) to Harriman (TN)**

Tennessee Central Railway: History Through the Miles

Tennessee Central Eastern Division
Nashville (TN) to Harriman (TN)

The Eastern Division of the Tennessee Central Railway included the tracks from Nashville, Tennessee, to Harriman, Tennessee. Most of this Division is still in service, operated by the Nashville & Eastern Railroad, Lhoist, and Norfolk Southern. Regular passenger service is offered on the western end of the Division by the *Music City Star* commuter service, and the Tennessee Central Railway Museum operates regular excursion service between Nashville and Monterey.

The route guide for the Eastern Division covers all of the rail lines that existed between Nashville and Harriman. The guide includes a history of the lines and the locations that they pass through. It should be noted that this guide is not designed to be a complete history of the railroad, but instead it provides a great deal of information for those who like to ask, "Where are we and what once happened here?" Because of this, the guide includes information about current as well as former station locations, historic towns, and major stream crossings along the line.

Directions on this railroad will be based upon the railroad's own terminology. A train heading from Nashville to Harriman is heading east, so to the left is railroad-north, and to the right is railroad-south. To make matters easier, north and south directions will generally be used for the direction from the mainline.

Throughout this guide, locations will be identified by mileposts. Railroads, just like highways, use mileposts to identify locations and to show the distances between them. On the mainline between Nashville and Harriman, the mileposts are generally on the south side of the tracks. Look for the short concrete markers with milepost numbers painted on them.

As stated elsewhere, this Division was initially divided between the Louisville & Nashville Railroad and the Southern Railway in late 1968. The dividing line was just west of Crossville, Tennessee, giving the L&N the business from the DuPont complex at Old Hickory and other industries on the west side of the Cumberland Plateau. The Southern Railway wound up with the limestone quarry at Crab Orchard and what foundry business remained at

Rockwood, plus access to the Tennessee Valley Authority (TVA) power plant at Emory Gap. The histories of these operations are detailed further within the route guide materials.

Louisville & Nashville Railroad (1968 – 1982)
Seaboard System (1982 – 1986)
CSX Transportation (1986)
Nashville & Eastern Railroad (1986 – current)

With the breakup of the Tennessee Central Railway, the route between Nashville and Crossville became the property of the Louisville & Nashville Railroad for $525,000. Like the other two railroads, the Louisville & Nashville (L&N) didn't seem to know exactly what to do with their part of the Tennessee Central. The L&N kept most of the line, but it abandoned the portion between Monterey and Crossville to prevent through traffic, although little existed. From the earliest days, the biggest fear of the L&N about the Tennessee Central was its use by the Southern Railway to break the rail monopoly at Nashville.

For the L&N, the Tennessee Central was a railroad that they didn't really want, but they didn't want anyone else to have it either. The Tennessee Central had some valuable property on the east side of Nashville, and much of the real estate was sold or leased off. Industry in the Old Hickory area produced some nice revenue, but east of there the railroad was lightly built and freight levels were also pretty light. Trains basically operated as needed over the line. For example, *Nashville Division Time-Table No. 10*, dated October 22, 1978, showed a Crossville to Radnor via Vine Hill line, but there were no scheduled trains on the route. Interestingly enough, the details for the line called it the "Nashville and Eastern Sub-division." There were also two agencies listed, Old Hickory and Lebanon, both open daytime on weekdays.

The Louisville & Nashville was acquired by the Seaboard Coast Line Railroad in 1971, but it was allowed to run independently until 1982 when it was merged into the new Seaboard System. As the railroad got larger, the route east out of Nashville became even less important. Studies were underway to look at selling the line. In 1986, the Seaboard System was merged with the Chessie System to form the new CSX Transportation. This simply increased the interest in selling the line, and it was soon sold off becoming the Nashville & Eastern Railroad, which still operates the route today.

Southern Railway (1968 – 1982)
Norfolk Southern Railway (1982 – 2000)
Franklin Industrial Minerals / Lhoist (2000 – current)

When the Southern Railway acquired the Tennessee Central from Crossville east for $340,000, it assigned the property to the Harriman & Northeastern Railroad subsidiary. This continued through the merger with Norfolk & Western that created Norfolk Southern. In 1970, not long after the line was acquired, Southern Railway had train #37 depart Harriman at 8:05am and arrive at Crossville at 10:00am. It would return as #38, leaving Crossville at 11:00am and arriving back at Harriman at 12:15pm. Both operated daily except Saturday. In 1983, the Southern still operated a daily except Saturday roundtrip to Crossville. Train #37 was scheduled to depart Emory Gap at 4:45pm and arrive at Crossville at 6:00pm. Returning as train #38, it had a scheduled departure at 7:00pm and arrival at Emory Gap at 8:15pm. The schedule showed plenty of work time allowed at Crab Orchard. By 1988, Norfolk Southern was running the railroad and there were no scheduled trains over the line, instead operating as needed.

Through the 1970s and 1980s, the line between Emory Gap and Crossville was popular for fall excursion trips out of Chattanooga. For years, the train was headed up by steam locomotives, but by the mid-1980s, the trips were pulled by diesel locomotives. However, as the line's business continued to decline, the excursion trains stopped running by the late 1980s. In 1989, the line from Crossville to Crab Orchard was abandoned, ending these trips for good.

A major change came about in 2000 when Norfolk Southern decided to officially abandon the line and sell it to the only major customer still left on the line – Franklin Industrial Minerals. On July 28, 2000, the Cincinnati, New Orleans & Texas Pacific Railway Company (CNO&TP), a wholly owned subsidiary of Norfolk Southern, filed with the Surface Transportation Board a petition to abandon the Crab Orchard Line between milepost 141.5-H at Crab Orchard and milepost 156.9-H at Rockwood. After receiving approval, the line was sold to Franklin Industrial Minerals, which operated it as a long industrial railroad. The company began a number of improvement projects along the line, rebuilding several bridges and the tunnel, as well as installing ties and rail along the line.

In 2005, Norfolk Southern through its Cincinnati, New Orleans & Texas Pacific Railway Company, decided to extend the track operated by Franklin to allow more room for interchanging freight. On August 15, 2005, and again on November 6, 2006, NS applied to abandon an approximately 1.1-mile line of railroad, extending from milepost 156.9-H to milepost 158.0-H. An interesting part of this application was the need to continue service to Horsehead Resource Development at Rockwood. The final application stated that Horsehead had its own locomotive and would handle its own switching, with the CNO&TP continuing "to use the line, under an agreement with Franklin, as an interchange track to interchange freight traffic with both Franklin and Horsehead." Today, Lhoist operates the line after acquiring Franklin Industrial Minerals.

Tennessee Central Eastern Division
Nashville (TN) to Monterey (TN)
Nashville & Eastern Railroad

Nashville & Eastern Railroad

The Nashville & Eastern Railroad (NERR) operates the former Tennessee Central Eastern Division tracks from Nashville to Monterey. The NERR was created in 1986 by three partners with the intent of acquiring the rights to operate the former Tennessee Central route east of Nashville, Tennessee. The railroad originally focused on providing service from Nashville east to industries in Old Hickory and Lebanon, and east of there as needed. In early 1989, it added a dinner train to the operations on the line. Operating from near where today's *Music City Star* commuter train departs Nashville, the Broadway Dinner Train operated to Old Hickory on a regular basis. This operation reached a reported peak of 33,250 riders in 1993, but dropped to just more than 10,000 in 1998, before shutting down on July 19, 1999.

To acquire and rebuild the railroad, several area counties created the Nashville and Eastern Railroad Authority (NERA) to handle grant money from the Tennessee Department of Transportation. According to documents of the Authority, they "originally entered into a ten-year lease, dated August 28, 1986, with Nashville and Eastern Railroad Corporation to operate the line." According to the agreement, rehabilitation of the line is the responsibility of the Authority. Since the beginning of this effort, more than $90 million in shortline assistance money has been spent to rebuild much of the railroad and its bridges. According to several sources, this rebuild has included 130 miles of track, of which 110 miles is main line. Industry tracks and spurs were also upgraded to handle modern freight cars. Three miles of new branchline have been built. Also, 85 bridges have been upgraded or replaced.

The Nashville & Eastern Railroad is responsible for standard maintenance of the line, and the lease payments are based upon gross freight revenues. The Authority also receives a percentage of the payments from the commuter operations as well as lease payments for the locomotive shops at Lebanon. Several sources state that the lease agreement between the Authority and the railroad has been extended until 2053 to provide a stable agreement for the commuter trains.

Today, the railroad operates 110 miles of mainline and four branches: the Vine Hill Branch from Southern Junction that connects with CSX, the Old Hickory Branch, the Carthage Branch, and the new Crawford Branch. More than 30 customers are served, shipping and receiving products such as metals, plastics, aggregates, sand, lumber, corn syrup, aluminum, pulpboard and scrap paper. Additionally, commuter service between Lebanon and Nashville began in 2006, funded by the Tennessee Regional Transportation Authority, which today handles more than 1200 passengers daily on its *Music City Star*. Finally, regular excursion trains operate along the line, sponsored by the Tennessee Central Railway Museum.

The Nashville & Eastern operates several trains during weekdays, "hauling bulk merchandise and unit train traffic for over 30 industrial customers," according to the railroad. The *Music City Star* (MCS) operates their trains west of Lebanon on weekdays. Finally, the Tennessee Central Railway Museum operates excursion trains from their Nashville base to a number of destinations many weekends. To control the movement of these trains, CTC signaling has been installed between Nashville and Lebanon. CTC – Centralized Traffic Control – is a signaling system where a centralized train dispatcher can see where all trains are, using a computer screen, and direct their movement using colored signals along the route. Additionally, they can control the switches to direct trains down different routes.

East of Lebanon, trains operate using blocks – watch for the signs alongside the tracks that separate the blocks. Blocks are Watertown, Silver Point, and Cookeville. The east end of the NERR has a sign identifying it as the "Monterey Branch."

Tennessee Central Railway Museum

The Tennessee Central Railway Museum (TCRM) is based in the former Tennessee Central Railway Master Mechanic's office at 220 Willow Street, just east of downtown Nashville. The Museum includes a library and artifacts collection, including what is considered to be the largest collection of Tennessee Central Railway artifacts to be found anywhere. There are also several model railroads as a part of the collection. The Museum dates back to the Cumberland Division of the Southeast Region – National Model Railroad Association. Today, the two groups still maintain a close relationship, explaining the model trains and hobby shop that are a part of the Museum.

Beginning in 1989, the Tennessee Central Railway Museum began operating excursion trains over parts of the Nashville & Eastern. Trips routinely operate to Lebanon, Watertown, the Del-Monaco Winery at Baxter, Cookeville, and Monterey. With the trips came the ability to collect a roster of passenger cars, many of them former Atchison, Topeka & Santa Fe Railway (Santa Fe, or ATSF) cars built by Budd. A collection of locomotives and freight cars is also a part of the TCRM, most stored at the yard near their Master Mechanic's office headquarters.

The TCRM uses a fleet of stainless steel passenger cars that can be operated in all weather conditions. Photo by Barton Jennings.

The Tennessee Central Railway Museum operates their trips 12 months a year, often starting in January and February with Valentine and winery trips and ending with a series of Santa trips in December. They also operate special events such as trips with

Thomas the Tank Engine, and charters for various organizations. Details can be found at www.tcry.org, and the organization maintains an e-mail notification list for those interested in riding.

Music City Star

The *Music City Star* (MCS, reporting mark NRTX) uses what is hoped to be the first of many commuter rail routes serving Nashville, Tennessee. The commuter railroad's operations date back to the 1988 creation of the Regional Transportation Authority (RTA) of Middle Tennessee. Created by Tennessee statute, the purpose of the RTA was to create a regional transit system for Middle Tennessee. RTA included Cheatham, Davidson, Dickson, Montgomery, Robertson, Rutherford, Sumner, Williamson and Wilson counties. Among the projects started by RTA include the largest commuter vanpool program in the Southeast, the coordination of thousands of carpools, and nine regional express bus routes.

On September 18, 2006, commuter rail service was added to this list. The trains of this route serve Davidson and Wilson counties to the east of Nashville, using a 32-mile section of track belonging to the Nashville & Eastern Railroad Authority. A managerial change happened at RTA in December 2008 when the managers of the Nashville Metropolitan Transit Authority (MTA) became the managers of the RTA's regional services.

To make the commuter service possible, various public funds were used to replace or upgrade track, bridges, grade crossings, and signals. Six stations were built: Riverfront (Nashville), Donelson, Hermitage, Mt. Juliet, Martha and Lebanon. For equipment, the organization acquired four rebuilt ex-Amtrak EMD F40PH locomotives and seven former Chicago Metra bi-level gallery coaches, as well as four cab control bi-level gallery coaches. Because of the willingness to operate with second-hand equipment and to operate at relatively low speeds on a single-track route, costs were kept very low. Reports indicate that the route initially cost only $41 million, or just under $1.3 million per mile. This low cost has been praised as being the "most cost efficient commuter rail start-up in the nation."

The operator of the commuter train is Transit Solutions Group (TSG), a sister company to the Nashville & Eastern Railroad, that has operated the trains since the start of commuter service in 2006. As the NERR website states, "TSG provides train service and equipment maintenance in Lebanon, Tennessee, and is able to draw upon a wealth of knowledge and resources from its affiliated freight and construction companies."

As of 2018, the trains run during weekday morning and evening rush hour, operating four Nashville-Lebanon roundtrips, plus two Nashville-Mt. Juliet roundtrips, each day, plus an evening roundtrip on Fridays. Ridership on the Lebanon line has never been high. The first full year (2007) saw 104,785 passenger trips. Ridership reached a peak of 277,148 in 2012 and has held steady to slightly lower since. The record single-day ridership was 1,374 on April 19, 2011. Nevertheless, the RTA has plans for as many as six more commuter train routes. The destinations of these routes are in all directions from Nashville and would mostly require operations on heavy freight mainlines of CSX. These hoped-for destinations include Murfreesboro (southeast), Columbia (southwest), Dickson (west), Ashland City-Clarksville (northwest), Springfield (north), and Gallatin (northeast). The routes in all directions look like a star on the map, hence the name for the commuter system – The *Music City Star*. It also plays on the fame of the country music industry in Nashville.

0.0 MCS RIVERFRONT – Riverfront is the name of the Nashville terminal station for the *Music City Star* commuter train. The station is located just east of the north end of Broadway at 108 1st Avenue South, next to the Cumberland River.

A Tennessee Central Railroad map dated June 30, 1918, shows that the area just east of Broadway and north of First Avenue was once full of Tennessee Central tracks. These included tracks that served a passenger station at First Avenue and Sparkman, near the south end of the former Sparkman Street Bridge, now the John Seigenthaler Pedestrian Bridge. The railroad's offices and freight depot were a block further east at the end of Demonbreum Street. Much of this land was actually owned by the Tennessee Central Station Company and the Nashville Terminal Company, parts of the railroad. An interesting note dated August 3, 1936, stated that the railroad installed "electric wiring at Passenger Station to serve air-conditioned Pullmans." The facilities here had the telegraph call letters of DS and MS.

The original freight house burned down in 1942 and was replaced by a new concrete building. It was torn down after the railroad shut down. The rambling passenger station complex is also long gone, having been torn down in 1963. A new station was built along Broadway about 1990 to handle the business of the *Broadway Dinner Train*.

To the west of Broadway, the railroad had a long track down First Avenue to Union Street, serving a number of customers in buildings marked "Brick Wholesale Buildings" on various railroad valuation maps. There were also several tracks to a wharf and "River & Rail Warehouse" on the shore of the Cumberland River. Today, this area is a network of clubs and bars in the many old buildings, along with some open land awaiting development.

Music City Star station in downtown Nashville. Photo by Barton Jennings.

Eastern Division – Nashville to Monterey

Old warehouse district in downtown Nashville. Photo by Barton Jennings.

City of Nashville, Tennessee

Nashville is the capital of Tennessee and the county seat of Davidson County. Nashville, with its government partner Davidson County (there is a joint city-county government), has a population of approximately 700,000, with the 13-county Nashville metropolitan area having about 1.75 million residents, making it the largest city in the state.

Nashville was founded by James Robertson, John Donelson, and a party of Overmountain Men in 1779. An earlier settlement, Fort Nashborough, stood nearby on the Cumberland River. Francis Nash, an American Revolutionary War hero, was the inspiration for the town's name. The community was incorporated as a city and became the county seat of Davidson County in 1806. It became the capital of Tennessee in 1843. Its location on the Cumberland River, and the number of railroads built to the docks, made Nashville a very prosperous city. During the Civil War, it was an early target for Union forces, and during February 1862 became the first southern capital to fall to northern forces. It soon became the major supply point for Union forces across the region. After the war, the facilities built by the Union Army soon hosted commercial businesses, and the economy again boomed in Nashville. The money moving through the city led to the construction of a number of grand classical-style buildings, many of which still stand throughout Nashville.

The capitol building for Tennessee is on the northwest side of downtown, standing on a low hill above an industrial area once served by the railroad. Standing in front of the capitol is a 1927 bronze statue of Edward Ward Carmack, placed there by the Women's Christian Temperance Union. Carmack was a newspaper editor, U.S. Senator (1901-1907), and temperance leader, who was murdered by a political rival on the streets of Nashville in what is still considered to be the city's most notorious murder. While Carmack was not directly involved with the Tennessee Central, he impacted it and all of the railroads in the United States with the passage of the Carmack Amendment in 1906. The amendment held a carrier responsible for proving it wasn't negligent in its handling of in-transit cargo that was lost or damaged.

Nashville is famous for its country music, and it is one of the major economic factors in the city. All of the Big Four record labels, plus many independent labels, are located in Nashville. Since the 1960s, Nashville has been the second-largest music production center in the country. Guitar company Gibson is also based here. Estimates state that the music industry employs approximately 20,000 people and pumps nearly $7 billion a year into the local economy.

However, this is not all that drives Nashville. It is also a center for the healthcare, publishing, banking and transportation industries. Healthcare accounts for 200,000 jobs in the area and contributes $30 billion to the economy. Nashville is home to more than 300 health care companies, including Hospital Corporation of America (HCA), the largest private operator of hospitals in the world.

Eastern Division – Nashville to Monterey

Fortune 500 companies with offices within Nashville include companies such as Bridgestone, Nissan North America, Tractor Supply Company, and Dollar General. It is the home of Goo Goo Clusters (made in Nashville since 1912). The economic environment of the area has placed Nashville on many business lists, including *Forbes* Best Places for Business and Careers (#10 in 2017), *Forbes* Best City for White Collar Jobs (#1 in 2016), and *Business Facilities* Cities for Economic Growth Potential (#5 in 2017).

Nashville is a major railroad hub, with CSX lines heading in multiple directions. However, Nashville is not served by Amtrak, making it the third-largest metropolitan area in the country without such passenger service (behind Las Vegas and Columbus).

0.2 CP NASHVILLE – This location is also known as CP Riverfront. The railroad passes under the Shelby Street bridge, now the John Seigenthaler Pedestrian Bridge over the Cumberland River. Today, this is a single-track line, but was a two-track railroad before 1920. Just east of here at Milepost 0.6, located under the new Korean Veterans Boulevard bridge, the railroad has a switch to a siding.

1.0 SOUTHERN JUNCTION – This is a switch located under Interstate 24 that connects into the former Tennessee Central "Shops and Yards" complex, also known as Southern Junction Yard or East Yard. This line also connects to the Vine Hill Subdivision, which curves south to connect with CSX about three miles south of here. The timetable of the Nashville & Eastern shows that there is a 4500-foot siding here. The Vine Hill Subdivision was once the route that Tennessee Central trains took to reach Hopkinsville, and the wye still exists at the east end of the yard near Milepost 1.8. East of the wye, the railroad was single-track in 1918. **For information on the Vine Hill Subdivision, see page 207.**

This area was originally known as Belt Line Junction. However, in 1905, the line east of here was leased to the Southern Railway and the tracks west of here to the Illinois Central. With this, the junction location was renamed Southern Junction.

Old Tennessee Central timetables show the station of Shops (telegraph call YD) at Milepost 1.7. Much of this yard still exists, but the large roundhouse (burned down on June 7, 1970), turntable, and other shop facilities to the south are gone. The former Tennessee Central Railway Master Mechanic's office today houses the Tennessee Central Railway Museum. The museum operates excursions over today's Nashville & Eastern, and much of their passenger equipment is generally stored in the yard.

The former Tennessee Central Master Mechanic's office today houses the Tennessee Central Railway Museum, and serves as the origin of its excursion trains. Photo by Sarah Jennings.

Eastern Division – Nashville to Monterey

N&E 5343 prepares to pull a January 2003 charter from the Tennessee Central Railway Museum at Southern Junction. Photo by Barton Jennings.

On the north side of the yard, a new mainline has been built to allow *Music City Star* commuter trains to bypass the congestion in the yard. Many documents show that it is named the Southern Junction By-Pass.

At the east end of the yard at Southern Junction, the Nashville & Eastern has an office and engine track next to Stanley Street. Locomotive 5938 was found here in 2017. Photo by Sarah Jennings.

2.2 BROWNS CREEK BRIDGE – Originally a timber trestle, it is now a new concrete ballast deck bridge, built for the heavier traffic from the commuter and freight railroads. In this area, Browns Creek has been re-channeled directly north to the Cumberland River, where it once flowed to the east just north of the railroad. The change in the stream's route allowed the area to be used for industry and manufacturing.

3.3 **NASHVILLE WATERWORKS** – This red brick building facility is on both sides of the track, but what may be the most beautiful building is to the north. Note the "Nashville Pumping Station 1888" lettering. Much of the complex is on the National Register of Historic Places.

This facility is old, more than 100 years old, but it still supplies Nashville with drinking water. The plant has been known as the Omohundro Water Filtration Plant and is located at 1400 Pumping Station Road. According to several sources, the Omohundro plant originally opened as the George Reyer Pumping Station in 1889. However, that wasn't the first pumping station here; reports show that the first pumps date from the 1870s and that some are still in use pumping water out of the Cumberland River. Initially the water was cleaned by running it through a gravel and sand filter, but a full filtering system was installed in 1929. The plant was powered by steam until 1953. For many years, the Tennessee Central had several business tracks serving the waterworks.

High above is the ex-Louisville & Nashville Radnor Cutoff. This route was built by the Lewisburg & Northern Railroad as a bypass around Nashville, connecting to their Brentwood, Tennessee, to Athens, Alabama, line. A small quarry was once operated here by Foster, Creighton and Gould, used to provide materials for the construction work on the Lewisburg & Northern. Documents show the route running 10.61 miles from Maplewood (north of Nashville) to Mayton (just south of Nashville). What became known as the Radnor Cutoff opened on January 1, 1918. The name Radnor Cutoff came from the new Radnor yard and shops built as part of the project. This bypass around Nashville allowed freight trains to go directly in and out of the yard and shops without having to pass through the congested passenger station area in downtown Nashville.

4.3 **MILL CREEK BRIDGE** – Look for the large (124-foot-long) Warren through truss span, known by the Tennessee Central as Bridge No. 4.27. The bridge was once much longer, but 974 feet of the west approach was officially retired July 20, 1923.

Mill Creek is about 28 miles long, forming near Nolensville, Tennessee, and flowing north before entering the Cumberland River just north of here. Because it covers a large watershed and flows through a number of new subdivisions, it has developed a reputation for flooding. In the 2010 Tennessee Floods, Mill Creek was the first stream to experience major flooding. Mill Creek is also known worldwide as the only known habitat for the endangered Nashville Crayfish.

At the west end of the bridge is a large building that is served by the Nashville & Eastern. Several companies have space in the building, including SCP Distributors – the world's largest wholesale distributor of swimming pool supplies, equipment and related leisure products – and Haldex Brake Products, a Swedish company that dates from 1887 when it started making clocks and typewriters.

Just east of the bridge, there was once a spur track to the south into a quarry known as the Mill Creek Crusher. There are several closed quarries still in this area. One of these was the Joseph Lightman limestone quarry that was used for road construction during the 1910s.

The railroad was very busy in 1924 improving its route. In that year, bridges at mileposts 5.28, 5.45, 5.79, and 6.43 were all retired and filled in. These bridges were all more than 100 feet long and were replaced by culverts.

5.4 **BRILEY PARKWAY BRIDGE** – This large modern concrete ballast deck bridge was built to span Briley Parkway, also known as Tennessee Highway 155. This bridge was part of a 3.2-mile-long railroad main line realignment which eliminated several grade crossings and allowed for higher train speeds.

The bridge also allowed the widening of Briley Parkway to eight lanes. Briley Parkway was built around Nashville as a divided highway to connect most of the roads in and out of town. It also provides access to landmarks such as the Grand Ole Opry House, Opry Mills, the Opryland Hotel, and the Nashville International Airport. The road was named for former Nashville mayor Beverly Briley.

For trains heading east, their speeds can reach 60 miles per hour due to the track upgrades and the CTC signal system installed for the commuter trains. These higher speeds last until the last *Music City Star* station at Lebanon, where speeds drop to between 10 and 40 mph on east to Monterey.

6.6 **HARDING** – During the early part of the 1900s, Harding was a flag stop on the Tennessee Central. Records from the Tennessee Comptroller of the Treasury show that the passenger shed at Harding was retired on May 26, 1930. The building was just west of today's McGavock Pike, known many years ago as Central Pike. A short spur track was located on the north side of the track just east of the passenger shed.

The Harding name likely came from the family of Thomas Harding, a military veteran from Virginia who bought a great deal of land in the area starting in 1799, after he and his brother Giles Harding arrived in the Nashville area. He continued to buy land locally until his death in 1805, and then the land was divided among his children on June 27, 1806.

Several miles south of here is the Hall-Harding-McCampbell House, known also simply as the McCampbell House, and listed on the National Register of Historic Places. The house was started about 1800 after William Hall purchased the property. The house was built in the Federal style with the traditional hall-and-parlor design (one large entertaining room and one small room on each floor). The house was reportedly sold to the Harding family in 1820 and enlarged. It then was sold to James Anderson in 1847, and then Thomas McCampbell in 1852.

7.8 **MCS DONELSON** – This is the new *Music City Star* commuter train station. Located at 2705 Lebanon Pike on the north side of the tracks, there are approximately 230 parking spaces here.

Donelson is a neighborhood of Nashville, known by many as "'Hip Donelson" and considered to be among Nashville's most desirable suburbs. The community was named for John Donelson, co-founder of Nashville and father-in-law of Andrew Jackson, the seventh President of the United States. John Donelson reached this location on April 24, 1780, after a four-month, 1000-mile boat and overland move. His record of the trip includes references to Indian attacks, a smallpox outbreak, hunger, exhaustion, extreme cold, swift currents, and treacherous shoals. He soon became a political leader and was a signer of the Cumberland Compact, a forerunner of the Tennessee State Constitution. The document was signed by settlers when they arrived at Fort Nashborough (Nashville) on the Cumberland River and was designed to recognize land claims and encourage lawful behavior.

The first suburban development in the area was Bluefields, started in 1929 by the Bransford Realty Company. There were more than fifty houses in the suburb by 1938. Most of the development happened after World War II, and especially after the start of the Nashville boom of the 1980s. Driving around, you can see a number of mid-century red brick, detached ranch-style homes. Donelson is also the home of Donelson Plaza, one of the earliest strip mall shopping centers in the country.

Records of the Tennessee Central show that on July 31, 1936, the railroad retired "2 car body laborer's dwellings" at Donelson. Two years later on March 16, 1939, the railroad did work to "replace Comb. Station with 6' x 14' Comb. Pass. & Frt. Shed."

7.9 **CP WEST DONELSON** – This is the west switch for a 1000-foot siding, built for the *Music City Star* commuter train operations.

8.1 **CP EAST DONELSON** – This is the east switch of the siding. In the curve just east of here, the abandoned right-of-way of the NC&StL branch to Lebanon comes in immediately to the south and follows the Tennessee Central eastward. A short spur for the State of Tennessee once existed at Milepost 8.5 at the Stewarts Ferry Pike grade crossing. The spur into the utility yard to the south actually uses part of the old NC&StL grade.

9.3 **STONES RIVER BRIDGE** – This is former Tennessee Central Bridge No. 9.33. It is 439 feet long with a 200-foot-long Warren through truss with all verticals in the middle and a deck plate girder span on each end. Just upstream to the south are several stone piers from the original Nashville, Chattanooga, & St. Louis Railroad. This was their Bridge No. 30.6 on the Stones River-Chattanooga Division Main line, according to some early railroad documents. The bridge appeared on topographical maps in 1932 but was gone by 1956.

The Stones River is actually Stone's River, named after early explorer Uriah Stone who navigated the river in 1767. Stones River consists of three major forks: the West, Middle, and East forks. The largest and longest of these is the East Fork at more than fifty miles in length. It starts west of McMinnville on Short Mountain, a part of the Cumberland Plateau, in Cannon County. The Middle Fork is only about twenty miles long and forms near Hoovers Gap in Bedford County. It flows north from a series of small hills, basically following Interstate 24 until it enters the West Fork near Murfreesboro. The route of the Middle Fork has long been used by travelers and was an important military route during the Civil War. The West Fork is about forty miles long and starts south of Murfreesboro and follows U.S. Highway 231 into Murfreesboro where it meets the

Middle Fork. The West Fork was the scene of a major Civil War battle when forces met and fought December 31, 1862, to January 2, 1863, at what became known as the Battle of Stones River just north of Murfreesboro.

The East and West Forks merge to the south of here and are then dammed by the J. Percy Priest Dam, named for a Nashville Congressman. The Army Corps of Engineers developed the lake in the 1960s, creating a series of waterfront suburbs on the east side of Nashville. A number of boat docks, marinas, parks, campgrounds, and beaches encircle the lake, with the dam located just south of Interstate 40. From the lake, the river winds its way north, flowing into the Cumberland River about a mile north of here.

Just east of the Stones River Bridge, the Nashville & Eastern curves on a "new" grade, measuring 2400 feet, realigned by the Tennessee Central in 1918 and officially opened on July 26th. The west end of Stones River Siding is in this area. Trains heading west climb grades of more than 1%, while heading east, they have about one mile of flat track before beginning several climbs which peak at almost 1.75%.

9.7 **STONES RIVER** – The Tennessee Central showed Stones River as being at Milepost 9.9, but the Nashville & Eastern uses Milepost 9.7 as its location. Some know the location as CP Stones River. This is the junction with the Old Hickory Subdivision, which heads north about eight miles to the DuPont plant. The 2300-foot-long siding and small yard is named for the nearby river. **For information on the Old Hickory Branch, see page 165.**

On December 15, 1923, the Tennessee Central bought the U.S. Government Tracks at Stones River, including the "Interlocker Tower, Interlocker Shed & Freight Shed." The interlocking was part of a series of tracks that crossed the Tennessee Central to become the "Monsanto Track" on the former NC&StL track to the south. The interlocking was retired in 1928. Many of the Stones River yard tracks acquired were retired within a year. On May 23, 1930, the "frame Freight Depot" was officially retired.

To the south is Brandau Road, which uses the grade of the former NC&StL branch to Lebanon. To the north is Stoners Creek, named for explorer Michael Stoner who scouted the area in the late 1760s. A bit further east is a large Vulcan Materials Company.

10.6 HERMITAGE – This was the location of the Tennessee Central Hermitage station, at the grade crossing with Central Pike. There was a short siding to the south of the mainline and the depot was on the north side of the mainline just east of Central Pike. Railroad records indicate that the company retired their "car body Freight Depot at Hermitage" on June 18, 1930. During World War I, the U.S. Government built a temporary rail line northward from here. It was soon retired.

Hermitage was named for Andrew Jackson's nearby home, The Hermitage. Jackson was the seventh President of the United States and his father-in-law was John Donelson. This was a rural farming area until the 1960s. Today, the area is a popular mix of suburbs and shopping. It is also the technology headquarters of Deloitte Touche Tohmatsu, one of the Big Four auditors.

11.3 DRY FORK CREEK BRIDGE – This stream is not always dry as it drains about five miles of country to the southeast. It flows into Stoners Creek just to the north.

11.8 MCS HERMITAGE – Today's *Music City Star* Hermitage Station has almost 280 parking spaces and is served by area buses. It is located at 4121 Andrew Jackson Parkway, a major roadway in the area, on the north side of the tracks. This station is in a residential area as opposed to the more industrial areas to the west. The road to the south is located on the grade of the former NC&StL branch to Lebanon. The former grade is immediately to the south of the Tennessee Central track for the next seven miles.

12.7 TULIP GROVE – The small depot and flag stop of Tulip Grove was named for the nearby mansion of Andrew Jackson Donelson. The team track at Tulip Grove was retired on March 22, 1924, while the passenger station was retired on March 14, 1933. Both were just west of the grade crossing here with the team track on the north side of the mainline while the depot was on the south side.

Listed on the National Register of Historic Places in 1970, Tulip Grove is an antebellum house built near The Hermitage in 1836 for Andrew Jackson Donelson, who was President Jackson's private secretary and the nephew of Jackson's wife Rachel. It was originally known as Poplar Grove, but was renamed Tulip Grove in 1841, reportedly at the suggestion of President Martin Van Buren. In 1858, the property was sold to the parents of painter Mayna Treanor Avent, who grew up at Tulip Grove. The estate and house went through a number of owners until 1964 when it was acquired by the Ladies' Hermitage Association.

13.3 STONERS CREEK BRIDGE – The railroad crosses Stoners Creek on a seven-span concrete bridge. Stoners Creek was named for explorer Michael Stoner who scouted the area in the late 1760s. Stoner and his family have an interesting history. His family moved to North America in 1710 with a promise to produce tar and pitch for the British navy. The plans failed and they moved west to develop land, which was then confiscated from them by British leaders. The family then moved to near Philadelphia where they changed their name from Holsteiner to Holstein. In 1748, George Michael Holstein was born. His parents soon died and George Michael Holstein was apprenticed to a saddle maker. At age 16 he left the field, changed his name to Michael Stoner, and traveled to New River, Virginia, where he joined up with Daniel Boone. Stoner traveled with Boone through Cumberland Gap into Kentucky, where they split up. Stoner then explored to the southwest, covering Central Kentucky and the Cumberland River to near today's

Nashville, Tennessee. He eventually joined back up with Boone and traveled back to Virginia.

Stoner later was a resident of Boonesborough, Kentucky, fighting in several western battles of the Revolutionary War and later Indian wars. He often traveled and explored with Daniel Boone into their 60s, heading as far west as Missouri. Three of Stoner's children married Boone family members, demonstrating the closeness of the two families. Stoner died in 1815 and was buried near Monticello, Kentucky. Several streams were named for him over the years, including this one.

13.6 **COUNTY LINE** – This is the county line between Davidson County (to the west) and Wilson County (to the east).

Davidson County dates back to when this area was part of North Carolina. In 1783, the legislature of North Carolina created the county. It was named for General William Lee Davidson, who was killed while trying to prevent a British crossing of the Catawba River on February 1, 1781. Nashville is its county seat. Davidson County and Nashville were the first European settlements and governments in Middle Tennessee. Much of its early law was set by the Cumberland Compact, a document created to establish a basic rule of law and to protect the land titles of the settlers.

Wilson County was created on October 26, 1799, from parts of Sumner County. The name reportedly honored Major David Wilson, a Revolutionary War veteran and statesman. When the railroads arrived, the county became a temporary center of logging and lumber. Its county seat is Lebanon.

15.0 **GREEN HILL** – Green Hill was settled in the late 1790s when several families moved away from Nashville during a smallpox outbreak. A post office was located here from the 1830s through 1904. Today, this area is a suburb of Nashville. There are no clear records of how the community's name came about. Some sources say that it came from a description of the green rolling hills in the area. Other

Eastern Division – Nashville to Monterey

sources say that it was named for a former state treasurer of North Carolina.

There are no railroad facilities here today, but there was once a short siding used to serve a set of stock pens. The siding was on the north side of the mainline just east of South Greenhill Road, with a cinder platform and depot between the road and siding. Just to the south was the depot for the Nashville, Chattanooga & St. Louis, also located to the east of the road and between the lines of the two railroads on a short siding. The Tennessee Central passenger depot and cinder platform was retired on May 23, 1930. A number of small stations along the line were retired on that date.

17.0 MOUNT JULIET – While generally a flag stop for passenger trains, there was once a depot here (telegraph call MJ), torn down and replaced by a shelter in 1942. The Tennessee Central also had a siding, a team track, and a number of section houses at Mount Juliet, probably explaining the need for a depot. Historically, the community was spelled Mount Juliet, but most modern sources use Mt. Juliet.

Mt. Juliet is generally believed to have been named for Mount Juliet Estate, a manor house in County Kilkenny, Ireland. However, some sources insist that it was named for Julia Gleaves, a local citizen who was well known for her care of the needy in the community. Either way, it is the only city in the United States with the name. The community was first organized in 1835, and was incorporated as a city in 1972. Being close to Nashville, the city has boomed with the growth of Middle Tennessee.

17.3 CP MT. JULIET – This control point is designed to protect passenger trains stopped at the Mt. Juliet passenger station.

17.4 MCS MT. JULIET – Located to the south, this is the new *Music City Star* station for Mt. Juliet, located at 22 East Division Street. It has approximately 220 parking spaces.

Heading east, the country suddenly becomes more rural. The tracks of the Nashville & Eastern climb up and over several small ridges east of here, often with short grades easily exceeding 1%. To the south is still the former NC&StL grade, which curves off to the south about milepost 19.8.

20.2   CEDAR CREEK BRIDGE – Tennessee Central Bridge No. 20.24 is approximately 210 feet long. Cedar Creek starts on the west side of Lebanon on Hickory Ridge. The area was initially one of the most prosperous in the region. The first water powered gristmill in the area was built on Cedar Creek in 1799, and a sawmill was later added. Cedar Creek was named for the plentiful cedars and flows generally northward into the Cumberland river.

20.9   BECKWITH – Some sources show this to be Curd's Station. There was a small depot on the north side of the tracks just east of the Beckwith Road grade crossing. There was once a short siding to the south. Today, there is a spur into the TVA (Tennessee Valley Authority) electrical substation to the north.

Heading east, the railroad climbs a 1.38% grade all the way to Milepost 22. It then drops at the same grade to near Martha. Much of this area is a mix of woods and pasture.

22.1   KENWAL SPUR – Over the years, there have been several quarries and related facilities in this area. However, today, to the north is a mile-long spur track that serves the Kenwal Steel facility. Kenwal cuts, treats, and prepares steel for the specific needs of various customers. Their "Lebanon facility is 100,000 square feet with rail access and two 72-inch slitters." It has a slitting capacity of 350,000 tons/year, making it a sizeable customer for the railroad. Dozens of coiled steel cars are often located on the several tracks at the site. The plant opened in 2007.

Tennessee Central valuation maps from the 1920s and 1930s show this location to be the Franklin Limestone Company. There was a series of tracks to the north

Eastern Division – Nashville to Monterey

about where today's Kenwal Spur exists, as well as a short siding. Tennessee Central records show that the railroad built an additional "682' spur for Franklin Limestone Co." in April 1939. Track charts later showed this to be Marquette Cement, also known as Martha Quarry Cement. A now-flooded quarry marks this location.

23.4 **MCS MARTHA** – Martha Station is another of the new *Music City Star* stations, opened in February 2011 on the north side of the mainline. Located at 65 Martha Circle off of Tennessee Highway 109, Martha was originally served by a temporary station before Highway 109 was improved.

Much of the railroad in this area has been rebuilt. Crouch Engineering of Nashville "designed a 3.2-mile realignment of the Nashville and Eastern mainline in conjunction with the US 70 highway widening project and the SR 109 highway widening project, eliminating 2 major grade crossings, on behalf of Nashville and Eastern Railroad Authority (NERA). The project included design of a grade separation at SR 109, two concrete and steel 3-span ballast deck bridges over streams, and a steel through plate girder bridge over US 70." The widening of Tennessee Highway 109 was an important part of road improvements in Middle Tennessee. It "has been identified as a strategic corridor, serving as the primary north-south connector between I-65 in Sumner County and I-40 in Wilson County."

The 1930s were a busy time for Martha as facilities were added and subtracted. On March 11, 1931, the railroad retired the old tool house and built a new 10' x 12' tool house. It was retired the next year on March 31st. The stock pens were retired on July 13, 1937, and then a month later the station was retired on August 23rd. A new 6' x 10' passenger shed was constructed and went into service on May 31, 1939. For many years, the Tennessee Central had a siding here from just west of the depot all the way east to the Spence Creek Bridge, located on the south side of the mainline. In November 1928, the siding was extended more than 1000 feet to the east. A second siding apparently also existed on the north side of the mainline, according to a Tennessee Central track chart, which shows that "Hiway 109" ran through the middle of the sidings.

The Tennessee Central was famous with rail enthusiasts as being an Alco railroad, using locomotives built by the American Locomotive Company, which exited the business in the late 1960s. Martha was the scene of near destruction of two of these locomotives when a truck driver failed to yield to a train in July 1958. Diesels 257 (Alco RS3) and 801 (Alco FA1) were derailed and heavily damaged in the accident. They were later sent back to Alco for rebuilding. Many pictures of the scene were taken as it took several days and two large railroad wrecking cranes to clean up the mess.

23.5 **CP EAST MARTHA** – This is the east end of the new siding at Martha.

23.8 **MARTHA BRANCH BRIDGE** – A Tennessee Central June 30, 1918, Valuation Map shows this to be Spence Creek. It is Bridge No. 23.76. Martha Branch forms from several small streams about five miles south of here and flows into Spencer Creek just to the north.

23.9 **U.S. HIGHWAY 70 BRIDGE** – The Nashville & Eastern crosses Highway 70 on a new three-span through plate girder bridge. A Tennessee Central map dated 1918 shows this road to be the "Lebanon & Nashville T. P. Co."

On October 24, 1840, Gideon J. Pillow, President of the Columbia Central Turnpike Company, sent a letter to "His Excellency James K Polk" about plans "to incorporate a company to be called the Lebanon and Nashville Turnpike Company" and asking for the "appointment of three commissioners to view said road and make report to your Excellency with the view to the erection of two additional Toll Gates." In fact, a bill had actually been passed in 1835-1836 to allow the incorporation, but it took several years to raise the funds to do the actual construction.

Eastern Division – Nashville to Monterey

U.S. Highway 70 was originally commissioned in 1926, routed from Beaufort, North Carolina, to Holbrook, Arizona. Soon after, it took on the name of "Broadway of America" due to its heavy use across the center of the country. Today, the highway is 2,385 miles long, stretching from eastern North Carolina to east-central Arizona.

24.0 **SPENCER CREEK BRIDGE** – Many early settlers built along Spencer Creek, which forms on Hickory Ridge west of Lebanon. Spencer Creek flows to the west before turning north near here. Eventually it flows into the Cumberland River.

According to the *Early History of Middle Tennessee*, by Edward Albright, Spencer Creek was named for Thomas Sharp "Bigfoot" Spencer. Spencer was born in Virginia on March 29, 1754, and came here to check out reports about good land with plenty of big game. Spencer reportedly spent much of the rest of his life in the area, even living for some time in "a hollow upright Sycamore tree in what is now Castalian Springs, then known as Bledsoe's Lick." Spencer Creek was reportedly the favorite hunting location for Spencer. Legend has it that Spencer initially scared the local Native Americans when they saw his strength and the size of his footprints. Several sources state that Spencer was killed in an ambush on April 1, 1794, as he returned from selling his furs in Virginia. Reportedly, he was shot by a local tribesman, scalped, and then robbed of $2,000.

24.2 **BROOKWOOD** – Look for the farm crossing. A waiting shed was once located here on the north side of the original mainline. This area was realigned as part of the U.S. Highway 70 bridge project. The original grade is to the south a short distance. Brookwood was in the middle of a short tangent between two five-degree curves. The new line is now a single curve, longer but less sharp, allowing for higher train speeds and less track maintenance.

Brookwood is at the bottom of another pair of grades. Heading east, grades again reach at least 1.2% before cresting near Horn Springs.

25.2 **CAIRO BEND** – Cairo Bend was basically closed in the 1930s. On March 11, 1931, the passenger shelter was officially retired, and the spur track on the north side of the mainline was removed on December 1, 1933. The station was just east of today's Cairo Bend Road. There are several new subdivisions in this area.

Cairo Bend is actually located about ten miles north of here on the Cumberland River. The Cairo Bend Ferry once crossed the river there, making the road to the north important during the 1800s.

26.9 **HORN SPRINGS** – The top of the grade is just west of here at milepost 26.3, so eastbound trains are again descending. East to Lebanon there are a number of stretches of track like this that climb over low ridges and then drop down to small streams.

Early Tennessee Central maps show that there was a cinder platform and mail crane on the north side of the tracks. Records also show that the spur track here was retired on July 18, 1924. The spur track was to the west of the Old Horn Springs Road grade crossing while the rest of the facilities were just to the east.

The station of Horn Springs was named for the resort and mineral water bottling plant nearby. The Horn family moved into the area about 1800, receiving a 640-acre farm from the State of North Carolina. The original owner was Ethelred Horn, a veteran of the Revolutionary War. About 1870, James Horn discovered a spring on his property and the water tasted and smelled odd. Curious, he sent samples to nearby Vanderbilt University, which reported that the water had several trace minerals in it that could possibly cure things like liver and blood problems. Horn immediately began bottling the water for sale across the country, and opened the Horn Springs Resort for those wanting to experience the waters at their source.

Changes took place in 1893 when James Horn died and his son Jim took control of the resort. The Tennessee Central Railway opened that year with a line just a few hundred yards from the resort, so Jim expanded the resort hotel by adding a dance hall, bowling alley, dining room and more guest rooms. To fill the rooms, a national advertising campaign began, attracting people from across the country. Among the most famous were Harry Truman (33rd President of the United States), H. L. Davis (Pulitzer Prize Winning Author), and Virginia Frazier Boyle (Poet Laureate of the Confederacy).

Competition started up at nearby Hamilton Springs in 1898, but the resort and water plant stayed successful until the depression of 1929. Joseph Horn acquired the hotel in the 1930s after his father died, and he quickly downsized the hotel, lowered the rates, and added the Horn Springs Pool in 1935. Joseph also began to market the resort as an event center, hosting meetings, meals, and dances. Dr. R. D. Wilkerson acquired the hotel in 1937 and remodeled it, adding a miniature golf course. During the 1950s, the Horn Springs Hotel burned. Recent efforts have been made by Cumberland University students and researchers to conduct an archeological dig to document more about the history of the site.

27.4 **HAMILTON SPRINGS** – Hamilton Springs was the nearby competitor of Horn Springs. In 1898, Jim Hamilton opened his own resort just to the east of the Horn Springs Hotel. With visitors coming to the new hotel, a train stop for each was operated. From the beginning, there was a war over the water rights with Hamilton claiming that Horn's water was actually coming from his spring.

The Hamilton Springs Hotel burned during the 1930s and was never rebuilt, while the Horn Springs Hotel struggled through the next several decades. The land around the old Hamilton Springs Hotel is now the Hamilton Station

Apartments, a growing suburban development that is part of the Hamilton Springs Subdivision.

Early maps show a cinder platform at Hamilton Springs, located on the south side of the tracks.

28.6 **EGANVILLE** – There was once a siding on the south side of the mainline at Eganville, located just west of today's Maple Hill Road, shown as Sharon Road in 1918. The siding was extended 689 feet eastward on November 28, 1931, but fully retired on March 29, 1933. A waiting shed also once existed here, located on the north side of the tracks just west of the road crossing. Apparently, there were once plans for more because the railroad had a much wider right-of-way through here. Today, this is where the railroad really starts to enter Lebanon.

While Eganville doesn't seem to exist today, Egan does have some recognition. It is reported to be at an elevation of 558 feet. Jesse Eagan moved to this area in the early 1800s. Several members of the family still owned land in the area during the early 1900s.

29.8 **PENNVILLE** – There was once a small waiting shed on the north side of the track just east of today's Babb Drive. A short spur to the south serves a local farm co-op. Just to the east, a much longer track – a one-mile spur known as the City Track – serves several shippers in an industrial park to the north.

30.5 **BARTONS CREEK BRIDGE** – The railroad bridge is a seven-span deck plate girder structure. Bartons Creek, originally Barton's Creek, was named for Samuel Barton, a frequent visitor to the area. It is believed that Samuel Barton first arrived in the area as a part of the Henry Scraggins party of 1765, a rough survey that led Daniel Boone to check out the area a year later. Barton eventually acquired a great deal of land along the creek, which he named for himself. Bartons Creek flows off of Hickory Ridge and forms the

Eastern Division – Nashville to Monterey

west side of historic Lebanon, before heading on north about six miles to the Cumberland River.

Reportedly, the first water mill built in today's Wilson County was established on Bartons Creek by Thomas Conyer about 1796. Its location was about three miles to the northwest of downtown Lebanon, not far from here.

Just east of Bartons Creek is the Don Fox Community Park. The park includes a jogging trail, wading pool, a 25,000 square foot playground, and a number of pavilions.

31.2   CP WEST LEBANON – This location is just east of the Castle Heights Avenue grade crossing. It also marks the east end of the Nashville Subdivision and the west end of the Lebanon Subdivision, stretching all the way to Monterey. For eastbound trains, this location is marked "Yard Limit" and "End CTC." West of here to Nashville, the railroad uses CTC (Centralized Traffic Control) signaling, controlled by the railroad's dispatchers. From here to Milepost 35.0 trains operate under Yard Limits rules. This means that train speeds are limited and they must be able to stop short of any obstruction such as an open switch or another train.

31.6   MCS LEBANON – This is the modern *Music City Star* (MCS) passenger station for the Lebanon area. This location was once a factory, replaced by the current 140 parking spaces and station at 334 W. Baddour Parkway. There is also a 1200-foot siding on the south side of the mainline, allowing trains to pass passenger trains serving the station. The siding begins on the west end near Milepost 31.4, where a siding was extended to on September 3, 1902. The east end of today's complex is at the grade crossing for Greenwood Street, which was once Barton's Lane. In the 1920s, the siding continued to a location east of the Lebanon Depot.

The *Music City Star* stations feature small but ornate shelters, such as this one at Lebanon. Photo by Sarah Jennings.

31.7 LEBANON WOOLEN MILLS – There was once a track heading off to the northeast at this location, serving the Lebanon Woolen Mills complex. Until 1998, this was a major business and employer in Lebanon. The mill opened ninety years earlier when Dr. Howard K. Edgerton found himself with an excess of livestock, payment for many of his medical services. He realized that if he could create a demand for sheep and wool, he could turn much of his barter into cash.

Today, the rail spur is gone and the woolen mill is now the Mill at Lebanon, an events, retail and business office facility.

Eastern Division – Nashville to Monterey

The former Lebanon Woolen Mills is a noted landmark as trains enter Lebanon from the west. Photo by Sarah Jennings.

32.0 LEBANON – To the north (compass east) is the former Tennessee Central Lebanon station, once serving both passengers and freight. Located just south of Gay Street and a block west of downtown, this white wooden building is still used by the Nashville & Eastern.

The former Tennessee Central Lebanon Station stands next to the tracks. Photo by Sarah Jennings.

Various telegraph call letters were used at Lebanon, including BO and BN. A block east at 121 South Cumberland Avenue is the former NC&StL station, built of brick in 1916 and today used by Shenandoah Mills. Shenandoah Mills is a custom dry mix manufacturer, producing products such as biscuit mixes, pancake mixes, cornbread mixes, and fish and chicken batters.

The NC&StL station still stands on South Cumberland Avenue in Lebanon. Photo by Sarah Jennings.

The NC&StL had several spur tracks into the east side of their station and Shenandoah Mills sits on the site of the small railroad yard that was once here. On July 15, 1935, the Tennessee Central bought the Lebanon area tracks of the "NC&StL Ry. Co." Tennessee Central maps also show that the NC&StL had an "old depot" on the mainline between Cumberland and College Streets.

The Tennessee Central had a small but busy rail yard at Lebanon. There was a series of stock pens here and livestock loading was common almost until the end of the railroad. Local factories also kept the railroad busy. In 1903, a siding was built for the Fakes Coal & Lumber Company. Fakes & Hooker Lumber Company still exists in downtown Lebanon. Today, most of the rail activity is east of town.

Fakes & Hooker Lumber has been a customer of the railroad since 1903. Photo by Sarah Jennings.

Lebanon was founded in 1802. Reportedly the location was chosen due to the excellent water and timber in the area. The name Lebanon came from the cedars in the area, referencing the biblical cedars of Lebanon. Early landowners included Neddy Jacobs, who reportedly built the first cabin in Lebanon, James Meneis, who owned much of the area land, and John Impson, who built the first house after the town was laid out. The first lots sold for thirteen dollars each. The first store, hotel, jail, and court house opened in Lebanon in 1803. Lebanon was officially incorporated in 1807.

Today, Lebanon has a population of about 30,000 and serves as the county seat of Wilson County. It is the corporate home of Cracker Barrel and is where Dan Evins started the restaurant chain in 1969.

32.3 **SINKING CREEK BRIDGE** – This timber bridge sits on a series of concrete piers. Sinking Creek is channeled through much of Lebanon, often using tunnels under buildings. It eventually flows to the northwest where it enters Bartons Creek. Sinking Creek has also used the name of Town Creek.

Just across Cumberland Street was once a switch that connected to a series of tracks that ran north along Cumberland and served the NC&StL station. Trains heading east from Sinking Creek start climbing grades of up to 1.9%. The grades last for almost ten miles to near Cherry Valley.

32.8   N&K JUNCTION – This was once the junction with the NC&StL, named for the Nashville & Knoxville Railroad which, being chartered in 1884, was the start of the Tennessee Central Railway. This area was a network of tracks as both railroads served area shippers. The NC&StL had a spur track up Cumberland Street, with a wye near where it hit their mainline. With the track now gone, Tennessee Boulevard and Leeville Pike now use the railroad's grade through town.

33.2   NERR/MCS MECHANICAL FACILITY – To the south are the shops and servicing facilities for the Nashville & Eastern and the *Music City Star*.

The *Music City Star* shares mechanical facilities with the Nashville & Eastern just east of Lebanon. Photo by Sarah Jennings.

Eastern Division – Nashville to Monterey

To compass east is the Wilson County Fairground. Among the facilities there is the Fiddlers Grove Historic Village. Among the collection of buildings is the former NC&StL Tucker's Gap Depot, bought at auction in 2005. Tucker's Gap was located southwest of Lebanon on the original line between Nashville and Lebanon.

34.0 EAST LEBANON – Look for where the railroad passes under Interstate 40, which stretches from Barstow, California, to Wilmington, North Carolina. Sources say that the Interstate Highway is 2555 miles long. There are more miles of I-40 in Tennessee than in any other state – 455 miles. It also passes through the three largest cities in the state: Memphis, Nashville and Knoxville.

Just east of here the railroad has a short siding to the north and an industrial lead to the south into a large industrial park full of distribution centers. The siding is 1500 feet long. Heading east, the railroad becomes very rural for most of the rest of the way to Monterey.

At Milepost 35.0, look for the sign reading "Enter Watertown Block" for eastbound trains.

The Tennessee Central Railway Museum operates trips all year long, as shown by this train near East Lebanon on January 18, 2003. Photo by Barton Jennings.

37.3   SPRING CREEK BRIDGE – As with many streams in the area, Spring Creek forms in the low hills to the south and west and then flows about ten miles to the north to the Cumberland River.

The community of Spring Creek once existed in this area, but it is considered to be a ghost town today. The first area settlement was in 1799 and soon after there was at least one gristmill on Spring Creek.

37.5   GREENWOOD – Greenwood was once a busy station, created by the Nashville & Knoxville Railroad in the middle of a mile-long flat spot of the climb to Cherry Valley. Its stock pens were enlarged in April 1919 but were retired on March 17, 1930. Two months later on May 31, 1930, the combination passenger and freight station was retired. Maps show that a short spur once served the stock pens and that a mail crane also stood here. All were just west of today's Greenwood Road grade crossing.

39.3   SHOP SPRINGS – The community of Shop Springs was established in 1850 when a post office was located here on the land of Thomas Waters at the junction of a Spring Creek tributary and the Lebanon & Sparta Pike. Within a few decades, the community consisted of about 75 inhabitants, two stores, two blacksmith shops, one wagon shop, one cooper shop, a wool carding factory, school house, and two physicians. Today this area is a cluster of houses and a local café.

There was a passing siding on the north side of the mainline at Shop Springs. On November 19, 1921, it was officially extended 336 feet west, making it 2290 feet long. It was further extended eastward on December 31, 1923. There was a depot on the north side of the siding just east of Young Road. It was later replaced by a passenger shelter.

The grade heading east stiffens at Shop Springs, being as much as 2.0% when it reaches the peak of the grade near Milepost 42, at an elevation of 790 feet.

43.0 BUCK LEG CREEK BRIDGE – This large culvert was once a bridge. On November 16, 1923, the railroad built a new 32-foot-long ballast deck trestle here. The next year, on March 10th, the Tennessee Central noted that it retired a bridge at the same location. There is no record explaining the name of Buck Leg Creek, but records and maps of the Tennessee Central clearly show the name for this small stream. However, many current maps and documents show it to be Beech Log Creek. You have to wonder if it was an accent issue, a poorly written note, or a change to make it more appealing. Some later Tennessee Central track charts show the stream to be Round Lick Creek. Also in this area is a Buckley Creek, which Tennessee Central track charts show the railroad crosses at Milepost 43.9.

43.4 CHERRY VALLEY – The station here was once just west of the grade crossing with Beech Log Road – the old Cherry Valley & Statesville Road. A passenger shelter was built here on October 30, 1920, made from "1/2 box car body." A new "Passenger Shelter" was built on June 14, 1934, replacing the "half car body Pass. Station."

Cherry Valley was established in 1848 on land owned by Wilson T. Cartwright. Its location on the Lebanon & Sparta Pike made it a local center for commerce. Today it is a suburb of nearby Watertown.

Less than a mile to the north is the Stardust Drive-In Theatre. This is a two-screen drive-in built in 2003. The theatre operates from the "first weekend in March (weather permitting) through the end of November."

45.0 WATERTOWN – The first building at Watertown was a fort built in 1780 by Captain Thomas Thompson of North Carolina. The fort was built to provide protection for travelers on the Holstein Trail, and stood near where three small streams converged to form Round Lick Creek. Watertown, originally known as Three Forks, was created on a Revolutionary War grant to Colonel Archibald Lytle and his brother William. The Waters family also moved here about 1790. Eventually, Wilson L. Waters opened a store, and in 1845 the post office at Three Forks relocated to the Waters store. Waters soon opened businesses on his farm, including a sawmill, gristmill and blacksmith shop. This was the start of today's Watertown. The village more than doubled in size soon after the Nashville & Knoxville Railroad built a depot in 1885. The current downtown is mostly brick buildings, resulting from the 1903 fire that burned most of town. Much of the downtown area is now the Watertown Commercial Historic District, listed on the National Register of Historic Places. The population is currently about 1500.

During the early 1900s, Watertown was a significant shipping center on the railroad. Industries included the Watertown Milling Company, the W. E. Stephens Manufacturing Company, the Wilson County Garment Company, Moer's Hosiery Mill, and the Williams Pin Mill Manufacturing Company. For many years there was also a Carnation Company Milk Plant at Watertown, supported by a large number of local dairy cattle. A small brick kiln was also in operation in 1913, producing brick for local construction.

Watertown has seen more than its fair share of cameras and events over the years. It was the location of filming for *Dark Harvest 3: Skarecrow*, as well as the music video for Darius Rucker's *Wagon Wheel*. Watertown is also part of the spring and fall "Mile-Long Yard Sale," which attracts shoppers from across the region. The Tennessee Central Railway Museum runs trips to this event and operates several other trips to and from Watertown.

Railroad

As already stated, Watertown was once a busy railroad town. There were a number of tracks here, many located near the south end of Depot Street. A 1900-foot long siding still exists. Located on the north side of the tracks, there is a long station platform for the excursion trains. Stock

Eastern Division – Nashville to Monterey

pens and a scales track were also once at this location. In early 1922, the railroad installed a new 60,000-gallon water tank, a 10' x 16' frame pump house, and an automatic pumping unit. During March 1923, the depot burned and was officially retired on March 22nd. On January 5, 1924, the railroad replaced two boxcar body tool houses and built a new 14' x 20' tool house. Two days later on January 7, 1924, the railroad opened its new brick combination station measuring 23' x 150' x 15' with two platforms measuring 16' x 23' and 8' x 120'. This station was torn down in 1972.

About 1915, the railroad moved a turntable from Lebanon to Watertown. The turntable is an interesting part of the railroad history of Watertown as it was here to turn the locomotive operating the Watertown to Nashville daily train, a train basically used as a commuter train by locals. The railroad retired its turntable and turntable track at Watertown on February 28, 1924. The remains of the turntable can still be seen if you know where to look.

In 1903, the Tennessee Central operated train #8 from Carthage Junction (5:40am) to Nashville (8:00am), then train #7 back from Nashville (4:30pm) to Carthage Junction (7:00pm). At the same time, train #5 operated from Nashville (10:30am) to Lebanon (11:45am), with train #6 departing at 1:15pm and arriving back at Nashville at 2:30pm. By 1908, #7/#8 were based in Lebanon, making a morning roundtrip, and then made a second afternoon round trip as #9/#10.

45.2 ROUND LICK CREEK BRIDGE – This 96-foot bridge consists of two through plate girder spans. The town of Watertown started here due to the mills located on this stream. The stream flows north to the Cumberland River. At one time, the community of Round Lick was located several miles north of Watertown.

48.5 QUARRY – In 1926, the Tennessee Central approved an Authorization for Expenditure (AFE) for a track to a rock crusher at this location. It also included plans for a rock crushing plant, bins, engine house, store house, and other facilities. A great deal of new ballast and fill material from this quarry was placed along the railroad in the late 1920s. The rock crushing plant was retired on May 13, 1930.

49.5 HOLMES GAP – Just west of the former station location of Holmes Gap, the railroad makes a sharp 135-degree turn using a five-degree curve where eastbound trains going northeast are suddenly heading south. Records of the Tennessee Central show that on April 26, 1919, the railroad built a frame passenger shelter measuring 12' x 13' x 8', as well as a 4' x 140' cinder platform at Holmes Gap. There was also once a spur track here, located just railroad-east of the shelter.

Records show little about the name Holmes Gap except that there was a post office here in the late 1800s and also a Holmes Gap School. The location is listed on several birdwatching websites as a great place to look for Eastern Bluebirds and Indigo Buntings.

50.1 COUNTY LINE – This is the county line between Wilson County (to the west) and Smith County (to the east). Look for the small grade crossing which was once the junction between Brush Creek & Commerce Road to the east and Commerce & Alexandria Road to the south. Today, it is Holmes Gap Road.

Wilson County was created on October 26, 1799, from parts of Sumner County. The name reportedly honored Major David Wilson, a Revolutionary War veteran and statesman. When the railroads arrived, the county became a temporary center of logging and lumber. Its county seat is Lebanon.

Smith County was also created from Sumner County on October 26, 1799. The name honors Daniel Smith – Revolutionary War veteran, Secretary of the Southwest Territory, and U.S. Senator. Daniel Smith is also credited with making the first map of Tennessee. Carthage is the county seat, a location once known as William Walton's ferry and tavern site. In 1804, it was chosen by a vote over Bledsoesborough.

51.5   BRUSH CREEK BRIDGE – This small 26-foot-long trestle crosses Brush Creek, which closely follows the railroad in this area. Heading east, the railroad is steadily dropping at grades between 0.4% and 0.9%. It crosses Brush Creek four times in approximately one-half mile. The other crossings are at Mileposts 51.6 (26-foot-long trestle), 51.9 (43-foot trestle), and 52.0 (85 feet long).

52.6   NORTH ALEXANDRIA – North Alexandria, known as Brush Creek by the railroad before 1923 (explaining its telegraph call letters of BC), was an important station in the area. The larger community of Alexandria is located about three miles south and Brush Creek/North Alexandria served as its rail station. The area around Brush Creek figures prominently in the early history of the area. The first Baptist Church in the area was started here on May 29, 1802, by Cantrell Bethel. The church grew over the years and supported other area churches in their growth by training a number of preachers.

As the railroad was built through the area, Brush Creek received a post office in 1879. In 1896, the post office was renamed Tuxedo for a few months before going back to Brush Creek in early 1897. The post office was renamed North Alexandria in 1923, but went back to the Brush Creek name in 1926. A post office is still here and the Brush Creek community remains, but is unincorporated.

Brush Creek had a short 750-foot-long siding on the south side of the mainline with a spur off of it. The spur still exists, serving a propane facility. A stock pen once stood here, replaced in February 1937, and later removed. The station of the original Nashville & Knoxville was replaced in 1910, and the new station received electric lights on June 5, 1920. The tool house at North Alexandria was replaced with a frame tool house measuring 12' x 14' x 10' located on the south side of the mainline. None of these structures exist at North Alexandria today.

54.3 NORTH FORK BRUSH CREEK BRIDGE – This bridge was replaced in September 1930 with a "ballast deck bridge 40' long on stone and concrete abutments and piers." According to maps of the Tennessee Central, the North Fork comes in from the north and flows into Brush Creek just south of here. Brush Creek then flows east a short distance before pouring into Hickman Creek

55.7 SYKES – Sykes was named for the Sykes family, decedents of Joshua Sykes Sr., who was born in Norfolk County, Virginia, in 1749 and moved here about 1800. Even though the Sykes family was here by that time, the community seems to have originally been known as Bairdsville. The *Tennessee State Gazetteer and Business Directory for 1860-61* stated that Bairdsville was "A post office of Smith county in the northeast central part of the State about 50 miles east from Nashville." Records show that the Bairdsville post office opened in 1855 and closed in 1860.

A new post office opened here on April 9, 1886, as Sykes, about the time the community changed its name from Bairdsville to Sykes. The post office finally closed on August 31, 1957. The center of the community was across Hickman Creek to the south. In 1920, the first road bridge was built across the creek, described as the "one lane Sykes bridge." At the railroad, there was once a small cinder platform and a mail crane, with trains stopping only when flagged.

Little remains of Sykes today. To the south are the remains of the old stone general store, almost completely overgrown with vegetation.

55.8 HICKMAN CREEK BRIDGE – This 101-foot-long, deck plate girder bridge consists of two spans. That is Sykes Road to the north, and on a Tennessee Central map dated

1918 the land in this area is shown to belong to W. E. Sykes, apparently William Elias (Buck) Sykes.

Hickman Creek forms a few miles west of Alexandria, Tennessee, flows east to merge with Goose Creek at Alexandria, and then flows north to near here. It then flows to the northeast another ten miles before entering the Caney Fork River east of Gordonsville. It passes through Hickman, Tennessee, and both were named for members of the Hickman family.

56.2   HICKMAN CREEK BRIDGE – After passing through open pasture in the horseshoe bend of Hickman Creek, the railroad again uses a two-span deck plate girder bridge to cross the creek. Railroad records show it to be 102 feet long.

East of here, the railroad cuts through more pastures while Hickman Creek curves to the south. Near Milepost 56.9, the railroad and creek come back together. Here, the creek has a history of washing out the railroad grade, so notice the retaining walls and stone rip-rap that have been placed to prevent this from happening. The grade makes a steady drop heading east, with the track dropping between 0.3% and 0.9%. A sudden and short drop of 1.34% happens just west of Hickman.

The late 1920s was a good time for the railroad and a number of improvements were made along the entire railroad. In this area, the former cinder ballast was removed and replaced with slag ballast. Many of the smaller wooden trestles also received additional stringers while steel bridges were strengthened to handle heavier train loads.

58.6   HICKMAN – Hickman was once a small community supporting area farmers. It had a canning factory, stock pens, and the Hickman Milling Company. The depot was modernized in 1920 when electric lights were installed. Tennessee Central records state that "the 514' Hickman Mill spur track" was retired on June 10, 1929. The siding on the north side of the mainline has also been retired, and in 1940, the passenger/freight station was retired and replaced with a 6' x 14' passenger shelter. Today, the stock pens and canning factory are also gone.

Records show that the Hickman post office opened in 1886. The community was located on Hickman Creek and named for Colonel Thomas Hickman. Today, Hickman is a rural community spread out on both banks of Hickman Creek, named for Edwin Hickman who helped do the original surveys in the area during the 1780s and 1790s. Thomas and Edwin were brothers who fought in the Revolutionary War and later moved to this area.

60.4 WEST SWITCH CARTHAGE SIDING – This is the western limits of the Carthage Junction complex. There is a 2100-foot siding here that has existed since March 1919. The siding, located on the south side of the mainline, ends just before the actual junction. When built, it was 2515 feet long, but was shortened on the east end. The railroad operates under Yard Limits from Milepost 60.0 to 61.0 to allow for switching and to protect freight trains going on or coming off the Carthage Subdivision.

For photographers or those wanting to photograph the train they are riding, this is a favorite spot as the train makes several long curves while passing through open fields.

An eastbound excursion train approaches Carthage Junction in 2016. Photo by Barton Jennings.

Eastern Division – Nashville to Monterey

60.8 CARTHAGE JUNCTION – This junction, known initially as Gordonsville, then Hickman Creek Junction, then simply Hickman Junction and then Junction, connects the mainline of the Nashville & Eastern with the Carthage Subdivision, which heads north about seven miles to serve several major customers near Carthage, Tennessee. The name Carthage Junction was in use by 1902 and the telegraph code was simply J. **For information on the Carthage Branch, see page 177.**

The Carthage Junction switch is still busy due to the industries on the Carthage Branch. Photo by Sarah Jennings.

The railroad has always had a number of facilities at Carthage Junction. There was once a wye here, but it was removed many years ago. A depot stood between the mainline and the branchline at the southwest switch, built in the early 1900s. A fire extinguisher was installed in the depot in 1925, electric lights went in during November 1927, and a desk phone updated the facilities in November 1928. An oil house stood across the branchline where a short spur track exists today, the remains of a short siding.

The station was active with a train order semaphore for many years. The station was rebuilt in the mid-1960s with a number of improvements, but it soon closed with the end of the Tennessee Central. It was eventually sold and moved to Interstate 40 at the Highway 56 exit. It was used by several businesses, including the Gordonsville Motor Company. It was again abandoned and sat empty for a number of years. Preservationists from the area took interest and have acquired the building, with it being donated by the developers of the Taco Bell® at the site. The station was moved three miles further north to South Carthage on October 23, 2014. It now sits across the street from the end of a rails-to-trails path. During late 2017, the station was being rebuilt with plans to use it as an "internet café, train and history museum, and local arts gallery."

A standard section house was built here in late 1923, just north of the depot. It measured 26' x 13' x 10-1/2' with a wing measuring 13' x 11' x 10-1/2'. In September 1927, the section house had a porch and shed room added. In November, electric lights were also installed. Railroad maps show that there were at least three section houses here at one time. There were also several tool houses in the area.

Heading east, the railroad climbs over several ridges, slowly gaining elevation from 507 feet at Carthage Junction to 580 feet east of Lancaster and then back down to 518 feet at Buffalo Valley. Grades along this section are generally mild, but some do peak at 2.15%. This explains why many trains during the steam era picked up a helper here. These helpers were based at Monterey and would run to here, turn, and then shove trains east up Silver Point Hill. When no longer needed, the helper would cut off and follow the freight on in to Monterey. A number of locomotive servicing facilities once were in the Carthage Junction area to support these helpers and the trains that faced the challenging climb eastward.

61.1 HICKMAN CREEK BRIDGE – Less than a mile north of here, Hickman Creek flows into the Caney Fork River.

Eastern Division – Nashville to Monterey

The railroad crosses Hickman Creek on a relatively new bridge consisting of deck plate girder spans sitting on tall concrete piers. It replaced the original timber trestle bridge in 1998, allowing heavier trains to operate east of here.

Just east of the bridge stood a water tower, and then a coaling and sand station. The original water tower was replaced in November 1928 with a new 20' x 24' redwood tank. At least three coaling stations were in this area. The first was retired in 1923 when the Tennessee Central reported the opening of a new "coaling and sand station and coal chute spur track 371' long." Details about this new complex included an 11' x 19' engine house and a sand house measuring 10' x 12-1/2'. Reportedly, a dwelling for the caretaker was also retired at the time. A fire extinguisher was installed at the coal chute in January 1925. In June 1937, the coal chute had electric lights installed. A fire destroyed the second coaling tower and sand house and a replacement went into service in April 1946.

For trains heading east, the Yard Limits end at Milepost 61.0. Look for the "Enter Silver Point" block sign. This block is short and just covers the climb to Silver Point, allowing trains to double the hill (make multiple trips to get their entire train to the top of the hill) if needed.

62.1   BOLDENS BRANCH BRIDGE – Most modern maps show this to be Bolling or Boiling Branch, while older maps show it as Boldens Branch. Based upon some birth documents, Boldens Branch could have also been a small community in the area. The railroad crosses the stream and local roadway using a series of deck plate girder spans topped with concrete decks, sitting on cut stone piers.

Boldens Branch, or more historically Bolden's Branch, starts about five miles to the south and flows due north to here, and then another mile north where it enters the Caney Fork River. For the several miles just south of here, Boldens Branch, or Bolling Branch, flows immediately adjacent to the Lancaster Highway, also known as Tennessee Highway 141.

63.5 STEWARTS – J. W. Stewart once owned a great deal of land in this area, divided through the family over the years. Nearby is the Stewart Cemetery. There doesn't seem to have been any railroad facilities here, but crews knew the location because heading east, the railroad comes beside the Caney Fork River. The river is to the north while a long rock bluff is very close to the train to the south.

64.4 SEBOWISHA – For a number of years, a lodge operated for the owners and management of the Tennessee Central reportedly stood on a hillside at Sebowisha. A small cinder platform once stood on the south side of the track just west of the Smith Fork bridge. A post office opened here in 1910 but closed in 1912.

"Mineral Products Along the Tennessee Central Railroad" discussed the dark-blue limestone in the area, visible in several cuts along the railroad. The report has several interesting comments, including that "many of the strata have a strong petroleum smell when freshly broken" and that a second seam of limestone contains "enough phosphatic material to constitute a commercial blue phosphate rock."

A local complication is that numerous area signs use different spellings of the Sebowisha name. There is also a great deal of confusion about the name. Some credit it to an early name for the area while others try to make it the name of someone who lived nearby or an Indian name. A tale sometimes told is that a local railroad worker would walk the tracks here, looking for fallen rocks, with his two dogs Sebo and Wisha. No documentation has ever been found for any of these theories.

The name Sebowisha is found in Henry Wadsworth Longfellow's *The Song of Hiawatha* where it refers to a brook by that name that teaches its waves to "flow in music." Some doubt whether a name from a poem is the source, but the owners of the railroad were well educated and the poem was a favorite across the country at the time. The name Sebowisha was used in several places nationwide, generally for property along small streams. Longfellow's poem also played a significant role in the railroad industry as the Chicago, Milwaukee, St. Paul & Pacific Railroad (known as the Milwaukee Road) named its major trains Hiawatha starting in 1935.

64.5 **SMITH FORK BRIDGE** – Alternate names for this stream include Smith Fork Creek, Smiths Fork, and the Smith Fork of the Caney Fork River. The creek flows into the Caney Fork River just north of the bridge, built of several deck plate girder spans on tall concrete piers. Legend has it that the stream is called Smith Fork Creek instead of Smith Fork River because it is only 99 miles long. Reportedly, early standards said that a river had to be 100 miles long.

A Tennessee Central map from 1918 shows that much of the land east of the bridge was owned by various members of the Lancaster family, but mostly by Henry Lancaster.

Just west of the bridge, look for the Louisville & Nashville wood chip car over the railroad embankment to the south. Sometimes when a car derails like this and it is near the end of its useable life, it is just left where it winds up.

65.6 **LANCASTER** – The Lancaster family obtained a great deal of land in this area, located between the Smiths Fork and the Caney Fork. John Lancaster operated a mill on Smith Fork, and the town of Lancaster was laid out nearby in 1817 on property belonging to either Richard or John Lancaster. The Lancaster family still lives in the area and their farm has been recognized as a Tennessee Century Farm.

Over the years, the post office at Lancaster has opened and closed a number of times. The first post office opened on May 18, 1821, but closed soon after the end of the Civil War on December 22, 1866. The post office reopened for much of the 1870s (October, 1874 - July 28, 1879) and then again during the late 1880s (October 27, 1885 - October 28, 1887) before reopening again on December 28,

1888. The post office again closed on March 4, 2011. The Lancaster school closed almost eighty years earlier in 1932. Today's population is less than 400.

In December 1918, the Lancaster depot was enlarged with the existing 18' x 18' freight section extended with a 20' x 18' addition. The station had a new 12' x 134' dirt and cinder platform installed, replacing a much smaller platform. The station received a company telephone on November 17, 1928, appropriate for a regular passenger train stop. Besides the depot, there were a number of other facilities at Lancaster. The section house was retired in 1925, the spur track in September 1934, and the stock pens in July 1937.

East of Lancaster at Milepost 66.2, the Lancaster & Buffalo Valley Road once crossed the railroad. Little remains of this road except for a trace through the fields and woods to the north. Further east, the Caney Fork River is immediately adjacent to the railroad. East of this, the grade of the Lancaster & Buffalo Valley Road is again immediately to the north, before crossing the railroad about Milepost 68.

Heading east, the railroad runs on a narrow ledge with bluffs to the north, while the Caney Fork River is again close to the railroad below and to the south.

68.9 CANEY FORK – Look for the open pasture lands just west of the Caney Fork River bridge. Until the late 1930s, this was the station location of Caney Fork, Tennessee. Records show that the first station was a car body, but later a small passenger shelter was built. It was finally officially retired on August 13, 1937. A short passing siding once existed on the south side of the mainline, shortened during July 1918. The 744-foot siding was fully retired during January 1929.

69.1 CANEY FORK RIVER BRIDGE – This well-photographed five-span bridge, located just south of the Interstate 40 rest area, is actually a mix of bridge designs and eras. The original bridge likely dates from the 1880s or 1890s and was built with lighter pin-connected beams with ornamental portal bracing. Today, the three through truss spans from this era are all reinforced with various types of steel and timber bents added under the floorbeams to carry today's heavier railroad loads. The two heavier through truss spans were ordered by the Southern Railway (during its temporary lease of the Tennessee Central) and installed in 1907 by the Virginia Bridge & Iron Company. These two spans replaced a swing span, once used to open the bridge whenever steamboat service operated on the Caney Fork River. The swing span washed out in flooding in 1902 and a series of timber trestles were used until the new bridge spans were installed.

Tennessee Central 5764E pulls an excursion train eastbound across the Caney Fork River Bridge in 1999. Photo by Barton Jennings.

The Virginia Bridge & Iron Company was incorporated in Roanoke, Virginia, in 1895. Initially it designed and built lightweight highway bridges, but soon grew into heavyweight railroad bridges. Its products primarily were used by railroads in the southern part of the United States, in Mexico, and in a number of Caribbean and Central American countries. J. P. Morgan's American Bridge

Company eventually acquired the Virginia Bridge & Iron Company.

The Caney Fork River is shown to be 143 miles long and is dammed twice to form Center Hill Lake and Great Falls Lake. The river forms to the northwest of Crossville and heads generally west to exit the Cumberland Plateau. A number of area streams flow into the Caney Fork, and its waters are popular for canoeing and kayaking. The name Caney Fork comes from the large number of dense canebrakes that once grew along the river's shoreline.

The Caney Fork River was once an important source of income – the pearl industry. The mussels in the river were an early source of food, but pearls were discovered by the 1870s, the first reportedly near Sebowisha. The industry was very profitable by the 1880s, with the best pearls selling for $200 to $300 each. Reports state that a yellow mussel locally known as the lake mussel was considered to contain the best pearls. There were also attempts to use the mussel shells to make buttons, but without the success of the pearl business.

At this location, the Caney Fork River is the county line between **Smith County**, to the west, and **Putnam County** to the east. Putnam County has a complicated history. It was first created on February 2, 1842, from parts of Jackson, Overton, Fentress, and White Counties. However, in 1844, an injunction charged that it violated state constitutional requirements, making some of the counties involved too small to meet legal requirements. Because of this, the Tennessee general assembly reestablished the county in 1854, but Putnam County's borders were still disputed for decades. The name Putnam comes from General Israel Putnam, a general in the American Revolutionary War who earlier was a hero in the French and Indian War.

The Lancaster & Buffalo Valley Road once passed under the east end of the bridge. Today's more modern Medley Amonette Road (Highway 96) is just to the south and crosses the railroad at grade a few hundred yards to the east.

Eastern Division – Nashville to Monterey

For those who have seen the movie *The Green Mile*, this is the filming location where John Coffey is discovered with the bodies of the two little girls. The movie was mostly filmed in and around Nashville.

70.0 **BUFFALO VALLEY** – Today, Buffalo Valley is a small community dominated by a large sand and gravel facility. The railroad once had greater plans for the community, designing a town of 24 lots on three streets (1st, 2nd, and 3rd Streets) along the railroad, with Indian Creek and Farmers Spring Branch to the west and north, respectively. A long siding (1122 feet long thanks to an extension in 1926) once existed on the north side of the mainline along with a short spur track to serve a series of stock pens. The original stock pens were replaced in September, 1926, with three new pens and chutes, each measuring 24' x 32'.

Buffalo Valley was a maintenance-of-way center for the railroad, with several section houses and tool houses. A note dated December 1929 states that the railroad retired four toilets and constructed one double toilet and three single toilets at the section houses. A water well was also built at the west end of the community near Indian Creek. Documents state that the railroad installed a new well and pump in September of 1930 and retired the old pumphouse, then built a new one in November 1931. An automatic electric water pump was installed in 1939. The original oil house was retired in November 1931, but a new underground gasoline tank was installed at the tool house in January 1939. A water tank stood in the same area on the south side of the tracks

The depot at Buffalo Valley, once located on the north side of the mainline, received a fire extinguisher in January of 1925 and a company telephone in May 1927. Its telegraph call letters were BY. The depot was built about 1897 and reportedly had a metal floor in the freight storeroom. The reason for the metal floor were the shipments of barrels of whiskey to the community. Apparently, someone had once crawled under the station and drilled upwards through the floor to tap into one of the barrels. The station was torn down in 1940 and replaced with a small passenger shelter.

Little remains of the once-booming downtown of Buffalo Valley. Photo by Sarah Jennings.

There are no clear records as to who settled the area first, but it is known that Robert King sold land in this area to David Young in 1803. Many early land deeds refer to the South Fork of Indian Creek and the fact that it flows into Caney Fork. It actually enters the Caney Fork just north of the railroad bridge just west of here.

Interviews and stories show that Buffalo Valley was a fairly important business center. It once had a tobacco warehouse where tobacco was sold and shipped out by rail. It was also a livestock center, with cattle sold and shipped by the trainload, and mules and hogs being shipped routinely by rail. Other livestock, such as turkeys, were sold to buyers who used the railroad to ship them to cities across the country. Reports also state that Buffalo Valley once had a bank, four stores, a drug store, a restaurant, a car dealership, two sawmills, and two gristmills. The former Buffalo Valley School, now used as a community center and library, is listed on the National Register of Historic Places.

For trains heading east, the grade stiffens to 1% or more, with several locations showing 3%. This five-mile-long grade is known as Silver Point Hill. The siding at Buffalo Valley, located at about 528 feet above sea level, was often used to double the hill (make multiple trips to get their entire train to the top of the hill) when helper locomotives were not available. Even during diesel days, doubling the hill was a common activity.

While downtown Buffalo Valley was once a busy place, today it is mostly a collection of abandoned store buildings. Photo by Sarah Jennings.

71.7 ALCORN SIDING – The property here was once owned by Robert Simpson Alcorn. There was a siding here for a number of years, but only a wide grade exists today. There is a farmhouse and barn to the south at the Alcorn Cemetery Road grade crossing. Heading east, trains are climbing grades between 1.31% and 1.93%.

The following history of Alcorn Siding comes from *Alcorn Family History*, written in 1975 by Georgia Alcorn Bly. "The railroad company surveyed the track to be built across some of the choice land of the Alcorn farm. They could use the land with the stipulation that the railroad company put in a side track for placing cars for the loading of corn and livestock. They also agreed to provide a flag or whistle stop called Alcorn Siding to take passengers on and off. My grandfather visualized this flag stop would one day develop into a railroad station with a town growing around it. This agreement was never put into writing. It was just a gentlemen's agreement, which lasted as long as Robert Alcorn lived. This flag stop was abandoned, the railroad company saying it lost money on the run. It took too much coal to get the steam up to make the Silver Point hill after the stop. A few years later the side track was taken up and the Alcorn Siding passed into history."

74.6 CENTER HILL DAM ROAD – The railroad passes under Highway 141, also known as Center Hill Dam Road. Center Hill Dam is located a few miles to the west and creates Center Hill Lake from the Caney Fork River. The dam was built in 1948 to produce electricity and prevent flooding. The dam stands 260 feet high and creates a lake 64 miles long. The grades heading east are 2.7%, made even more challenging by the number of curves required to climb the hill.

75.2 SILVER POINT – Silver Point, which used the telegraph code of X, was a major railroad terminal with a freight house (enlarged by 1911), station (remodeled and enlarged in 1926, it also received a telephone in 1927), stock pens

Eastern Division – Nashville to Monterey

(built in 1929 and retired in 1937), and log yard. Located at the top of Silver Point Hill, a five-mile grade ranging between 1% and 3%, the facility was often used to double freight trains, or to service helper locomotives helping trains up the hill. The elevation here is 1043 feet, more than 500 feet higher than nearby Buffalo Valley.

Tennessee Central 5764 reaches the top of Silver Point Hill on a 1999 excursion trip to Cookeville. Photo by Barton Jennings.

There was a siding at Silver Point, located on the north side of the mainline and extended to 2209 feet long in March 1926. The east end still exists as a short spur track. The climb up to Silver Point can still require doubling the hill and the use of the spur track. For eastbound trains, look for the "Exit Silver Point Block" and "Enter Cookeville Block" signs at Milepost 75.0.

There are several versions of how Silver Point received its name. This area, located at the top of the hill leading out of Buffalo Valley, was originally known as "the head of the valley." The name was too long for the Post Office and instructions were sent that the name must include only one or two words. Reportedly, a debate over the name took place on the front porch of Walter Jones' general store. The debate ended when Dr. W. S. Farmer rode up and suggested the name Silver Point. Another version simply states that is was named for the legend of there being silver ore in the surrounding hills.

Today, the businesses here are the several gas stations and convenience stores serving traffic off of adjacent Interstate 40. Silver Point is unincorporated.

77.8 INTERSTATE 40 – The railroad bridges over Interstate 40 using four deck plate girder spans. For years, this bridge was a popular photo location for those chasing the train due to its L&N signs.

An eastbound excursion train in 1999 crosses Interstate 40 using former Pennsylvania Railroad E8A 5764. Photo by Barton Jennings.

78.1 ROBERTS SPUR – There was once a short spur track to the south here. Measuring 267 feet long, it was officially retired on April 2, 1925. Much of the land in this area was once owned by Francis Marion Roberts. Roberts was a member of the 5th Tennessee Calvary (USA). Records show that he deserted in 1863, was captured and then returned to his unit in 1864, promoted to corporal, then deserted again and was recaptured and reduced in rank in 1865.

79.3 BOMA – Boma was clearly a temporary railroad stop that grew beyond the railroad's original plans. Car bodies were originally used for the passenger shelter, freight house and tool house. The car body was replaced with a new frame (12' x 13') passenger shelter with a 4' x 115' cinder platform in January, 1919. The tool house car body was retired in May 1927 and replaced with a 12' x 14' frame tool house. The new tool house was retired in early 1932. The 1930s weren't kind to Boma, and the passenger shelter, along with the car body freight house, were retired in October 1935. There is no information on when the mail crane was retired. All of the facilities were on the north side of the tracks.

This community was originally known as Lee's Field when it was settled soon after the Civil War. Tennessee Central records show that the land in this area once belonged to A. B. Lee, thus the original name for the community. The community grew when the Nashville & Knoxville Railroad arrived in 1890, and a post office soon opened with Pierce Fisher as postmaster. The name Boma reportedly is a misspelling of Andrew J. Boman, an early resident of the area. Some other sources report that the name comes from a town in Africa. The Boma Cemetery, located to the south of the tracks, is now known as the New Home Baptist Church Cemetery.

To the south of the tracks is the New Home Baptist Church Cemetary. Photo by Sarah Jennings.

Boma is located at 1050 feet above sea level and was described in an early geology report as being the location of the only mines which worked the black phosphate found in the area. The mines were located to the south along Mine Lick Creek. The ore was hauled up a 160-foot hill to reach the railroad.

82.1   MINE LICK CREEK BRIDGE – This bridge was built 85 feet long. It has since been filled and replaced with a large culvert. The name Mine Lick Creek dates at least as far back as the 1850s as it is used in several legal documents in 1854 defining the limits of Putnam County.

82.4   BAXTER – The wooden Baxter depot, which was assigned telegraph call letters BX, was once located on the north side of the tracks at 3rd Avenue. For many years the area was a gravel parking lot, across from a series of storefronts. In 2013, a new brick replica train depot opened as a visitors center and museum.

Baxter now features a new brick station, built as a visitors center and regional museum. Photo by Sarah Jennings.

Eastern Division – Nashville to Monterey

A short spur track once looped around the station. There was also a 700-foot siding to the east of here on the south side of the mainline. A set of stock pens, built in 1925 and measuring 32' x 48', were served from this siding. A spur off of the west end of the siding was built in late 1924 to serve Standard Oil. It was retired in April 1934.

This area was originally known as Aiyee (pronounced as Ay-Eye), and sometimes spelled Ai. It then acquired the name Mine Lick from Mine Lick Creek. In 1902, the name was changed to honor Jere Baxter, the builder of the Tennessee Central. The Town of Baxter was originally chartered on March 12, 1915.

A report about Baxter, dating from 1924, stated that Baxter was "a great shipping point. Last year there was shipped to various parts of the United States and Europe 125 cars of pulp wood, 100 cars of acid wood, 150 cars of poles, 200 cars of crossties, 50 cars of lumber and spokes, 35 cars of handles, 30 cars of eggs, 40 cars of poultry, and 25 cars of hogs and cattle." At the same time, Baxter had a bank, an electric light plant, a grocery store, a telephone exchange with "one long distance service with copper circuit," a Western Union Telegraph office, six general stores, a number of boarding houses, and a flour exchange.

Ex-PRR E8A #5764 pulled an excursion train eastward through Baxter, Tennessee, in 1999. Photo by Barton Jennings.

Baxter is at the bottom of grades from both east and west. Located at 1022 feet, grades in both directions are as much as 1.5% to 2.0%. The population in 2010 was 1365 and much of the business has moved south to Interstate 40 at a place known as Baxter Junction. However, most of the historic storefronts still stand along the tracks.

83.5 **BLOOMINGTON** – Bloomington was also known by locals as Blumington and Bloomington Springs, but the railroad used the name Bloomington. The railroad retired the spur track here in July 1938, but a newer siding and industry track exists on the south side of the tracks just west of the station's historic location. Look to the south to see the DelMonaco Winery. This is about where the passenger shelter stood next to the tracks until 1930.

This area was originally owned by Matthew Kuykendall and Ridley Draper. There was a post office here from October 16, 1835, to June 21, 1843, known as Draper Springs. The town took its first step toward developing into a real community in 1865 when Ridley Draper developed a nearby spring into a summer resort. The development, also known as Draper Springs, included a number of cabins and a guest hotel for 200. However, when the post office reopened in 1878, it was named Bloomington. On December 28, 1907, the post office name was changed to Bloomington Springs. In 1925, Bloomington Springs had three stores, two gristmills, a sawmill, two churches, and a school.

84.0 **DELMONACO WINERY & VINEYARDS** – Just to the south of the tracks is DelMonaco Winery, a very popular destination for excursion trains on the railroad. The winery is relatively new; the 52-acre estate was purchased in 2006 and construction on the complex was completed on November 15, 2008. The winery offers a wide variety of dry, semi-sweet, and sweet dessert wines, having almost 30 acres in vineyards. Additionally, the company makes tra-

Eastern Division – Nashville to Monterey

ditional Tennessee and Southern wines using muscadines, peaches, and blackberries.

The DelMonaco Winery is a popular destination for passenger train trips over the Nashville & Eastern Railroad. Photo by Sarah Jennings.

85.1 DOUBLE SPRINGS – This area is known for its mineral springs; at least five have been identified. Look for the grade crossing with Double Springs Road. Also known as Two Springs, the community's claim to fame in the late 1800s was a distillery. Legend has it that the distillery was the only place to buy liquor along the railroad. For many years, passenger trains routinely made long stops here at the request of passengers. This finally ended with a new law in the early 1900s which banned the sale of this alcohol.

The original depot was replaced with a combination station measuring 20' x 64' in October 1926. The stock pens were extended in May 1927 and two new loading platforms were added. However, they were retired and removed in late 1937. An underground gasoline tank was installed at the tool house in January 1939.

Heading east, the railroad again crosses several ridges with grades of as much as 2.0%.

86.3   BROWN'S SPUR – J. W. Brown once owned a great deal of land in this area. While shown as a station location on maps from 1918, railroad records really never show any major facilities here. A short spur to the south is shown on an early track chart, but no stations or other facilities are noted at Brown's Spur, also known as Brown.

The railroad passes under Spring Street. In 1999, Tennessee Central 5764 pulls eastward with an excursion train. Photo by Barton Jennings.

90.0   PSC METALS SPUR – Look for the "Entering Cookeville Yard Limits" if you are heading east. In late 1937, the track from just west of the Spring Street overpass (Milepost 89.6) to Willow Avenue (Milepost 90.1) was realigned, straightening the track and moving it to the south. At the same time, a 1383-foot spur was built into the Whitson Lumber Company facility. In reality, the Whitson spur was the east end of the original mainline, a route that became unused with the track realignment. A spur track also headed to the south at the same location. Whitson Lumber still exists, operating out of their Clarksville, Tennessee, facility. They state that the company was founded in 1913 in Nashville, Tennessee, and still specializes in Appalachian hardwoods. Today, there is still a spur to the south, but now it is used for the loading of scrap metal by PSC Metals.

According to the December 30, 1922, issue of the *Southern Lumberman*, the H. T. Whitson Lumber Company started in Cookeville with a circular sawmill, but soon expanded by acquiring band mills at Algood and Livingston. In addition, the company created the Cookeville Planing Mills. During the 1910s, the company bought virgin hardwood lands across Tennessee, Kentucky, and West Virginia, and opened a number of sawmills to cut the wood. H. T. Whitson built a twenty-four-mile-long pole road (a railroad using logs to run on instead of steel rails) to connect to the Oneida & Western, allowing the cutting of timber of some of the most inaccessible areas of the Cumberland Mountains. *Southern Lumberman* stated that the pole road was the longest ever built. The company also had a large sorting yard at Erlanger, Kentucky, on the Southern Railroad, where "several million feet of soft-textured mountain hardwoods are usually kept for shipment."

90.3 **COOKEVILLE** – Cookeville (CK) was once a major station on the Tennessee Central Railway. A large depot was built just west of Cedar Street on the south side of the mainline (it received three toilets in 1939, indicating the slow progress in the area). Just west of the depot, there was a short siding with a wye off of it, heading to the south to the Cookeville Veneer Company at Spring Street, now the location of the Builders Supply facility. Between the siding and the mainline the railroad had their water tank, tool house, shop, and other facilities. A few blocks further west was a reservoir, once used to supply water to the water tank. The tank was connected to city water in August 1925, and the dam and pumphouse was retired in early 1929.

On the north side of the mainline, where there is now a parking lot, was a railroad freight depot. In 1920, the railroad extended the building by adding a 14' x 90' platform with a 20' ramp to the west end of the structure. On the north side of the freight depot was Butler Spur, a track more than 1000 feet long that served a number of warehouses, a roller mill facility, and the Cookeville Ice & Coal Company.

In the same area, there were spur tracks serving industries such as Gulf Refining, Columbia Produce (1929-1937), J. W. Dubois, and Eller & Olson (1937-1938). In 1928, the railroad installed a new 100-ton track scale and scale track to handle the growing business. However, many of the area industries closed during the 1930s, and even the spur into the Fairgrounds was retired in 1931. East of the depot over the next mile were once a number of rail spurs serving local shippers. These included Menzies Shoe Company, J. A. Isbell, the Fairgrounds, and the railroad stock pens (three new ones built in 1925 replacing the original pens).

Of all of these facilities, only the depot and the western end of the siding still remain. The first two-story frame depot was built in Cookeville by the Nashville & Knoxville Railroad in the 1890s. It was built "one half-mile west of the courthouse" and essentially created a new part of town. The N&K also built the reservoir, a two-story office building, and several repair shops in the area. In 1909, the current red brick station was built by the Tennessee Central. Today, this structure is listed on the National Register of Historic Places and houses the Cookeville Depot Museum. The area around it is known as Cookeville's west side district.

Eastern Division – Nashville to Monterey

The Cookeville station now houses the Depot Museum. Photo by Sarah Jennings.

Just west of the station is a display of railroad equipment that includes a steam locomotive and several cabooses. The steam locomotive is a Baldwin 4-6-0 originally used by the Louisiana & Arkansas Railway, but lettered as Tennessee Central #509. This locomotive was built in 1913 as #403 (later renumbered #509) and operated by the L&A until being sold to the Louisiana & Midland Railroad in 1950. When retired, it was sold to a private collector, and then was sold to the Tennessee Valley Railroad Museum in Chattanooga. In 2002, it was bought by the Friends of the Cookeville Depot Museum and moved here.

The cabooses are Tennessee Central #9828 and Louisville & Nashville #1066. The Tennessee Central caboose was built in the early 1900s and was rebuilt a number of times over the years. It was acquired from a private collector in 1993 and restored to an earlier appearance. The L&N caboose was actually the first piece of the collection acquired by Cookeville. It was donated to the City on December 30, 1985, by the Seaboard Systems. The L&N caboose was built in the 1950s and was retired from rail service in early 1980.

County Seat

When Putnam County was created, the law required that a new county seat be located and built with the name of Cookeville. The name Cookeville came from Richard F. Cooke, who served in the Tennessee Senate from 1851 to 1854. Cooke's efforts were essential in the second effort to create Putnam County. Officials from neighboring counties were selected to locate the county seat, and a relatively flat spot on a hilly tract of land owned by Charles Crook was selected.

Thanks to the position of county seat, Cookeville took on a regional role of importance. With the arrival of the railroad, Cookeville took on a larger role as a manufacturing center. It also became the home of the Tennessee Technological University, located on the north side of the tracks at the east end of town. Today, Cookeville is known as the "Hub of the Upper Cumberlands" and still serves as a center of small manufacturing. Due to its altitude, located a few hundred feet higher than either Nashville or Knoxville, it has a slightly cooler climate, leading to the area becoming a retirement area. Approximately 25,000 people work in Cookeville and its population is slightly more than 30,000.

From Cookeville east to Monterey, a number of organizations have been working to build a trail beside the railroad. Known as the Tennessee Central Heritage Rail Trail, this trail is almost 20 miles long and includes parking, three trail heads, and a paved route designed for "two-way bicycle traffic, low levels of walking and hiking, and equestrian use in designated areas."

While most people will be looking south at the train depot, you should take the time to look north at the classic "Cream City Ice Cream & Coffee House." This building features an iconic sign, leading to the area becoming known as the Cream City local historic district.

Eastern Division – Nashville to Monterey

The sign for the Cream City Ice Cream & Coffee House is a Cookeville landmark. Photo by Sarah Jennings.

92.0　J. ARNOLD SPUR – A short spur was once located to the north, just west of the grade crossing with Brown Avenue, serving land owned by J. Arnold. Just east of here at Milepost 92.4 is a spur to the north. One of the tracks here is often used by the Nashville & Eastern to park a locomotive that is used to switch area industries.

Heading east for the next several miles to Algood there are several marshy areas. Look for the beaver dams that are scattered through them.

94.4　ALGOOD – To the north of the mainline is a 1000-foot siding. The former Algood depot (AD) was on the south side of the mainline, just east of 2nd Avenue. A second siding once looped around the depot to the south. Communications to Algood improved in October 1922 when a telephone was installed at the depot. Stock pens once served local customers from a spur track to the east of the depot, but they were retired in June 1934. There were other spur tracks east of the station to serve several customers, but most were retired during the 1920s and 1930s.

New York Central 4080 (E8A) pulls westbound by the Algood First Freewill Baptist Church while turning an excursion train in 1999. Photo by Barton Jennings.

The first community in this area was White Plains, built around an antebellum plantation in the early 1800s. White Plains was located on the Nashville to Knoxville road, known as the Walton Road, making it an important area community. However, the arrival of the Nashville & Knoxville Railroad just to the north, and the erection of a depot at what became Algood, shifted the center of commerce. Algood was a common name in this area. For example, General Alfred Algood, known as "one of the ablest lawyers this section of the state has produced," was admitted to the Cookeville Bar about 1878. Joel Algood owned the land where the Algood depot was built in the 1880s. This area had been known as Algood's Old Fields, and Algood Mountain was nearby, so the name Algood made sense to the railroad.

With the arrival of the railroad, manufacturing moved to the community, especially businesses related to the local supply of timber. The first major industry was built in 1887 when the Pennock Brothers of Nashville started a spoke mill, which later became the Pennock-Walters Manufacturing Company. This business led to the organization of the community, with Algood being incorporated in 1901. The Pennock-Walters works installed an electric power system in 1908, soon selling electricity to the community, making Algood the first town in Putnam County with electric lights.

Other early industries at Algood included the Algood Column Company, the Speyer Lumber Company, and the Thompson Manufacturing Company (cedar furniture). The H. T. Whitson Lumber Company also had a sawmill here. For farmers, there was the J. B. Ferguson and J. C. Smith flour mill. This mill opened in 1897 and produced almost 100 barrels a day of "Imperial," "Cream of Wheat," and "Mountain Dew Flour." The mill became part of Cookeville Roller Mills in 1910. There was also the Algood Canning Factory during the 1920s, canning tomatoes, blackberries and wild berries. Finally, there was the Algood Produce Company which reportedly handled more poultry than any other business of that nature in the state of Tennessee, making Algood the "Chicken Capitol of the World." The report "Mineral Products Along the Tennessee Central Railroad" stated that, "There are several favorable sites along the Tennessee Central Railroad about two miles east of Algood where good lime quarries, which would contain an unlimited amount of material, with no overburden, could be opened." Rogers Group has operated a quarry in this area since 1970.

The Algood Post Office was established October 17, 1892, and still exists. While much of the industry is now gone, Algood still has a population of about 3500 and appears to be a prosperous little community. CSX abandoned operations of the line east of here in 1987. The line to Monterey has been rebuilt by the Nashville & Eastern.

94.8 OC JUNCTION – A particular track of note that was retired was the "Old Main Track," also known as the TK&N Connection. It was officially retired on January 17, 1936. Located at Milepost 94.8, this track once curved to the north to reach Livingston, Tennessee. The line was created in March, 1904, when a number of local investors organized the Overton County Railroad. The plans were to build a 17.1-mile-long railroad to Livingston to serve shippers in the area. The railroad was completed in early 1906, derailed on its first trip, and never turned a profit.

On August 13, 1912, the railroad was sold to a reorganization committee, which then sold it to the Cincinnati-Nashville Railway Company, which was incorporated on September 30, 1912. The railroad was then leased to the Tennessee, Kentucky & Northern Railroad, organized on August 14, 1912. A unique part of the company was that Mrs. Phebe E. Clark was company president, while C. P. Clark was vice-president and purchasing agent. The company's general offices were listed as being at 1012 Stahlman Building, Nashville, Tennessee.

Online sawmills and products from area farms kept the railroad running, but generally at little more than break-even. Photos show a Shay locomotive, as well as various small steam locomotives, operating on the line. A Shay locomotive is a unique steam locomotive, designed by logger Ephraim Shay in the late 1800s. The steam locomotive features trucks (wheel structures) that swivel like a freight or passenger car, giving them the ability to make sharper turns over rougher track. The trucks are powered by a drive shaft on the outside of the locomotive, driven by vertical cylinders. While slow, the steamers were very powerful and could climb steep grades pulling heavy loads, and became the most widely used geared steam locomotives anywhere.

The Shay, a class B42-2 two-truck locomotive, carried construction number 2561 and was built for the Overton County Railroad on June 27, 1912. It was #4 on the railroad and soon went to the TK&N. In November 1919, #4 was sold to Southern Iron & Equipment as their #1409, and then immediately sold to the Bolinger-Franklin Lumber Company through the General Equipment Company of McComb, Mississippi. In 1923, the Shay went back to Southern Iron & Equipment as their #1851. In 1929, the Shay was sold to the Eastman-Gardiner Hardwood Company in Sandersville, Mississippi. It was eventually scrapped.

The TK&N was an early user of internal combustion and mechanical traction, using motorcar #101 to handle passenger service between Algood and Livingston. Photos of the motorcar show it to be a small bus mounted on railroad wheels. Later photos show a McKeen motorcar #7 on the railroad. A turntable was used at Algood to turn the motorcar, a service which ended by 1928. The railroad eventually shut down in April 1934.

Heading east, the Nashville & Eastern passes the large Rogers Group quarry and plant. The company is headquartered in Nashville and was listed in 2014 as the eighth largest aggregates producer in the nation, as well as the largest privately-owned company in the aggregates industry. Surprisingly, the quarry isn't a rail customer and has no tracks into the plant. The railroad begins climbing a steep hill, curving left and right as it does, passing through a number of deep rock cuts as it climbs over the ridge. The elevation of Algood is 1119 feet, while the top of the hill at Paragon is 1426, requiring grades of up to 2.5%.

Heading east, there is a railroad sign stating "Enter Monterey Branch" at Milepost 95.0. The line east of here was rebuilt in 2008, with the first passenger train to Monterey operating on October 11, 2008. This is mountain country, and the train will be crawling on this part of the line as the tracks loop around Algood Mountain, located immediately to the south. To the north will be an occasional view down into the valley of Spring Creek.

97.9 **PARAGON** – Paragon, shown as Parragon on some maps and railroad track charts, was a short spur on the north side of the mainline on property belonging to Lee Paragon. A small booth had a telephone in it for the use of train crews, the only structure located at Paragon. In July 1924, this location was retired and a new spur track built off of the siding to the south side of the mainline at Milepost 98.3. The new Paragon Spur had its switch changed from the east end to the west end of the track so the east end could be extended to serve J. C. Hodge, making the track 993 feet long in May 1931. The track serving Hodge was removed in early 1936.

Just west of Paragon can be seen a derailed hopper car, off the fill to the south. This car has been here for many years and it will probably continue to rest here for many years to come.

99.8 **BROTHERTON** – Brotherton was a siding, built to allow trains to double the four-mile hill to Bilbrey. An interesting part of the local history is that Joseph Bilbrey once owned most of the land at Brotherton. The depot at Brotherton was once on the south side of the tracks, but later was located on the north side. A short spur track and a mail crane were also here. A railroad's laborer's dwelling was retired on May 15, 1939.

The elevation of Brotherton is 1427 feet. A state historical marker gives a bit of history about the area. It states, "Mount Granger was the western distribution point for all U.S. mail to the southwestern frontier. In 1806, Mount Granger was named in honor of the Hon. Gideon Granger, Postmaster General. This historic site is located in what is today known as the Brotherton Community."

To the south is Willet Mountain. Heading east, the railroad makes a number of sharp curves as it climbs up to Bilbrey on grades between 2.0% and 2.4%. At one time, the Tennessee Central had guard rails on a number of these curves to help maintain the track gauge. About halfway between Brotherton and Bilbrey the railroad goes through a long deep cut as it passes through Blaylock Mountain.

103.4 **WOODCLIFF ROAD** – The railroad passes under this road, what was once the Walton Road, the original road between Knoxville and Nashville. Just east of the overpass, the railroad had a small oil house used to store oil for lubricating the curves in this area.

In 1799, the General Assembly of Tennessee appointed William Walton, William Martin and Robert Kyle to establish a new east-west road between Southwest Point

(Kingston) and the Cumberland River near Carthage. Opened in 1801, officially it was the Cumberland Turnpike, but it was generally known as the Walton Road. The road was described as being level and fifteen feet wide with all stumps removed.

104.0 BILBREY – This is the top of the grade heading east from Brotherton, located at 1821 feet of elevation. In December, 1919, the former depot – built using a carbody – was replaced with a 12' x 20' frame depot. A telephone arrived in late 1922. The building was located on the south side of the tracks. A short siding was also in the same area.

William Bilbrey owned land here for a number of years. The Old Walton Road, now Woodcliff Road, is adjacent to the railroad and crosses it several times.

106.2 WOODCLIFF – There was a short siding at Woodcliff, located on the south side of the mainline and officially retired on December 19, 1922.

Woodcliff Road crosses the railroad here. Also look for the Woodcliff Baptist Church and cemetery to the north. To the south are several small pastures surrounded by thick woods.

108.3 MONTEREY – The Tennessee Central reached Monterey (telegraph MY) in 1894 – the town was renamed from Standing Stone and incorporated as Monterey on December 7, 1893. The name Monterey reportedly came from the nearby Monterey Coal Company.

At Milepost 108.23, the railroad bridges over Walnut Street. This underpass was long a timber trestle, but today's bridge is a modern concrete and steel stringer bridge. Just to the east, the Nashville & Eastern has a short siding to the north. Also in this area is the new Monterey replica depot (Monterey Depot Museum), built to resemble the earlier depot from 1903. Monterey was once a major railroad town, with stockyards, a coal chute and sand tower, and various mechanical shops. In 1912, the Tennessee Central moved its shop facilities and crew change point eastward from Cookeville to Monterey. The depot from 1903 was approximately where the new replica depot stands on the north side of the tracks.

This caboose is displayed at the Monterey Depot Museum, numbered for the birthdate of Ted Sheckler, who restored it. The caboose was originally Norfolk & Western 518532, built in February 1969 by International Railway Car Company. It later became # 555532. The caboose was moved here in 2015 from Oak Ridge, Tennessee. Photo by Sarah Jennings.

A block west on the same side of the tracks were the stock pens, and then just west of Poplar Street (where the post office now stands) was the water tower. At one time, Monterey had two wooden water tanks, but they were replaced with a 100,000-gallon steel tank in June 1940. Earlier, in June 1926, the railroad had built an additional 7.3 million gallons of reservoir for the increased water demands. In early 1929, the railroad installed a Dearborn water treatment plant, and then built a new frame house to house it in late 1930. Into the 1960s, there was a water column (used to water steam locomotives) on the mainline at the wye.

Across the tracks, the railroad had a tool house, along with a row of six company houses. None survive today. Between Chestnut and Elm, where the switch for the east end of the siding is now, the railroad had a series of shops, a coal chute and sand house, a cinder pit and conveyor, and a number of other servicing facilities. The remains of the concrete coal chute still stand, and the shop office still exists, used by the local Lions Club. A number of tracks were also in this area to service locomotives and allow work on freight cars.

Part of the former Tennessee Central coal chute still stands in Monterey. Photo by Sarah Jennings.

At Milepost 108.6 was the switch to the Crawford Branch, the west leg of the Monterey wye. Today, the west leg of the wye still exists as the mainline of the Nashville & Eastern. The Tennessee Central freight house stood just north of the switch, served by a spur track off the wye. Two water tanks stood just east of the switch to the wye.

Monterey has a reputation of being a coal mining town, but for most of its life, it has simply been a terminal of a railroad serving coal mines in the region. However, a number of sources state that Monterey was developed by the Cumberland Mountain Coal Company in 1893. The actual founders consisted of a group of local citizens, as well as coal mining officials from Oklahoma and Missouri. The coal company immediately opened a general store, but significant coal mining at Monterey didn't take place until the 1940s and 1950s. By that time, a number of coal mines were served out of Monterey on several different branches. Among these coal mines were the Bill Turner Ray Meadow Creek Mines, ABC Coal Company, Central Coal, Clinchfield Coal, Fentress Coal & Coke, Clear Creek Coal, and Lowe & Wall.

With the arrival of the railroad, a second industry developed – lumbering. During the 1920s, Monterey led the nation in the production of hickory golf sticks. About the same time, the J. H. Lumber Company and the Monterey Hardwood Flooring Company both had spurs off the Crawford Branch just north of the wye.

The third major industry of Monterey was the summer resort business. At its peak, there were seven resort hotels in Monterey, all providing a cooler environment for those from the nearby river valleys. The first major hotel was the West Crest Hotel, opening during the spring of 1894. Initially, the hotel was a failure and was sold in 1896 to Thomas Emmett Goff, a Seth Thomas clock salesman who had experience operating the Reed House in nearby Livingston. In 1903, a 20-room addition to the West Crest was built, but the entire hotel was destroyed by fire in 1905.

During the summer of 1898, the Monterey Hotel Company started construction on the Reagan Hotel. Standing on the southeast corner of Cleveland Avenue and Oak Street, the railroad provided special service to the hotel by stopping trains at the Oak Street crossing to let off passengers for the short walk to the hotel. The Monterey Hotel Company opened the three-story, 110-room Cumberland Hotel (originally known as the Ramsey Hotel) in 1902, and work on the three-story Dow Hotel started the same year. Other Monterey hotels included The Southern, The Commercial, and The Park. There were also two additional hotels, The Monterey Hotel and The Imperial Hotel, that were built as lodging for railroaders.

The Monterey resort business peaked about 1905, but held steady until World War I. However, the resort business quickly ended during the 1920s and 1930s as roads and private automobile ownership allowed the business to move to larger and fancier resorts across the country. Today, only the Imperial Hotel remains standing in Monterey, in spite of efforts by Monterey. A local family has spent years rebuilding the hotel with plans to open it back in its original resort style. However, as plans developed for the replica depot and the trail between Monterey and Cookeville, it was determined that the back stairs of the Imperial Hotel "extended four to eight inches on the rails to trails bike path, so the city tore down the stairs." This left the Imperial Hotel out of code, forcing its closure. Efforts are being made to reopen the hotel, so check locally for more information.

The Imperial Hotel is one of the last reminders of the resort era of Monterey. Photo by Sarah Jennings.

Today, Monterey is the east end of the Nashville & Eastern, with the railroad serving a large sand mining operation several miles up the former Crawford Branch. The population in 2010 was 2850. It should be mentioned that Monterey was once known as Standing Stone, named for a tall rock that once stood upright on a sandstone ledge in the area. Early reports stated that it marked the boundary between Cherokee and Shawnee territory and designated the Cherokee Tallonteeskee Trail. Reportedly the Cherokee called the stone "Nee Yah Kah Tah Kee," which means "Standing Stone." Many reports state that the stone was actually a monolith constructed of various rocks held together with iron oxide cement. Remnants of the stone have been moved and preserved in Monterey as a part of the Standing Stone Monument. The monument was dedicated on October 17, 1895. Each October there is a Standing Stone Celebration of Native American Heritage.

108.6 CRAWFORD BRANCH SWITCH – This switch, shown as Milepost 0.0 on the Crawford Branch, takes trains of the Nashville & Eastern (NERR) northward to serve Monterey Sand. A short stretch of the original Tennessee Central mainline continues to the east to about Milepost 109. The east leg of the wye is gone and the NERR considers the line north to be part of their Monterey Branch. **For information on the Crawford Branch, see page 185.**

Tennessee Central Eastern Division
Monterey (TN) to Crab Orchard (TN)
Abandoned

The former Tennessee Central route east of here is abandoned to Crab Orchard, Tennessee. The Louisville & Nashville Railroad acquired the line east to Milepost 129.0, just west of Crossville, Tennessee. Southern Railway acquired the track from Milepost 129.0 east to Harriman, Tennessee. In 1987, CSX (L&N) abandoned the line between Algood and near Crossville, but only removed the track east of here. In 1989, Norfolk Southern (technically the Cincinnati, New Orleans & Texas Pacific Railway Company, which acquired the track through Southern's Harriman & Northeastern Railroad) abandoned their part of the line from Crossville as far east as Crab Orchard. Little remains along this route except for some old grades and the train station at Crossville.

108.6 CRAWFORD BRANCH SWITCH – This switch, shown as Milepost 0.0 on the Crawford Branch, takes trains of the Nashville & Eastern (NERR) northward to serve Monterey Sand. A short stretch of the original Tennessee Central mainline continues to the east to about Milepost 109. The east leg of the wye is gone and the NERR considers the line north to be part of their Monterey Branch. The former Eastern Division track east of here is abandoned. **For information on the Crawford Branch, see page 185.**

111.3 FLAT ROCK – While most railroad histories state that Dripping Springs was the center of action in this area, Tennessee Central documents show that the Flat Rock area was once fairly complicated. First, it was at the top of a short hill from Monterey. To allow trains to double the hill, a short siding existed to the south of the mainline between Mileposts 111.7-112.0. Next, there were a number of coal spurs in this area. A track known as the Flat Rock Mud Spur was once here but was retired on November 22, 1920. Two years later, a 290-foot spur was built at Flat Rock for

107

A. H. Mercer. The track was retired on April 25, 1924. Two years later, the railroad extended its house track.

Several significant coal tracks were also near here. At Milepost 110.3, a short siding to the north was used to connect to a track that was less than a mile long. Tennessee Central documents indicate that this track was built in July 1953 to serve the Fentress Coal & Coke Company and the ABC Coal Company. The ABC Coal Company started as the A&B Coal Company. A&B (Allred and Brown) drilled a number of test holes in the area in 1947 and brought on new partners to fund the development. The new company became the ABC (Allred, Brown, Copeland) Mines, which operated until being sold to Bill Turner Ray in October 1954. The operation was then sold to Blue Diamond Coal, which operated the mine until 1957 when it lost its TVA contracts.

In March 1948, a track was built from Milepost 111.0 to reach the new Meadow Creek Coal Company mine. The Meadow Creek Coal Company began operating in 1935, reaching peak production during World War II. During WWII, a 2.7-mile railroad spur was built to the mine from Dripping Springs. The company had at least two mines, the first on Dripping Springs Creek, the second on Meadow Creek. This track looped north to serve the company's second mine, located near where Dripping Springs Creek flows into Meadow Creek, to the north of their original mine. Bill Turner Ray also operated Meadow Creek Coal until it was sold to the Clinchfield Coal Company in 1954, which operated the mine until the late 1960s. The grades of these lines can barely be made out on modern maps and aerial photos.

111.6 COUNTY LINE – This is the county line between **Putnam County** (to the west) and Cumberland County (to the east). **Cumberland County** has a population of about 60,000 over about 680 square miles. Cumberland County was created on November 16, 1855, from parts of eight other counties (Bledsoe, Roane, Morgan, Fentress, Rhea,

Putnam, Overton, and White). Cumberland's early settlements were based upon mining and supporting travelers on several roads that passed through the county. During the 1930s, the federal government's Subsistence Homesteads Division established the Cumberland Homesteads south of Crossville, moving 250 impoverished families into a government-planned community. Today, much of this project is the Cumberland Mountain State Park.

112.8 DRIPPING SPRINGS – The depot at Dripping Springs was located south of Interstate 40 (milepost 112.45) just about where the tall cell tower stands today. Tennessee Central records state that on September 18, 1920, the Dripping Springs passenger shelter was replaced by a combination station built from a boxcar body. It was located on the north side of the mainline. Dripping Springs has also been recorded as the highest point on the railroad at 2028 feet above sea level.

On May 15, 1924, the railroad built a 1039-foot spur track at Milepost 113 for the Putnam Mining Company. During March 1936, a track was built nearby for the Meadow Creek Coal Company. This line followed Dripping Springs Creek, and reportedly, there were several switchbacks on these tracks that made it difficult to move the coal. A clay pit also once operated at Dripping Springs, providing clay for the Harley Pottery Company of Nashville. There were two seams of clay, one used for red flowerpots and the other for cream-colored stoneware.

115.6 WELSH – The railroad used to have a small passenger shelter here to the south. It was officially retired on September 1, 1932. To the west at Milepost 115.3, the railroad used to have a cinder platform to the north and a short spur track to the south. The track was retired on March 12, 1926. About a mile east of here was the Blanchard Mills Company spur track.

117.3 MAYLAND – For many years, Mayland was a busy summer passenger station due to Camp Nakanawa, located north of town on Lake Aloaloa. Colonel L. L. Rice founded Nakanawa Camps for Girls in 1920, and the railroad replaced their carbody depot with a new 20' x 42' combination passenger and freight depot on January 27, 1921. The station was located on the south side of the tracks between Lee Street and Main Street, street names that do not exist today. After the station was closed, it was moved and turned into a home.

By 1946, Camp Nakanawa was the largest private camp for girls in the United States. Camp Nakanawa still exists as a girl's camp, consisting of one thousand acres of forest, fields, and a 150-acre private lake. However, the depot is long gone, as are the section houses and tool houses that were on the north side of the tracks. An interesting 1928 report by the Tennessee Central states that all of the railroad toilets (depot plus three section houses) were replaced that year. The railroad also had a short siding to the north here, with stock pens at the east end.

Mayland was once known as Johnsons Stand, for Robert Johnson. Johnson was one of the first settlers in Cumberland County, and he and his family built a log cabin inn that attracted a small community and many travelers. The name Goodwill was later used for the community, and the school that opened in 1885 was called Band Springs. In 1900, a post office opened with the name Maywood, reportedly at the suggestion of William Cooper, a local resident.

Over the years, several Utopian groups moved into the area, but few lasted long due to the poor soil for farming. However, today there are several Mennonite Communities in the area. One interesting story relates to a group from North Carolina that moved to the Mayland area. Reportedly, after clearing the land, they found farming would be rough and that few other local jobs were available. Many of the men left the area for work, leaving their wives to run the town. Because of this, Maggie Cross became Mayland's

Eastern Division – Monterey to Crab Orchard

Police Chief while Cora Cooper Doney became the Assistant Police Chief. Family legend states that the two had only one gun between them, that it was never loaded, and in fact Mrs. Cross was afraid of guns.

Today, Royal Oak has a charcoal production facility just west of Mayland.

118.8 CAMPBELL JUNCTION – This was a junction with the Isoline Branch, an 8.88-mile-long branch to a series of coal mines to the north. The location of Campbell Junction is easy to find as it is at a sharp curve of Highway 24, and the old railroad reservoir is still visible to the north. The railroad grade across this small lake is also still visible. A new pump house was built on the west leg of the wye on October 20, 1936, designed to pump water from the reservoir to the railroad water tower that was located just west of the wye on the north side of the tracks.

Campbell Junction was never a major passenger station, and its passenger shelter was retired in 1924. However, during the early 1900s, Campbell Junction was a major freight station. The junction came about when the Cumberland Plateau Railroad was chartered on January 22, 1901, by Richard Orme Campbell, who had been mining coal near Isoline for several years. With the arrival of the railroad, he hired the Cumberland Construction Company, who had built the line from Emory Gap to Monterey, to build his Cumberland Plateau Railroad to connect the mines to the outside world. Even as the line was being completed, it was purchased by the Tennessee Central on September 30, 1902, and operated as their Isoline Branch. The report entitled "Mineral Products Along the Tennessee Central Railroad" in the April 1913 issue of *The Resources of Tennessee* published by the State Geological Survey stated that the coal mine was being operated by the Clear Creek Coal & Lumber Company. The coal seam was reported to be 38 inches thick.

Tennessee Central documents show that the land around the junction was owned by the Union Land, Coal

& Coke Company. This was one of several companies that owned timber and mineral rights across the Cumberland Plateau. Business on the line was heavy for several decades, but the mixed passenger/freight train service ended on April 1, 1933. All service ended by 1939 and the branch was removed in June of that year. **For information on the Isoline Branch, see page 195.**

121.9 POMONA ROAD – Pomona Road was a long siding at the top of a 2-mile-long, 2% grade from the east. The siding was often used to double heavy freight trains. The siding was lengthened in 1927 and a business spur was added. While no depot was here, a mail crane and stock pens did exist in the early 1900s.

The town of Pomona was to the south and was known as a community of fruit groves. This station was used to ship out much of this production. During World War II, Pomona was used as a prisoner of war camp, holding German and Italian prisoners. Some of the prisoners were Italian generals, and Mayor Fiorello LaGuardia of New York made at least one visit to Pomona to meet with them.

124.1 WIDENER SPUR – A short spur track was located here from August 31, 1922, until August 20, 1923. It was built for P. V. Widener & Son. The November 15, 1909, issue of the *St. Louis Lumberman* stated that, "P. V. Widener, who has been manager of the Bluefield (W. Va.) office of J. A. Wilkinson, of this city, has resigned to enter the lumber business in that city on his own account." The November 22, 1922, issue of the *Crossville Chronicle* reported that P. V. Widener & Son was in the lumber and sawmill business in the Crossville area. Over the next few years, short articles about the travels of "Mr. and Mrs. P. V. Widener," including one with their "new Studebaker," were regularly seen in the *Crossville Chronicle*. P. V. stood for Phillip Valentine.

125.7 CRESTON – Creston was at the bottom of a hill, and eastbound trains often had to double the hill to Crossville.

There was a depot on the north side of the mainline and several section houses to the south. All received new toilets in 1928, according to a Tennessee Central report.

East of Creston at Milepost 127, the railroad realigned 0.7 miles of track in 1927, straightening out a sharp curve. Several area bridges were filled in at the same time.

127.8 DOUBLING SPUR – A 700-foot-long siding was here from October 1922 until August 1927. It was used for climbing the hill between Creston and Crossville but became unnecessary when the railroad acquired larger locomotives.

129.0 PROPERTY LINE – When the Tennessee Central was divided between the Louisville & Nashville Railroad and Southern Railway, this was the dividing line of their ownership. CSX abandoned the line west of here in 1987, while Norfolk Southern abandoned the line to the east as far as Crab Orchard in 1989.

129.6 PIGGYBACK RAMP – The former Tennessee Central piggyback ramp was to the south. This ramp was a late effort by the railroad to attract new business, but it ended after the Louisville & Nashville took over the route to the west.

130.1 CROSSVILLE SIDING – The siding at Crossville was located just west of town, built in November 1925. The 1970 Southern Railway timetable showed that it was 60 cars long, while their 1983 timetable showed that it held 40 cars.

130.8 CROSSVILLE – For years, Crossville was known as CS by Tennessee Central telegraph operators. Today, Crossville bills itself as "The Golf Capital of Tennessee" and has almost a dozen golf courses in the area. With a population of more than 10,000, Crossville is the county seat of Cumberland County. Its location atop the Cumberland Plateau makes it milder during the summer than nearby river valleys, and its location on Interstate 40 has made it a popular business and retirement community. The surrounding hills are full of planned communities and retirement villages, many with their own golf courses.

A major attraction in Crossville is the Cumberland County Playhouse, one of the ten largest professional theaters in rural America. More than 165,000 visitors attend a show here annually. Another attraction is the Palace Theatre, which opened in November of 1938. Built as a community entertainment center, the building has been restored and houses live entertainment and serves as Crossville's community auditorium and visitors' center. It was listed on the National Register of Historic Places on January 7, 1994.

Crossville also surprises many people as being the headquarters of the United States Chess Federation, which moved here in 2005. Crossville is also part of the World's Largest Yard Sale on Highway 127, the early home of the first African-American to play in an NBA basketball game (Earl Lloyd), and the base of one of the federal government's Subsistence Homestead Divisions during the 1930s. The homestead project provided small farms for several hundred impoverished families, and the recreational area later became the nucleus for Cumberland Mountain State Park.

Crossville started as a store, tavern and a cluster of buildings where the Knoxville-Nashville Great Stage Road crossed the Kentucky Stock Road, a cattle trail between central Kentucky and the Chattanooga area. The first name for the community was Lambeth's Crossroads, named after Samuel Lambeth and his store that opened here about 1800 close to the intersection of today's Main Street and Stanley Street, near the courthouse.

A post office opened with the name Crossville by the mid-1830s. During the early 1850s, Lambeth's store was bought by James Scott and it became the Scott's Tavern. When Cumberland County was formed in 1856, Scott's

Eastern Division – Monterey to Crab Orchard

Tavern was in the middle of the county and selected as the county seat, especially after Scott donated 40 acres for the courthouse and town square.

The late 1800s saw the construction of the railroad through Crossville, and road construction reached the town during the early 1900s. Both led to a development boom in the region, especially for coal mining and lumbering. Later, other small industries developed. Today, Crossville includes a collection of small specialty manufacturing. Crossville Ceramics, founded in 1986, and its 1/3-mile-long production plant that manufactures porcelain tile is an example of a modern company based in the area. Some of their major customers include Subway, McDonald's, Wendy's, Cracker Barrel, and Chick-Fil-A.

The 1920s was a busy time for the railroad in Crossville as a number of tracks were built, moved, and closed. Just a few of the companies mentioned include Harrison, Kimmer & Mitchell; Tennessee Electric Power Company; John Oman Jr.; Cookeville Veneer Company; Mountain Oak Stave & Lumber Company; and Gulf Refining Company. On March 10, 1926, new stock pens opened. One big change happened on February 15, 1925, when the Crossville passenger and freight station was retired after it burned. A new brick combination station opened on June 22, 1926. Southern's 1983 employee timetable showed that there was still a yard here at that time.

While the railroad into Crossville no longer exists, the 1926 Tennessee Central train station still stands. The station was restored thanks to the efforts of the Rotary Clubs of Cumberland County, using grants from the Federal Highway Administration and the Tennessee Department of Transportation. The station is located several blocks north of the county courthouse at the intersection of North Main Street and North Street. The building is used as a meeting room and gift shop. Next to the station is caboose #6100, built in 1963 for the Chicago & Eastern Illinois Railroad. The railroad closed soon after and the caboose was sold to the Louisville & Nashville Railroad. It was moved to Crossville about 2009 and restored by August 2013.

132.9 DAYTON SPUR – This was listed in Southern's 1983 timetable as a 14-car spur. The track was located to the south. The grade crossing here was for the road now known as Dayton Spur Road.

135.0 DORTON – In Southern Railway's 1983 Employee Timetable, the railroad listed a 40-car siding (built December 1928) and a 16-car spur at Dorton. Both were to the north of the mainline. Dorton, named to honor a prominent attorney of the era, was once a junction with the 10-mile-long railroad of the Cumberland Lumber Company. The junction was just east of town, and the line ran ten miles north to Peavine Mountain. It was organized as the Cumberland & Northern Railroad but was operated by the Tennessee Central. The line was built in 1909 and abandoned in 1922 after the end of lumbering. During September 1923, the combination station and dwelling at the junction was retired, but a mail crane remained. Tennessee Central records show that the interchange track was abandoned in 1926.

Although the C&N Railroad was torn out by the late 1920s, there is an interesting agreement between the Tennessee Central and the Cumberland Lumber Company about a lumber shipping depot in Dorton, dated October 1942. This was not the first such agreement. In February 1914, the railroad and Cumberland Lumber Company also reached an agreement for a depot and storehouse.

Several section houses stood in Dorton for a number of years, finally being torn down in 1940. Today, the location is the home of Tennessee Building Stone. East of Dorton, the railroad started to drop heading east to Crab Orchard with grades of as much as 1.7%.

137.1 OTTER CREEK – Also shown as Otter Creek Junction on many maps, this was a 14-car spur in the 1983 South-

Eastern Division – Monterey to Crab Orchard

ern Railway timetable. It was built in 1921 to serve D. M. Wheeler. In 1926, a spur track was built at Otter Creek to serve a rock quarry. The quarry track was soon merged with the Wheeler track. In April 1930, the spur track was extended west to serve the new Cumberland Stone Company crushing plant. Most of the west end of the spur was abandoned in 1937.

Today, this area is at the grade crossing with Detour Road. The remains of the quarry can still be seen just west of the road.

138.7 BIG DADDY'S CREEK BRIDGE – This was a 585-foot-long timber open deck trestle. In late 1927, this bridge received a fourth chord throughout the structure to strengthen it and had its deck covered in galvanized metal as fire protection. It received 60# (pounds per year) guard rails a year later. Look for the description of Mammys Creek (Milepost 148.9) for the explanation of this stream's name.

East of here, the railroad followed U.S. Highway 70 to Crab Orchard, passing under Interstate 40 along the way. During the 1920s, much of this land was owned by the Union Land, Coal & Coke Company.

141.3 WEST END OF LHOIST NORTH AMERICA TRACK – This is the physical end of track, but the 1989 abandonment notice stated it was at 141.5. West of here, the tracks have been removed. East of here, the line is still in operation to Harriman.

Tennessee Central Eastern Division
Crab Orchard (TN) to Rockwood (TN)
Lhoist North America

This part of the railroad is still in service. It is used to move freight for Lhoist North America to and from their Crab Orchard quarry facility. For many years, Southern Railway, later Norfolk Southern, operated regular trains from Emory Gap through Rockwood and on to Crab Orchard to serve the large limestone quarry there. However, as other shippers on the line closed, a plan was reached to turn the tracks west of Rockwood over to the quarry. A Surface Transportation Board statement read, "On July 28, 2000, the Cincinnati, New Orleans and Texas Pacific Railway Company (CNOTP), a wholly owned subsidiary of Norfolk Southern Railway Company, filed with the Surface Transportation Board (Board) a petition under 49 U.S.C. 10502 for exemption from the provisions of 49 U.S.C. 10903-05 to abandon a line of railroad known as the Crab Orchard Line, between milepost 141.5-H at Crab Orchard and milepost 156.9-H at Rockwood, a distance of 15.4 miles in Cumberland and Roane Counties, TN." Later this line was sold to Franklin Industrial Minerals, which operated the line as an industrial railroad. Today, Lhoist North America operates the line after acquiring Franklin Industrial Minerals.

During the last years of the Tennessee Central, this was an important part of the company as the coal moves produced much of the company's revenues. However, trains heading west from Rockwood faced a long climb up Walden Ridge and onto the Cumberland Plateau. The Tennessee Central took more than 50 miles to climb from an elevation of 785 feet at Harriman to the 2028-foot elevation at Dripping Springs, the highest elevation on the railroad. This is a total climb of 1243 feet, or about 24 feet per mile. However, that is not the whole story.

The actual climb up Walden Ridge begins about a mile and a half east of the old Rockwood depot near Milepost 158, at an elevation of 856 feet. The first major climb is to the Willet Hollow Tunnel at Milepost 153.3, at an elevation of 1362 feet. While the Harriman to Willet Hollow Tunnel grade gains 600 feet at a rate of about 75 feet per mile, or an average of 1.4%, the main five-mile stretch sees a climb of more than 500 feet, or an average of 2.0%, with some grades reaching a steady 2.4%. To make the climb, the railroad also seems to curve as much as it climbs. While modern railroads attempt to keep their mainline curves at 3 degrees or less, at least three of the curves between Rockwood and the tunnel are 10 degrees.

A 1986 Norfolk Southern excursion train approaches Crab Orchard from the west. Photo by Barton Jennings.

From the tunnel to Crossville, the elevation only increases 492 feet, an average of 0.4%. However, the line actually climbs and drops repeatedly due to the number of streams that are crossed. For example, between Daysville and Ozone, the maximum grade is 1.5% with a maximum curvature of 14 degrees. Another steep climb for westbound trains happens in the 2.5 miles from Renfro Hollow (1645 feet) to the Crab Orchard Gap (1730 feet). Additionally, there are two 10-degree curves in Renfro Hollow. The railroad then drops to the former station location in Crab Orchard (1675 feet). When the railroad went further west, it then dropped further to the Big Daddy's Creek bridge (1650 feet), before climbing through Dorton (1815 feet) to 1854 feet at the Crossville depot.

141.3 WEST END OF LHOIST NORTH AMERICA TRACK – This is the physical end of track, but the 1989 abandonment notice stated it was at 141.5. This location was also identified in the July 28, 2000, announcement about the closure of the line east of Crab Orchard. West of here, the tracks have been removed. East of here, the line is still in operation to Harriman.

141.6 CRAB ORCHARD – The Lhoist/Franklin Industrial Minerals mine and plant at Crab Orchard is the reason that any of this rail line still exists. When Norfolk Southern abandoned the line on into Crossville, the quarry, a small tie company, and a few other small shippers were all that were left. By 2000, the quarry was the last shipper and the line above Rockwood was sold to Franklin Industrial Minerals.

When the Tennessee Central still ran the railroad, the depot (telegraph call CD) was located just west of Market Street (141.65) on the north side of the mainline. Just to the west was a wye track, also to the north and located between Adams and Garrison (now Hebbertsburg Road) Streets. This wye was used to turn steam locomotives that helped trains up the grades from the east. Crab Orchard was also a base for track workers. In October 1925, the Tennessee Central retired "Section Foreman's Dwelling and East Laborer's Dwelling." Several shippers also had tracks here. For example, Pierpont-Paxton/J. H. Findley had their own spur track that was retired in 1926. In late 1928, the Tennessee Central built another spur track north of the mainline, but retired it in early 1939. Interestingly, there was an agreement for a coal loading track for the Alberta

Coal Mining Company, built in October 1947. In 1970, the Southern Railway listed a 40-car siding and a 56-car spur track. However, by 1983, the only thing left at Crab Orchard was the limestone quarry and a 56-car spur, often being used to load rail cars with fresh-cut railroad ties.

The community of Crab Orchard is at a gap in the Crab Orchard Mountains, named for the wild crab apple trees in the area. A road between East Tennessee and Nashville was built through the gap during the 1780s. Because the road used the bottom of the valley, the area was perfect for attacks by area Cherokee, Creek, and Shawnee warriors. These attacks lasted though the mid-1790s and included the defeat of several small military units. Nevertheless, the location was valuable, and on March 7, 1796, a land grant was issued to William Tyrell and Stockley Donelson, brother-in-law of Andrew Jackson. By 1800, the Indian attacks had ended and the road was improved as the Walton Road. About the same time, Sidnor's Inn opened at Crab Orchard to serve travelers, making Crab Orchard the oldest continually settled community in Cumberland County. In 1827, the Crab Orchard Inn also opened here, operated by the Burke family who also operated a tavern at nearby Ozone.

The railroad built through Crab Orchard in 1898, helping the community to grow. The arrival of Interstate 40 made the area busier but allowed the residents to move to nearby larger communities. Although dating from about 1800, the town didn't incorporate until 1973. Today, Crab Orchard has a population of about 750 and includes several convenience stores and a post office.

Crab Orchard is also known for the durable sandstone that took its name. The Cumberland Stone Company opened in 1903 to sell the sandstone. The stone was first used for area buildings, but was later cut and used in buildings across the region. The sandstone gained fame in 1926 when it was used for Southwestern University in Memphis. The stone is still being produced and was used in 2001 by the Country Music Hall of Fame in Nashville.

Under the sandstone and in other veins is a large supply of limestone. Much of this limestone is mined underground in large caves. In the *Development of Unused Lands – Letter from the Secretary of the Interior Transmitting Report on the Development of the Unused Lands of the Country to the House of Representative's Committee on the Public Lands* (October 6, 1919), the report stated that, "A large limestone quarry is located at Crab Orchard, Cumberland County, which limestone is well suited for both road metal or agricultural lime when sufficiently pulverized. This limestone analyses over 95 per cent calcium carbonate and many of the layers show an analysis of 99 per cent calcium carbonate." Reports indicate that by the 1930s, there were a number of lime kilns in Crab Orchard.

Cox Valley Railroad

When reading about Crab Orchard, there are several reports about a short-lived narrow gauge railroad that operated to the south serving several coal mines and sawmills. The route apparently headed southwest through Cox Valley, where the remains of a number of small mines still can be found. Reports state that the railroad served the Goodstock and Devilstep Hollow area at the top of Grassy Cove. Grassy Cove is a unique area, basically a small valley surrounded by mountains (2930-foot Brady Mountain to the west, 2930-foot Bear Den Mountain on the east, and 2828-foot Black Mountain to the north) that is drained entirely by underground streams. The area is well known for its sinkholes and caves, and has been designated as a National Natural Landmark.

Some reports state that the railroad was built about 1915. However, the coal mines in the area have an earlier history. The *State of Tennessee – Fourteenth Annual Report of the Mining Department* (1904) listed the Cox Valley Mine, located "2 miles south of Crab Orchard, Tenn., near head of Grassy Cove." The report stated that the mine was owned by the Cumberland Coal & Coke Company and was "a new opening and consists chiefly of prospect work, only five or six men being employed." The report also stated that "no shipments from this mine have as yet been made for want of railway facilities." However, by the *Nineteenth Annual Report* (1909), the Cox Valley Mine was not listed. No other mines were listed in this area, either.

Things changed in 1907 when a new player entered the area mining scene. The February 14, 1907, issue of *Manufacturers' Record* reported that the Southern Coal & Iron Company had been formed and had bought 10,000 acres in Cumberland and Bledsoe Counties. It also stated that these "Tennessee properties are said to include the Cox Valley and Crab Orchard coal mines in the Cumberland valley, already equipped for producing coal. The properties are well timbered, and several small sawmills have already been located." *The Engineering and Mining Journal*, dated February 23, 1907, also reported on the Southern Coal & Iron Company, stating that the company "is preparing to open two coal mines at Crab Orchard and Cox Valley and will need machinery."

The Coal Trade Journal also had several articles about the company in various 1907 issues. An interesting one stated that the company "has also what is known as the Cox Valley mine, which has an 11-foot seam of Sewanee coal opened up, and equipped with haulage engine ready for operation. An output of 1,000 tons per day can be had from this mine within six months after it is started up. The Southern Ry. runs within four miles of this mine and offers to build a spur into the mine any time the Southern C. & I. Co. is ready to commence mining." The *Journal* continued with more information, stating that "the Southern C & I Co. is entirely free from indebtedness, its entire capital stock of $10,000,000 is owned 50 per cent by John A. Shellito of Crossville, Tenn., and Donald Fitzgerald of 80 Wall Street, New York."

Apparently, besides the coal mine in Cox Valley, the company also bought the Crab Orchard Coal Mine. This mine had coal seams "of an average thickness of five feet which is fully equipped." This mine was equipped with "boiler, engine pumps, fan, tipple house, scales, shop, mine cars, two extra carloads of T-rails, water and steam piping, miners houses, store house, and hotel." The mine produced 250 to 300 tons of coal per day, loaded directly onto the tracks of the Tennessee Central/Southern Railway. An interesting statement about the coal said that the "average cost of mining coal in this section is 75 cents per ton and the average selling price at present is $1.75 per ton" at the mine.

Some statements about the narrow gauge railroad say that it was two miles long, but others state that it served the mines and sawmills almost five miles southwest of Crab Orchard. Little else is known about this railroad except that it delivered coal, lumber and stave bolts to Crab Orchard.

One final note about the railroad can be found in a November 1922 contract between the Tennessee Central Railway and J. H. Findley of Cox Valley. The agreement rented rail materials to Findley, owner of the Findley Coal Company. The same year, mine inspection reports indicate that the company's coal seam was seven feet thick. Findley Coal was still in business 1925, but little other information exists.

142.2 GAMBLE CONSTRUCTION – This 11-car spur was listed in the 1983 Southern Railway timetable for the line. Gamble Construction built roads across Tennessee, and the Tennessee Central produced a contract with the company to build a spur track at Crab Orchard in March 1950. Today, this switch is in the middle of the growing lime facility.

142.3 LHOIST NORTH AMERICA – This is the historic east switch to the large limestone quarry and processing facility at Crab Orchard. The limestone quarry has a long history in the area, and this huge complex is the result. An early Tennessee Central legal agreement shows that the railroad built a spur track in October 1908 for the Crab Orchard Lime Works. An additional contract for a spur track was written in December 1909 for the Southern White Lime Company. Other historic records show that the Southern States Lime Company had a limestone quarry with kilns active here by 1910. Photos from the era show company partner and general manager Newton D. Walker, Sr., giving a tour of the property to a photographer. Among the facilities documented were the large limestone caverns where limestone-filled rail carts were hauled by horses or mules to the nearby kilns; a cooperage factory to make barrels for shipping processed lime; and a number of kilns where the limestone was processed.

In May 1912, the Tennessee Central agreed to add another track for the Southern White Lime Company at Crab Orchard. This track was a spur with a coal trestle to deliver coal for the use in the kilns. Interest in the limestone continued, and the April 1913 *Resources of Tennessee* stated that the limestone at Crab Orchard was "very pure containing between 95 and 99 per cent lime carbonate and on burning make excellent lime. At present the Southern White Lime Corporation has a quarry and several kilns located at this place on the north side of the railroad. In 1912, they made 18,000 tons of lime."

An article in the August 29, 1922, *Building Supply News* stated that Southern States Lime Corporation was adding a new processing plant that would produce 30 tons of chemical hydrate per day. By 1925, the number of kilns had more than doubled. In May 1957, the Tennessee Central acquired ten 70-ton covered hoppers to handle bulk freight, and five of the cars were assigned to Southern States Lime to move agricultural limestone. The Southern States Lime Company continued to expand the business, and in 1967, Crab Orchard led the Tennessee Central's Cumberland Plateau area in originating total cars, tonnage, and revenue. This single station represented 61% of the freight originated on the eastern end of the railroad.

A change occurred on April 15, 1969, when Southern States Lime Company was sold to the Franklin Stone Company, based in Nashville, Tennessee. However, the

1983 Southern Railway employee timetable still showed the switch as serving Southern States Lime Corporation, stating that it was a 52-car spur. On January 1, 1992, the company changed its name to Franklin Industrial Minerals. Franklin Industrial Minerals indirectly dates back to 1911 when the Rodes family created the Franklin Limestone Company. The family sold the limestone company during the late 1940s and started Franklin Builders Supply Company. Rodes Hart, a nephew of a family leader, got back into the limestone business using the Franklin name. The company quietly grew under family control, adding other divisions related to mining and construction materials.

To preserve rail service to the limestone operation, the company bought the 15.4-mile railroad between Crab Orchard and Rockwood (Milepost 156.9) in 2000. This led the company to buy their own locomotives, hire their own crews, and build a locomotive shop at the processing plant in Crab Orchard. This purchase of the railroad by the Rodes-owned Franklin Industrial Minerals is a fascinating irony. Back in 1968, Allan Battle Rodes was appointed as the receiver of the Tennessee Central during its last bankruptcy. On February 12, 1968, Battle Rodes filed an abandonment petition with the Interstate Commerce Commission to close the railroad. After several attempts to sell the railroad in one piece, Rodes set a date of May 31st for the railroad's closure. However, Rodes continued to work to save the railroad and eventually worked out an agreement whereby the railroad was split between Illinois Central, Louisville & Nashville, and Southern railroads. With the line's purchase in 2000, the Rodes family indirectly owned the part of the Tennessee Central acquired by the Southern Railway.

At about the same time the track from Crab Orchard to Rockwood was being bought, Franklin Industrial Minerals began to sell off its assets. The first major sale was the Franklin Industries mica mining reserves, sold to Oglebay Norton Company of Ohio in 1999. The second major sale came in 2003 when Franklin Brick Company, then the largest brick distributor in the United States, was sold to Boral Limited, Australia's largest building and construction materials supplier.

A Franklin limestone train departs Crab Orchard for Rockwood. Photo by Barton Jennings.

Still, Franklin Industrial Minerals was the largest producer of high-calcium chemical limestone in the United States, operating a number of mines and processing plants in the Southeast. In late 2006, Franklin Industries sold its limestone operations to the Chemical Lime Company (CLC) of Fort Worth, Texas. CLC is owned by Lhoist North America (LNA), a part pf the Lhoist Group of Limelette, Belgium, and a global supplier of many industrial products. LNA is described as being a "major supplier of lime, limestone and clay products to the North American marketplace, with locations throughout the U.S. and in Canada." The company is also involved with other industries such as iron and steel, chemical production, pulp and paper, glass, and building materials. The company dates back to 1899 when Hippolyte Dumont opened a factory in Belgium. The firm added facilities in France in 1926, starting a global move. The Lhoist Group moved

Eastern Division – Crab Orchard to Rockwood

into North America during the 1980s, and across Europe and Asia during the next two decades.

Since the purchase, some of the signs have changed and the locomotives received new paint, but the mining and processing of limestone has continued.

Lhoist North America towers over the Crab Orchard area, and is a landmark along Interstate 40. Photo by Sarah Jennings.

142.5 INTERSTATE 40 – The railroad passes under I-40, which stretches from Barstow, California, to Wilmington, North Carolina. Sources say that the Interstate Highway is 2555 miles long. There are more miles of I-40 in Tennessee than in any other state – 455 miles. It also passes through the three largest cities in the state: Memphis, Nashville and Knoxville.

This is the location of Crab Orchard Gap, at an elevation of 1730 feet.

143.6 RENFRO CREEK BRIDGE – Renfro Creek is another small mountain stream that drains the surrounding hillsides. The railroad uses a 271-foot-long timber open deck trestle to cross the gorge that the stream created. While the name Renfro Creek has historically been used for the stream, many modern maps show it as Berks Creek.

143.9 RENFRO – Renfro was another small community along the Tennessee Central Railway that served as a connection to an area mine. The *State of Tennessee – Sixteenth Annual Report of the Mining Department* (1906) stated that the Wilson Mine at Renfro had been the Renfro Coal Mining Company, but in 1906 was being drained and prospected by the Wilson Coal Company. The *Eighteenth Annual Report of the Mining Department* (1908) reported that the mine was the Renfro Mine and was being operated by the Renfro Coal & Coke Company. The company was headquartered in Mauch Chunk, Pennsylvania, but was not producing in 1908. Chief Mine Inspector R. A. Shiflett reported that coal was hauled from the underground rooms "a distance of 400 feet by mules from slope to mine entrance" and then "from mine entrance to railroad, a distance of 300 feet, by incline."

The coal mine apparently got more productive over the years. In July 1918, the Tennessee Central built a spur track for the Renfro Coal Company. A freight house and cinder passenger platform had also been built by this time. The coal spur was retired in 1923, the freight house retired in August 1926, and a second spur track retired in November 1933.

To the south and across U.S. Highway 70, Renegade Mountain Parkway heads into a new housing development, using some of the former coal mine lands. This area is known by locals as Mine Cove to this day. Tennessee Central maps show that Robert Renfro owned much of the area. The Renfro family arrived here during the early 1800s, and the area is known as Renfro Hollow. Much of the hollow was created by Berks Creek, with Haley Mountain to the south.

144.9 BRIDGE – This curved, 539-foot-long timber open deck trestle is a popular photo location as it is alongside U.S. Highway 70.

146.0 OZONE – Today's Ozone is a rural unincorporated community located on U.S. Highway 70, much of which is the original stage route between Knoxville and Nashville from about the year 1800. A tavern was first built here about 1806 by the widow of Elijah Haley, an early Cumberland settler who died near Ozone while moving west. His name was used for several local land features such as Haley Mountain to the south. The community never grew much, but did receive a post office named Mammy in 1880. The name Mammy came from the local creek, but in 1896, the community and post office changed its name to Ozone to promote its mountain air.

Ozone is located at an altitude of 1648 feet and once had a railroad siding, depot (Tennessee Central telegraph code Z), and a number of section houses for the track workers. Railroad maps show that the station was on the south side of the tracks while an additional spur track was to the north. There were at least four section houses to the west of the station, and several more east of the Fall Creek bridge. The depression of the 1930s led to the removal of many of the structures here, with the tool house retired during July 1932. By 1983, Southern Railway only showed a 10-car spur at Ozone, although in 1970 the railroad said that it would hold 24 cars.

To the south is the Ozone Falls State Natural Area, created to protect Ozone Falls, a 110-foot-tall waterfall on Fall Creek. The Natural Area was established in 1973 and is managed by the Tennessee State Parks System. While only 43 acres in size, the park features the amphitheater and pool created by the falls, an old-growth forest, and native grasses and prairie plants. Visitors can take one of several trails that loop and climb through the oaks, pines, eastern hemlock, magnolia, yellow birch, sugar maple, tulip poplar, and rhododendron. Because of the mix of vegetation and terrains, Ozone Falls was used for filming several scenes for the movie *Jungle Book*.

Ozone Falls is a popular tourist attraction and part of an official Tennessee Natural Area. Photo by Barton Jennings.

146.1 FALL CREEK BRIDGE – This 197-foot-long open deck trestle, made with steel stringers on wood bents, crosses the source for the water that flows over Ozone Falls. Fall Creek starts from several sources about ten miles to the north in the Crab Orchard Mountains. It runs about ten miles to the south where it flows into Piney Creek at the point that

Roane County, Cumberland County, and Rhea County all meet.

The falls that are today known as Ozone Falls were documented by travelers from at least the late 1700s. Apparently, the area was a popular camping spot for travelers. Just south of the bridge, Fall Creek used to power a gristmill, built in the 1860s. Known as the McNair Mill, the falls soon became the McNair Falls. A sawmill later joined the gristmill, with both being washed out several times before the last mill was washed over the waterfall in 1900. By that time, the nearby railroad stop had begun using the name Ozone, and the falls soon took the name Ozone Falls.

146.2 OZONE BRANCH – The Ozone Branch, also known as the Fall Creek Branch, headed north to serve a significant coal mine. The Fall Creek Mine was a coal operation that lasted into the 1920s. Tennessee's *Sixteenth Annual Report of the Mining Department* (1906) stated that the mine's owner was Fall Creek Collieries, based in Ozone, Tennessee. The report stated that the Sewanee coal seam was 48 inches and that the mine was "developed on the double entry room and pillar system" and was served by the Southern Railway.

The *Eighteenth Annual Report of the Mining Department* (1908) stated that the headquarters of Fall Creek Collieries was in St. Louis, and that the mine was at an elevation of 1800 feet, "two and one half miles from Ozone." The mine was described as having a roof of slate and the floor of fire clay. A comment was made that the coal was moved from the rooms in the mine to the coal tipple, served by the Tennessee Central, by mules.

Tennessee Central records indicate that several contracts were written in November 1904 for specifications of spur tracks to serve the Fall Creek Collieries Ozone coal mine development. The contractor assigned to the project was W. J. Oliver of Knoxville, Tennessee. A track scale was added on the siding in August 1906. In early 1918, the Fall Creek Branch was leased to Paul Roberts of the Fall Creek Coal & Coke Company of Nashville. At the same time, the

Tennessee Central leased a locomotive (Tennessee Central #5, a small 0-4-0 built in 1883) to the coal company. *The Retail Coalman* of December 1917 noted the incorporation of the company by four owners, with Paul Roberts being one of these. Numerous advertisements in Nashville area newspapers promoted the coal, stating that it was the cleanest available. Additional contracts and agreements covering the operation of the Fall Creek Branch by the Fall Creek Coal & Coke Company were written in 1921 and 1922.

Maps show that there were several section houses near the Ozone Branch switch, generally known as the East Ozone section houses. The railroad branch was retired during the 1920s.

147.1 LITTLE ROCK BRANCH BRIDGE – This is one of several former Tennessee Central bridges that were visible from Interstate 40 until the forest grew back. This curved bridge was described as a 555-foot-long timber open deck trestle by Norfolk Southern in 1989. However, the east end of the bridge has been filled recently by Lhoist/Franklin Industrial Minerals.

147.4 MILLSTONE CREEK BRIDGE – This structure is well known to drivers on Interstate 40, as it is visible through the woods for much of the year. It was described as a 930-foot mixed span open deck bridge by Norfolk Southern in 1989.

Millstone Creek starts about five miles to the north and flows to the south into Mammys Creek. The community of Millstone shows on some maps about a mile north of Waldensia. Both towns were founded by coal companies working different parts of the Upper Sewanee coal seam.

147.5 MILLSTONE JUNCTION – This is another railroad junction with a track that served several coal mines. For trains heading west, the mainline curves to the south (left) and the branch used to curve north (right). Tennessee

Central records indicate that the coal line was built about 1900. Known as the Millstone Creek Spur, the track headed north about two miles along Millstone Creek and served several coal mines. Records also indicate that the line was removed about 1910 and the station name retired.

Records of the Tennessee Mining Department provide more information about the coal mines that the railroad served, known as the Millstone 4 and 5 Mines. The *Sixteenth Annual Report* (1906) stated that the Millstone Mine was owned and operated by the Cumberland Coal & Coke Company of St. Louis, Missouri. Located at an elevation of 2200 feet, the report stated that the new mine (opened in 1905) worked the Upper Sewanee seam that showed an average thickness of 36 inches. The report also stated that the "output is hauled to incline with mules; thence to railway, a distance of 3,600 feet over gravity plane." At the time, the report also stated that the serving railroad was the Southern Railway. The *Eighteenth Annual Report* (1908) noted that the Tennessee Central Railroad served the drift mines, but that the "developments have not been extended any since 1905."

During June 1923, almost 300 feet of the branch was rebuilt as a spur for Hamilton & Melvin. It was retired during November 1925.

147.8 FLAT ROCK CREEK BRIDGE – Flat Rock Creek, also shown as Flatrock Creek, forms just west of Waldensia and flows south to here. Further south, it merges with Millstone Creek just before entering Mammys Creek. The structure is a 541-foot-long timber open deck trestle.

148.7 LITTLE MAMMY CREEK BRIDGE – This 268-foot-long timber open deck trestle crosses this small stream, which forms just a few miles to the north.

148.8 WALDENSIA – Trains heading west pass through a long curve that turns 84 degrees, taking the train from heading northwest to southwest. Just several hundred feet to the north through the woods is Interstate 40, yet today this seems to be an isolated location. However, until 1930, it was a junction with a railroad to the north that served a number of coal mines and coke ovens.

In 1901, approximately 8000 acres was acquired by the Waldensia Coal & Coke Company, with plans to mine a number of eight-foot thick seams of coal. The company immediately logged the land and constructed a company town named Waldensia that included a lake, 80 employee cottages, commissary, hotel, boardinghouse, office, school, coal washer building, post office, train depot, and about 100 coke ovens. Also built was a railroad connecting to the Tennessee Central. The entire operation was sold to the Chicago-Tennessee Coal & Coke Company in 1908, which operated the mines and ovens until closing in 1921. In 1925, the Connellsville Coal & Coke Company acquired the operation and began operating again. However, it closed in 1929 and the railroad was soon abandoned. Today, Lake Waldensia still exists on private property, and the coke ovens are covered with vegetation. Little else exists of the former operations.

Records of the Tennessee Central indicate that lines were built or extended as needed as the mines changed their operations. At the mainline, the railroad built a wye so that coal trains could serve markets to the east or west, and to turn locomotives that helped trains up out of the valley in Roane County. The railroad had a small two-track yard just north of the wye. The wye was officially retired in December 1935. A depot using the telegraph code of V stood between the mainline switches of the wye, finally being retired and torn down in December 1940.

148.9 MAMMYS CREEK BRIDGE – The railroad crosses this stream on a tall, 452-foot-long timber open deck trestle, located in heavy woods. While originally noted as being Mammy's Creek, today the name is Mammy or Mammys Creek.

Mammys and nearby Daddy's Creek are interesting names. An article in the May 26, 1887, issue of the *Crossville Times* provides a story about the names. Apparently, the rigorous travel required to move through the mountains was taking a toll on a husband and wife. Reports were that the couple had been fighting for days, and when they stopped to water their horses, the husband "seized his loving partner tenderly by the nap [*sic*] of the neck and administrated to her a sound cuffing." In honor of the cuffing, he named the stream Daddy's Creek. Heading further east, the couple again stopped to water their livestock. This time the wife grabbed a large tree limb and beat her husband over the head with it. The stream then took the name of Mammy's Creek.

Several different versions of this story exist. Some state that the family was moving east to avoid Indian attacks in the Nashville area (which makes sense since Daddy's Creek is west of Mammy's Creek), while others said that the family was uncertain about heading home to Nashville or retreating east, and thus kept repeating their movements through this rugged country. Either way, there were reportedly a number of observers of the fights and the stories traveled throughout the region.

Mammy's Creek is one of several large streams that form on Luper Mountain to the north, a part of the Crab Orchard Mountains. The stream flows to the south, under the railroad here, and heads on south where it flows into Piney Creek at the junction of Cumberland, Roane and Rhea Counties. The name of Mammy's Creek had a more major impact upon the area. In 1880, a post office with the name of Mammy opened at what later became Ozone.

149.4 DAYSVILLE – Daysville was once the home of a 55-car siding (2486 feet long) built in April 1930 after the station at Waldensia was retired. The location was chosen as it was the top of a steep grade from the east at an elevation of 1540 feet. Besides the siding, a 1357-foot-long spur track was also built here in 1930. Neither of these tracks exist today, but their grades are easy to see to the north.

Daysville can be found thanks to the grade crossing with Daysville Road. Daysville is another small rural mountain community that developed due to the railroad. The first post office with the name Daysville opened here in 1901, reportedly with George Day as the first postmaster. The post office closed in 1927, opened again in 1930, and finally closed for good in 1936.

152.0 WETSEL – Wetsel is a community of rural homes and businesses at an elevation of 1370 feet. The name Wetsel, also spelled Wetzel, has been used by several families since at least the early 1800s. For many years, Wetsel was simply a short railroad spur. However, some improvements came about around 1920 as the boxcar-body depot was retired in November 1919, and a new frame combination station opened in October 1920. Wetsel was apparently a base for track workers on the Tennessee Central as railroad documents indicate that two section houses remained after the company retired the east section house during August 1928.

Early Tennessee Central documents show a spur track to the north and a station to the south at the grade crossing at Wetsel, today known as Wetsel Road. The timetables of Southern Railway show that in 1983, the spur held 14 cars. Today, the spur is shorter and has been used to load railroad ties and other timbers by area timber companies.

152.6 PINEY CREEK BRIDGE – The railroad bridge here (known as the "Time ZoneBridge") is a noted landmark with U.S. Highway 70 just to the south. Highway 70 was the first state highway between Memphis to Bristol and was once Tennessee Highway 1. The railroad's 600-foot-long bridge consists of a mix of deck plate girder spans, as well as approaches that once consisted of timber trestles, being replaced by new concrete bents supporting large I-beams. The views from the bridge are great.

Eastern Division – Crab Orchard to Rockwood

The Piney Creek Bridge towers over the narrow valley which forms the county line between Roane and Cumberland Counties. Photo by Sarah Jennings.

Piney Creek forms about five miles to the northwest from a number of smaller streams flowing off the Crab Orchard Mountains, a part of the Cumberland Plateau. Piney Creek can be floated from here to near the Tennessee River south of Rockwood. The stream is classified as Class III-V by American Whitewater, meaning that it can be extremely difficult, depending upon water levels.

At this location, Piney Creek is the county line between Roane County (to the east, in Eastern Time) and Cumberland County (to the west, in Central Time). **Roane County** was named for the second Governor of Tennessee, Archibald Roane, when it was created on November 6, 1801. Roane County was the original location selected for the capital of Tennessee, but it was still owned and controlled by the Cherokee, so the capital wound up at Nashville. The area boomed in the late 1800s and early 1900s thanks to the iron ore and coal along Walden Ridge on the west side of the county. Rockwood was created as a processing center, creating pig iron for national markets. Today, the county has a population of about 60,000 and features a mix of rural activities, small manufacturing, and commercial businesses over its 395 square miles. Kingston is the county seat.

Cumberland County also has a population of about 60,000, however it is a larger county with about 680 square miles. Cumberland County was created on November 16, 1855, from parts of eight other counties (Bledsoe, Roane, Morgan, Fentress, Rhea, Putnam, Overton, and White). Cumberland's early settlements were based upon mining and supporting travelers on several roads that passed through the county. During the 1930s, the federal government's Subsistence Homesteads Division established the Cumberland Homesteads south of Crossville, moving 250 impoverished families into a government-planned community. Today, much of this project is the Cumberland Mountain State Park. Crossville is the county seat.

153.1 McLEAN – McLean was once the location of a track to the south to serve the McLean coal mine, also known as the Elder Mine, Willet Mine, or the Roane Iron Company's Tunnel Mine. In *Bulletin 123: Analyses of Mine and Car Samples of Coal Collected in the Fiscal Years 1913 to 1916*, by the Department of the Interior's Bureau of Mines, the mine was described from a 1915 inspection. It stated that the McLean Mine produced bituminous coal from "a slope mine three-fourths mile south of McLean siding on the Tennessee Central RR." The report stated that the mine worked "4 feet 3 inches of crushed rashy coal at the top of the bed" with a roof made of Walden sandstone and a floor consisting of hard clay.

The name McLean comes from the McLean family. George Forsyth McLean was born in Scotland in 1841 and moved to Pennsylvania by the 1860s where he learned the iron and coal business. He moved to Tennessee by 1871 and settled near Rockwood, where he became involved with the Roane Iron Company. His obituary in 1908 stated that McLean "was an experienced miner and was thoroughly conversant of the coal formations in the mountains in and around this section."

Like many mines in the area, the depression of the late 1920s and 1930s ended the business. However, it is obvious that the McLean coal business was drawing to a close by the early 1920s. In 1924, business slowed enough that the Tennessee Central retired their mail crane and passenger shelter here. In August 1925, a small house was built at McLean for the tunnel watchman. The coal mine spur, located to the south down what is today known as Willet Mine Hollow, was retired in June 1929.

153.3 WILLET HOLLOW TUNNEL – This tunnel, also known as Walden Ridge Tunnel, was one of the last parts of the Tennessee Central mainline built between Nashville and Rockwood. The railroad passes under Mount Roosevelt at what is called Mount Roosevelt Gap, and the tunnel is reportedly 722 feet long. The stone portals have a large "TC" as a part of their design. When originally built, the tunnel passed through stone, using wood bracing where needed. During December 1924, the tunnel roof was strengthened, with the railroad adding additional bents and roof arches. However, the soft stone has continued to collapse and some openings have reportedly happened in the tunnel's roof. Because of this, the lining of the tunnel was rebuilt in 2013.

West of the tunnel, trains climb grades of as much as 2.0% as they work their way to Crab Orchard. Heading east from the tunnel, the railroad begins to drop with grades of as much as 3.6%. There is also a short maintenance spur track just east of the tunnel that generally houses equipment used to maintain the tunnel.

154.3 BIG GULCH BRIDGE – This bridge is a mix of timber trestles and deck plate girder spans, making the bridge 454 feet long. The bridge is surrounded by heavy forests as the railroad runs along the side of Walden Ridge. Railroad grades in this area run 2.0% or more, steep for many railroads.

Valuation maps of the Tennessee Central Railway show that the lands on both sides of the railroad from here east were owned by the Roane Iron Company during the 1920s. Much of this area was mined over the years for coal and iron ore to be used in the making of pig iron. The railroad heading east also serves as the city limits of Rockwood all the way to Coalbank Hollow.

155.5 SLIDE AREA – This location has a history of landslides. Because of this, the Tennessee Central moved the railroad in this area in September 1927. In October 1934, a large 6-foot-tall and 180-foot-long timber retaining wall was built here to hold the slope above the railroad. Almost all of this retaining wall was destroyed by a slide in December 1936.

To the south and at the bottom of the hillside is the Horsehead Corporation Rockwood facility. Horsehead Corporation (also known as Horsehead Resource Development) is based in Pittsburgh, Pennsylvania, and is the largest zinc producer in the United States. The company makes zinc, zinc oxide and zinc powder from recycled products such as electric arc furnace (EAF) dust, batteries, and other nickel and zinc wastes. The Rockwood facility was built in 1978, acquired by Horsehead in 1989, and started processing EAF dust in 1990. The plant uses nearly 100,000 tons of EAF dust annually to manufacture Crude Zinc Oxide (CZO) and Iron-Rich Material (IRM). Horsehead receives some of the materials via the railroad, and some railcars are stored on the site until their cargo is needed.

156.2 COALBANK HOLLOW BRIDGE – This 461-foot-long mixed span bridge curves across a former Roane Iron Company road that was used to reach one of several coal mines they operated along the side of Walden Ridge. To the north of the bridge was once a coal washer, with a series of narrow gauge railroads moving the coal to a number of coke oven banks just south of the bridge, all serving Roane Iron. This area during the 1930s was a part of the Tennessee Products & Chemical Corporation blast furnace complex.

A Norfolk Southern excursion train passes over Coalbank Hollow Bridge in 1986. Photo by Barton Jennings.

The narrow gauge railroad that once existed here was a part of the much larger Rockwood & Tennessee River Railroad, built by the Roane Iron Company to move raw materials to the furnace and finished materials to boats operating on the Tennessee River. Originally, the railroad was built to a gauge of five feet and was built from the furnace at Rockwood to the King Creek landing on the Tennessee River. When several other branches were built upstream that connected to some iron ore mines, the gauge was changed to three feet in 1877 so that the smaller cars could be loaded on a steamboat and barge and moved between the lines. The Rockwood & Tennessee River Railroad was actually a common carrier railroad, but after the Cincinnati Southern (today's Norfolk Southern mainline between Cincinnati and Chattanooga) built through Rockwood about 1880, most of the line's purpose went away. However, the railroad survived for some time, finally dropping its common carrier status in 1898. The line was finally abandoned by 1911 when the ore and coal shipments were moved to the mainline railroad.

156.9 ROCKWOOD – Near here, the first rail on the east end of the Tennessee Central was laid on August 22, 1899, according to the September 7, 1899, issue of *Engineering News*. The same source reported in their December 21, 1899, issue that "a force of over 3600 men is now engaged in grading and tracklaying on this new road between Emory Gap and Monterey, Tenn., 60 miles. Most of the work is being done near Crab Orchard between Rockwood and Crossville. A 1000 ft. steel trestle has just been completed across the property of the Roane Iron Co. at Rockwood." As construction commenced, a number of industry tracks were built in the area, including a spur to Roane Iron's Wright Slope mine up the hillside to the north of the station in August 1900.

The Tennessee Central Railway's Rockwood station was on the south side of the tracks and just west of the grade crossing with Furnace Avenue. The original station built by the railroad finally had electric lights installed in March 1920. In January 1925, a fire extinguisher was installed in the station, prophetic since the combination passenger and freight station burned in early April 1926. The railroad was slow to respond, but finally constructed a freight and passenger depot made from two coach bodies by August 1933. An additional car body was added in October 1935 as a new freight depot. In November 1937, the railroad opened a new passenger and freight station at Rockwood. In the 1960s, a piggyback ramp was built at the same location.

In October 1920, the railroad installed an 11,900-gallon water tank just west of the station, using a water supply from the Roane Iron Company. This location is also the west end of the Rockwood siding, described by the Southern Railway in 1983 as 42 cars long. An industry track curves off to the south, serving the Horsehead Corporation Rockwood facility. This track once passed through downtown Rockwood and connected with Southern Railway near the former freight depot at the Rathburn Street grade crossing.

History of Rockwood

The area around Rockwood has long been home for various groups of settlers. One of the best documented uses before the settlement by Europeans was as the village home of Cherokee Chief Tallentuskie during the late 1700s and early 1800s. The route of the Knoxville-Nashville Walton Road passed through the area, and the Indians quickly began to demand a toll for travelers to pass through their lands. In 1799, a new road was built around the village to reduce the conflicts, but the large number of home-seekers heading west made the situation even worse.

By the time the Treaty of Tellico was signed on October 25, 1805, and the former Indian land was sold, the area had already been claimed by numerous settlers. What became Rockwood was split between the claim of Stockley Donaldson and James Wood Lackey of North Carolina, and a mile square reserve of land (today's Brick Yard Springs) that remained owned by Chief Tullentuskie. Eventually, Tullentuskie leased his land and moved to Missouri, leaving the area to Donaldson and Lackey.

Over the next decade, the Donaldson-Lackey grant began to be split up between various settlers, most of whom became farmers and operators of small stores and businesses, with the community using the name Kimbrough's Landing for one of the local business owners. However, what became Rockwood didn't really begin to develop until after the Civil War. This development happened because Union General John T. Wilder, who had earlier worked in the iron industry in Indiana, commanded troops in this area during the Civil War. During this time, he noted the coal and iron ore on the slopes of Walden Ridge. Months after the war was over, Wilder bought almost 800 acres of land and started making plans for a new iron furnace. He soon teamed up with Hiram Chamberlain (founder of the Knoxville Iron Company) and several other investors to charter the Roane Iron Company on June 18, 1867.

Materials for a new furnace and sawmill were purchased and shipped by river to Kimbrough's Landing, arriving near a post office that carried the name Bells on March 11, 1868. However, with the arrival of the supplies, a move was made to rename the area Rockwood, after W. O. Rockwood, the new president of the Roane Iron Company. The first cast in the new furnace was made on December 8, 1868. By the next year, the furnace was producing 15 tons a day, with the iron being shipped to rolling mills in Knoxville and Chattanooga on the nearby Tennessee River.

To house the many workers needed by the furnace, and to support the growth in coal and iron ore mining, the community of Rockwood was formally developed with company housing, a community church, and a school. By 1875, Rockwood had the only two public schools in all of Roane County.

During the early 1880s, the Cincinnati Southern Railroad was being built to the east of Roane Iron, and what was essentially a second "new" Rockwood was created alongside the tracks. An important part of this development was the opening of several taverns in this new part of town. General Wilder was a prohibitionist and had banned alcoholic beverages on company property. This new development caused problems as Roane Iron began to struggle with absenteeism due to alcoholism. The company thought that their problems had been solved when in 1887, Tennessee passed what was called the "Four-Mile" law that prohibited alcohol-selling saloons from operating in unincorporated areas. However, almost immediately, East Rockwood incorporated to again allow alcohol sales. To again settle the issue, the town of Rockwood was incorporated in 1890 and soon banned the sale of alcohol.

As a part of the incorporation, Roane Iron auctioned off parts of its land and encouraged the development of homes and businesses. This move is credited with the company surviving the Panic of 1893. Major fires in 1894 did set the community back, but the sale of land allowed the development of other area manufacturing, including Rockwood Mills (hosiery) and the Rockwood Stove Works. The Tennessee Central Railroad built around the north and west side of Rockwood in 1900, adding new sources of supplies and new markets. However, after a boom in sales during World War I, the depletion of area coal and iron, as well as higher labor costs and a 1926 mine explosion, forced Roane Iron to close in 1929. The need for iron and steel products before and during World War II caused the Tennessee Products & Chemical Corporation to reopen parts of the Roane Iron Company facility, producing ferromanganese and other products well into the 1960s.

Unlike many similar towns, Rockwood never experienced a major population boom and bust. Its population was about 1000 through the 1870s and 1880s, and grew to 2305 by 1890. By 2010, the town had grown to 5562 residents. Rockwood serves as a regional shopping and residential community, just a mile off Interstate 40. Rockwood has been the home of a number of famous and important people, including Harry T. Burn (Tennessee legislator who broke the deadlock on the 19th Amendment giving women the right to vote), C. M. Newton (member of the Basketball Hall of Fame and a former player, coach and administrator), Nancy-Ann DeParle (Rhodes Scholar and former director of the White House Office of Health Reform), and Megan Fox (*Transformers* movie actress).

158.0 LHOIST/NORFOLK SOUTHERN PROPERTY LINE – In 2005, the railroad operated by the limestone company was extended to here to allow cars to be more easily interchanged in the Rockwood area.

Tennessee Central Eastern Division
Rockwood (TN) to Harriman (TN)
Norfolk Southern Railway

In 1969, Southern Railway acquired the eastern end of the Tennessee Central Railway's Eastern Division, from Crossville to Harriman. The track was assigned to the Southern subsidiary Harriman & Northeastern, which later became part of Norfolk Southern's Cincinnati, New Orleans & Texas Pacific Railway Company. Much of this ex-Tennessee Central route closely paralleled the larger Cincinnati, New Orleans & Texas Pacific Railway, and over the years, parts have been consolidated between the two railroads. Norfolk Southern operates these lines today.

158.0 LHOIST/NORFOLK SOUTHERN PROPERTY LINE – In 2005, the railroad operated by the limestone company was extended to here to allow cars to be interchanged more easily in the Rockwood area.

158.4 BLACK HOLLOW SIDING – A short siding has been located to the south since almost the date of the railroad's construction. This track is often used to interchange cars between Norfolk Southern and Franklin Industrial Minerals. This area is the west end of the Roane County Industrial Park. To the north is a spur track into Proton Power, a company that manufactures low-cost hydrogen from biomass. To the south is Toho Tenax America, a manufacturer of continuous carbon fiber and other related fiber products.

For years, several spur tracks headed north from here. One served the Patton Slope Mine and another went to the Howard Slope Mine.

159.2 ROANE METALS – To the north is a spur track into the Roane Metals facility. The company recycles ferrous and non-ferrous scrap metals, including aluminum, copper, brass, and nickel. Just to the west, but not served by the railroad, is Thermo Fisher Scientific, a custom manufacturer for scientific research and manufacturing.

Just to the south is the Cincinnati, Ohio – Chattanooga, Tennessee, mainline of Norfolk Southern. This line is actually the Cincinnati Southern Railway, created on May 4, 1869, and owned by the City of Cincinnati. It is reportedly the only interstate railroad in the United States owned by a municipality. The railroad was built to attract business to the manufacturing firms in Cincinnati, and the railroad was built south across Kentucky and Tennessee. The last of the rails was laid on December 10, 1879. However, additional work and improvements meant that the first freight train between Cincinnati and Chattanooga didn't run until February 21, 1880, and the first passenger train made the trip on March 8, 1880.

On September 7, 1881, the Cincinnati, New Orleans & Texas Pacific Railway (CNO&TP) won a 25-year lease to operate the railroad, making it possible to form the *Queen & Crescent Route* between Cincinnati and New Orleans. Over the years, the CNO&TP became part of Southern Railway, and then Norfolk Southern. The railroad is still leased, has been improved to a totally modern railroad by the operating railroad, and has paid yearly lease payments to the City of Cincinnati.

160.1 CARDIFF – The Tennessee Central Railway never had many facilities at Cardiff. At one time, there was a short siding that became a simple seven-car spur track by 1983. Maps of the railroad did show a small cinder platform on the north side of the mainline. A note in the January 1904 *Official Guide of Railways* stated that the stations of the Tennessee Central and the *Queen & Crescent Route* were adjacent. This implied that passengers could actually transfer from one railroad to the other here.

There was also a spur track to the north to serve what was called the Chamberlain Slope coal mine. Tennessee's *Twentieth Annual Report of the Mining Department* (1910) stated that the mine was the McLean Mine, owned and operated by the Roane Iron Company, with H. S. Chamberlain as president. The mine worked the 48-inch-thick Sewanee coal seam. The report stated that coal was moved 400 feet from the coal face to the slope by mules, then a final 1200 feet to the tipple by rope.

To the north is a reminder of the iron days of Rockwood. The large plant is the Bayou Steel Group Harriman Mill, bought in 2008 and now the ArcelorMittal Harriman Plant. The facility was built as a long product finishing facility. The facility receives billets from the ArcelorMittal LaPlace, Louisiana, plant and then reheats the billets to roll them into various commercial shapes and sizes. The plant closed 2011-2014 due to a lack of demand, but reopened in 2014 to manufacture one- to three-inch angles and one- to four-inch flats. On the north side of the complex, and also served by the railroad, is PSC Metals. PSC is a national metal recycler and accepts everything from complete automobiles to home appliances to aluminum cans, and almost everything in between.

Cardiff was planned as a second community to support area mining and manufacturing. In some ways, it was a sister community of Rockwood with the idea of locating workers closer to the mines that they would work. In other ways, it was a competitor, with Rockwood being the temperance town and Cardiff being more tolerant of alcohol.

Cardiff was created by the Cardiff Coal & Iron Company in 1890. The name Cardiff came from the mining town of Cardiff, Wales. The company was created by a number of prominent New Englanders, including Maine businessman W. P. Rice, Maine governor Joshua Chamberlain, former Vermont governor Samuel Pingree, and several Knoxville businessmen who had contacts in the area. The group borrowed several million dollars to buy 50,000 acres and to build the mines, coke ovens, iron furnace, and town required. Just as construction and production was under way, a number of creditors who had bought property in Cardiff were unable to pay their bills. This forced the Cardiff Coal & Iron Company into receivership in June 1891, and with the Panic of 1893, forced it into bankruptcy. Today, very little of Cardiff remains.

161.3 CANEY CREEK BRIDGE – This small bridge crosses Caney Creek, which the railroad follows on to Emory Gap. Just to the south is the Norfolk Southern mainline, and then U.S. Highway 27. This location is at the bottom of the grade from each direction, with grades of more than 0.5% heading west, and as much as 2.0% heading east.

162.7 INTERSTATE 40 – The railroad again passes under Interstate 40. The west switch of Emory Gap is located under this highway.

This is Exit 347 on Interstate 40, meaning that the west border of Tennessee is 347 miles away. U.S. Highway 27 is the north-south highway here that justifies all of the hotels and restaurants. Highway 27 extends from Fort Wayne, Indiana, all the way south to Miami, Florida. It was once much longer than its current 1373 miles in length, as its northern end was once St. Ignace, and then Mackinaw City, Michigan. Through Kentucky and Tennessee, Highway 27 follows the Cincinnati, New Orleans & Texas Pacific Railway, today's Norfolk Southern.

A spur track to the north used to leave the mainline here to serve the Prospect Slope Mine. A water tank was also located here.

163.5 EMORY GAP – Emory Gap is actually part of Harriman, Tennessee. This area has also historically been known as South Harriman. Over the years, Harriman has expanded to the south and north along U.S. Highway 27, and east in the developing lands along Interstate 40. The historic Emory Gap is several miles to the north and is where the Emory River formed a gap through Walden Ridge. This gap was used for centuries by Indians and then settlers moving through the area. In the late 1700s, it was known as a gateway to the Cumberland Plateau.

The Tennessee Central wasn't supposed to have a terminal here. Instead, Glen Mary (Glenmary) was the chartered location for an interchange with the Cincinnati, New Orleans & Texas Pacific Railway. However, the railroad couldn't find an easy route to Glen Mary, so Emory Gap became a substitute. Emory Gap was not the only name used by the railroad for this area, as the name South Harriman was also used. In fact, records show that the Tennessee Central Railroad officially began operating between Nashville and South Harriman on June 2, 1902.

From the west, there was a crossover between the Tennessee Central and CNO&TP at Milepost 163.1, which allowed trains to use either railroad's yard at Emory Gap. After the Southern Railway acquired the east end of the Tennessee Central, several other tracks were built at Emory Gap to connect the two adjacent railroads and their yards.

In 1901, the Tennessee Central reached an agreement to use the CNO&TP scales and shop. However, over the next few years, the railroad built a number of their own facilities, including a scale that was rebuilt from a 60-ton to an 80-ton capacity in 1919, and a coaling tower that was retired in April 1920. The oil house was also retired in 1920, but a new supply house was added using a box car body. In December 1924, electric lights were added in all of the railroad's buildings and throughout the yard. Next, in 1926, the Tennessee Central built their own shop complex as part of a redesign of the yard and mainline, allowing a wye to be installed at the east end of the yard. These facilities were improved in 1940 with a new engine shed, allowing many of the smaller buildings to be retired, and the addition of a 27,600-gallon water tower. The water system had a Dearborn Chemical Company water treatment plant installed in 1942, and then it was connected to the Emory Gap city water main in November 1944.

An interesting item reported to the Interstate Commerce Commission in May 1940 is that the Tennessee Central had 12 new toilets built throughout the yard and offices by the WPA (Work Projects Administration), with all of the old ones retired.

The cinder block yard office still stands, painted blue and used as the NS mechanical building. Little else except the yard tracks of the Tennessee Central remain today at Emory Gap. In fact, the former Tennessee Central mainline east of Emory Gap towards Harriman has been abandoned for a short distance between about Milepost 164.0 and Milepost 164.6. This abandonment eliminated a bridge over the Norfolk Southern mainline and a duplicate rail line that served the TVA Kingston power plant.

The ex-Tennessee Central yard office building still stands at Emory Gap, now used by the mechanical forces of Norfolk Southern. Photo by Sarah Jennings.

164.1 BRIDGE OVER CNO&TP – During February 1921, an agreement was reached with the Cincinnati, New Orleans & Texas Pacific Railway to construct an "overhead crossing at Emory Gap." This would allow the Tennessee Central to cross the larger railroad and operate their line to the Emory River and on to Harriman, located just south of today's NS line, without the conflicts of an at-grade crossing. Norfolk Southern records show that this bridge was a 75-foot through plate girder span.

As previously stated, this bridge has been retired as part of a consolidation of tracks through this area.

164.2 SOUTH HARRIMAN – While this area has long carried the name of South Harriman, it is technically part of the City of Harriman. The Tennessee Central Railway had a wye here that connected to a short branch to what it showed as Kingston. In reality, this branch was an important source of revenue for the railroad as it connected with the TVA (Tennessee Valley Authority) Kingston Fossil Plant, generally known as the Kingston Steam Plant. Construction on the plant began in 1951, with units 1-4 going into service in 1954, and units 5-9 starting up in 1955. When it was completed in 1955, it was proclaimed to be the largest coal-fired power plant in the world. The plant was justified by the need for electrical power at the nearby Oak Ridge National Laboratory, and at its peak, it produced about ten billion kilowatt hours of electricity each year, consuming about five million tons of coal to do so.

The branch line crossed Highway 27 and then curved south and followed Baumgarter Road to a wye junction with the TVA line along Caney Creek. Initially when built, the Tennessee Central delivered coal to the TVA's Caney Creek Yard, where it was switched and then delivered to the plant by TVA's own railroad. This plant was an important source of business for the Tennessee Central Railway. Initially, much of the coal that the plant burned came from mines around Monterey, meaning that the railroad received all of the transportation revenue. Later, coal contracts were won by other mines on other railroads (primarily today's CSX), and the Tennessee Central simply received revenue from the short movements from Harriman.

During the 1960s, even with the loss of the long-haul coal movements, Emory Gap/South Harriman was very important to the railroad. According to multiple sources, in 1965, 222,768 tons of coal were delivered to Emory Gap. This accounted for almost half of the shipment deliveries in the Cumberland region of the railroad.

However, after the acquisition of the eastern end of the railroad by Southern Railway, through movements of coal from Monterey to Emory Gap almost ended. With two railroads involved, and better coal sources on the Louisville & Nashville north of Knoxville, coal stopped moving on this line. Instead, coal came directly from mines on the Southern Railway or was delivered by L&N trains at Harriman and shuttled on to TVA by Southern Railway locals.

This pattern held steady until a 1997 review of coal movements by TVA. The study (*1997 Final Environmental Impact Statement: Kingston Fossil Plant Alternative Coal Receiving Systems*) stated that coal "is now shipped to Harriman by both NS and CSX, and is then transported over a short NS spur to NS's Emory Gap rail yard or to TVA's Caney Creek rail yard. TVA then moves the coal via a TVA-owned line into the rail yard at the Kingston plant. NS has direct access to the Caney Creek yard. CSX must deliver trains to the NS yard; NS then charges a fee to interchange the train to the plant via the NS spur. This switching fee is approximately $2 million annually, and is expected to increase as TVA purchases more coal from CSX origin mines."

This review and its final report in 1999 resulted in the move to unit coal trains, the construction of a unit coal train unloading facility at the power plant, and the abandonment of the Tennessee Central route to Caney Creek Yard, which was also abandoned. Another part of the change was the abandonment of the Tennessee Central mainline from Milepost 164.0 to Milepost 164.6, with a switch and upgraded line built from the Norfolk Southern mainline to connect to the former Tennessee Central Emory River bridge to allow CSX trains to deliver coal.

165.2 EMORY RIVER BRIDGE – The Tennessee Central Emory River Bridge was authorized on June 30, 1902, by the Fifty-Seventh Congress. In *An Act To authorize the construction of a bridge across the Emory River, in the State of Tennessee, by the Tennessee Central Railway or its successors*, Congress stated that, "the Tennessee Central Railway, a corporation created and organized under the laws of the State of Tennessee, and its successors be, and it and they are hereby, authorized to construct and maintain a bridge and approaches there to over the Emory River, in the State of Tennessee, at such point at or near the city of Harriman as said company or its successors may deem suitable for the passage of its or their railroad over said river." It gave two years for the bridge to be completed. Apparently, the railroad was ready for the bill as the plans were approved by the Secretary of War on July 30, 1902.

This expansion of the railroad from South Harriman across the Emory River and into Harriman was one of the causes cited for the 1904 bankruptcy of the company. In the May 27, 1904, issue of *The Railway Age*, there was a report that the Tennessee Central had been appointed a receiver due to a number of unpaid bills and liabilities. Specifically, the article stated that M. N. Elkan & Company of South Carolina was owed a balance of $44,000 for extending the road from Emory Gap to Harriman.

The bridge today, from west to east, crosses Riggs Chapel Road, the Emory River, and the old Harriman & Northeastern Railroad (H&NE) mainline. The H&NE depot was located just to the north of the east end of the bridge. The center span is a large Warren Camelback span. Each end of the bridge features four-pile steel bents and short steel beam spans, replacing the former timber spans that were once here. Built about 1910, the entire bridge was shown to be about 1000 feet long, although some Norfolk Southern sources say 1440 feet.

In December 1926, the east approach timber span was replaced with 350 feet of new creosoted ballast decked timber trestle, and the 56-foot-long I-beam span over the Harriman & Northeastern was replaced by a 53-foot through plate girder span. Three years later in August, 350 feet of the west end of the bridge was replaced with a new creosoted ballast deck trestle.

A big part of the purpose of this bridge was to reach downtown Harriman. About 1900, Harriman was a rail terminal, with service by the Southern, CNO&TP, Harriman & Northeastern, and Louisville & Nashville, in addition to the Tennessee Central. This bridge allowed the Tennessee Central to reach the Louisville & Nashville in Harriman, and to serve the main passenger station there. For many years, the Tennessee Central was unable to turn their trains at Harriman, so the passenger trains would wye at Emory Gap and then back the last several miles to the Harriman station. Today, the bridge is used by trains running between Knoxville and Emory Gap, and by CSX trains bringing coal to the TVA Kingston plant.

Emory River

The Emory River is not a long river, starting about 45 miles north of here on Fork Mountain. It flows a bit to the west and then turns south, being used by Norfolk Southern as a steady grade through the mountains. The river flows into the Clinch River next to the Kingston Steam Plant, and then almost immediately into the Tennessee River about five miles downstream. The Emory River wraps around the west, south, and east side of Harriman.

The name Emory is believed to have come from William Emery, who drowned crossing the river during the 1779 action to destroy war supplies given to the Indians at Chickamauga by British forces. Some early articles called the river William Emeries River, while others used Emery River. It is not clear how it became Emory River. Before white settlers, the river was called "Babahatchie," which reportedly means "babbling waters."

165.8 HARRIMAN – Harriman was the east end of the Tennessee Central Railway. The last several miles into Harriman were the last part of the mainline built by the railroad. Harriman was built near the Emory River Gap through Walden Ridge, a traveling route for generations. Because of the coal nearby and limited routes through the area, Harriman became a railroad center with several railroads serving the community.

Eastern Division – Rockwood to Harriman

Today's Harriman began officially in 1889 with the East Tennessee Land Company, chartered in May of that year. The plan was created by the New England temperance movement headed by a minister named Frederick Gates, and the 1888 Prohibition Party presidential candidate General Clinton B. Fisk, who became the first president of the East Tennessee Land Company. Additional founders included Quaker Oats co-founder Ferdinand Schumacher, and publishers Isaac K. Funk and A. W. Wagnalls. The plan was to attract industry and hard-working individuals by preventing the sale and use of alcohol, and the pitfalls of a single-company controlled company town. Quickly, the company bought several hundred thousand acres of land and began to lay out a town, named Harriman, for Walter Harriman, a governor of New Hampshire. Reportedly, Harriman had marched through the area as a colonel with his 11th New Hampshire Regiment, and had commented that the location would be a good place for a town.

Besides the land company, several additional subsidiaries were formed to create jobs and industry. The companies were the East Tennessee Mining Company (coal and iron ore mining), Harriman Coal & Iron Railroad Company (local railroads), and the Harriman Manufacturing Company (an investment company to provide financial assistance in starting up area industries). A headquarters building was also built at the corner of Walden Avenue and Roane Street. This brick building with its four Norman towers still stands as part of the city office complex. In 2017, the building was under restoration.

The East Tennessee Land Company office building, also known as "The Temperance Building," still stands in Harriman, Tennessee. Photo by Sarah Jennings.

At the front door is a sign marking the structure's historic importance. The sign reads:

1890   2010
The Temperance Building
Originally the offices of the East Tennessee Land Co.
During the years 1897-1908 home of the American Temperance University.
Placed by
Avery Trace Chapter DAR 2010

To support these plans, more than one million dollars was borrowed from the Central Trust Company of New York. Harriman was planned in a manner that recognized that industry needed to be in one part of town, worker's houses in another, and homes for the professional class in another. Land along the Emory River was set aside for industry. Nearby were smaller lots that skilled laborers could afford, and land for apartments. For the wealthy and professional class, larger lots were set aside on Cumberland and Clinton streets in what became known as Cornstalk Heights.

By 1892, the plan was working and several rolling mills and factories were in operation, and housing lots were being built upon. However, the national economy was slowing with the approach of the Panic of 1893. Just as with Rockwood and Cardiff, the founders of Harriman found that they couldn't pay their debt and the East Tennessee Land Company was forced into bankruptcy during November 1893.

Harriman survived the financial panic and several industries continued to grow, including a paper mill and two hosiery mills that lasted into the 1980s. The temperance movement also didn't leave Harriman, as the American Temperance University was established in 1894. The idea was so ingrained in the community that the first liquor store didn't open until 1992.

Today, Harriman remains much as it was built, with several large Victorian neighborhoods. The Cornstalk Heights area is now the Cornstalk Heights Historic District, listed on the National Register of Historic Places on January 11, 1991. Also on the National Register is the former East Tennessee Land Company headquarters and the Roane Street Commercial Historic District.

Wilma Winifred Wyatt was born in Harriman on November 4, 1911. Wilma later changed her name to Dixie Lee, worked as a singer and actress, and was the first wife of Bing Crosby.

Harriman & Northeastern Railroad

As stated previously, the East Tennessee Land Company established the Harriman Coal & Iron Railroad Company (HC&I) to encourage the construction of railroads at Harriman. The Harriman Railway & Construction Company was incorporated on March 25, 1890, becoming the HC&I on January 10, 1891. The HC&I started construction almost immediately, building seven miles of track from Harriman to DeArmond, Tennessee, in 1891. Unfortunately, the railroad failed with the land company and entered receivership on November 21, 1893. However, the next year the railroad built another 15 miles northward to Petros, Tennessee, before being sold at foreclosure on July 22, 1895. The railroad property went to Isaac K. Funk, one of the original investors in the East Tennessee Land Company, who then sold the "19.614 miles" of railroad to the newly created Harriman & Northeastern Railroad (H&NE) on December 4, 1895, the same day the H&NE was officially incorporated.

At Harriman, the H&NE looped around town alongside the Emory River, with connections to the Southern Railway mainline on both ends. On the east end, there is still a wye next to U.S. Highway 27. The H&NE then turned south, following the river, and served several industries, such as the old American Kraft papermill and the American Fork & Hoe Company. The factory of American Fork was at the end of Morgan Street, near the location of the Louisville & Nashville depot on their parallel line.

The H&NE line passed under the Tennessee Central Emory River bridge. Just east of the Tennessee Central was once the H&NE engine house, and their Harriman depot was just to the west. The open area to the west housed the railroad's main rail yard, a wye, warehouse, car shed, coal yard, and icing platform. Much of this area was destroyed by a 1929 flood. Further west, the H&NE connected with the Southern Railway just east of their Harriman Junction with the CNO&TP.

Petros is historically a coal mining town and was at one time the home of Brushy Mountain State Penitentiary. Early records show that the coal mine was owned and operated by the State of Tennessee. It was felt that coal would be needed for the many industries that would build at Harriman, so this unserved mine was a logical destination for the railroad. Today, the mines are closed and the railroad is gone, but enough remains that some of the town and coal mine scenes in the movie *October Sky* were filmed in Petros.

Today, the Harriman & Northeastern is controlled by The Cincinnati, New Orleans & Texas Pacific Railway Company, making its remains part of Norfolk Southern. The Tennessee Central trackage in the Harriman and Emory Gap area was assigned to the H&NE.

166.0 END OF RAILROAD – The railroad ended at the Southern Railway station on Crescent Street. This was the junction with the Southern Railway line from Knoxville, today also used by CSX.

Tennessee Central Eastern Division
Old Hickory Branch
Stones River (TN) to DuPont (TN)
Nashville & Eastern Railroad

In January 1918, when DuPont was awarded the contract to build and operate a gunpowder plant near Hadley's Bend of the Cumberland River outside Nashville, the challenge was a lack of transportation for both the construction materials and the workers who would run the plant. With the construction project being planned, the Nashville, Chattanooga & St. Louis Railway surveyed a route from their line, across the Tennessee Central, and then on north to the plant location. Construction began on February 10, 1918. A month later, the first trains began running over the line, delivering materials to the site of the gunpowder plant. Reports indicate that the work set a record for new railroad construction, "moving 50,860 cubic yards of earth, 11,560 cubic yards of solid rock and 29,780 cubic yards of earth borrow; 10 acres of the right of way were cleared of trees and stumps, 624 lineal feet of pipe culvert were laid and 315 cubic yards of foundation excavation were moved."

The line was an immediate success, moving hundreds of carloads of material and thousands of laborers daily. The construction of a second track and two interchange yards at today's Stones River soon followed, being completed by late summer 1918. Reports state that by late 1918, as many as thirty-two trains operated daily over the line, hauling almost 300 freight cars and 17,000 passengers a day. This level of traffic didn't continue long as World War I ended on November 11, 1918, and the gunpowder plant was shut down. The plant site was eventually sold off to DuPont for a new Rayon plant. The government wasn't interested in operating a railroad, so they sold it to the Tennessee Central Railway on December 15, 1923. The line became a major source of freight revenue for the Tennessee Central, and when the Louisville & Nashville took over this part of the railroad, the Old Hickory Branch was the primary source of business on the line.

Today, this line is used to serve several large rail customers by the Nashville & Eastern. Known as the Old Hickory Subdivision,

Tennessee Central Railway: History Through the Miles

it sees almost daily service, generally by a local out of the Nashville area.

0.0   STONES RIVER – Stones River is 9.7 miles from Nashville and is the junction between the mainline of the Nashville & Eastern and the Old Hickory Subdivision, once known as the Old Hickory Branch. There is a small yard next to the mainline just west of the junction switch.

When the railroad was first built, there were two major yards constructed at Stones River, one to serve each railroad. Additionally, there was a diamond across the Tennessee Central which required an interlocker, signals, and a tower. During October 1924, the Tennessee Central retired many of the yard tracks, including Track #4 (1834'), Track #6 (2668'), Track #7 (793'), and Track #8 (876'). This left three tracks in the yard: Track #2 (2373'), Track #3 (2012'), and Track #9 (821'). Over the years, these tracks have been moved, lengthened and shortened, and modified as demand changed.

In 1928, the route over to the Nashville, Chattanooga & St. Louis Railway was removed, and a number of facilities were retired. They included the interlocker and interlocker shed, transfer interlocker tower, signals, and telegraph shed. On May 23, 1930, the railroad retired the frame freight depot at Stones River.

0.2   STONERS CREEK BRIDGE – This three-span deck plate girder bridge, originally built to handle two tracks, was known as Bridge O.H.-1 by the Tennessee Central, which showed that the bridge measured 244 feet long. Stoners Creek was named for explorer Michael Stoner who scouted the area in the late 1760s. Just downstream, Stoners Creek flows into Stones River, named for early explorer Uriah Stone.

0.7   CENTRAL PIKE BRIDGE – The railroad crosses Central Pike on a new three-span through plate girder bridge. This was Bridge O.H.-2 on the Tennessee Central.

Eastern Division – Old Hickory Branch

2.2 **TENNESSEE CONFEDERATE SOLDIERS' HOME** – To the east once stood the Tennessee Confederate Soldiers' Home, a large brick building that housed Confederate veterans from 1891 until 1933. Originally, the veterans were to be housed in the nearby empty Hermitage mansion, President Andrew Jackson's former plantation. Instead this complex was built nearby, featuring verandas stretching along two levels. The Home also included a hospital wing for medical care. Reportedly, this care included a daily dose of George Dickel whiskey.

By 1901, the Tennessee Confederate Soldiers' Home housed 126 disabled veterans. In 1933, the remaining veterans were moved to the Tennessee Industrial School, followed by another move in 1937 into private homes. Many of the veterans were buried in a cemetery on the Hermitage grounds, next to the Presbyterian Church. This church was built in 1824 on land donated by Andrew Jackson. The cemetery there has about 500 graves.

After the Home was closed in 1933, the Tennessee legislature deeded the site in 1935 to the Ladies' Hermitage Association, founded initially to prevent the Hermitage from being converted into the veteran's home. Almost immediately, the main entrance to the home and its largest wing was torn down as part of a Works Progress Administration federal project. The remaining part of the Home was used as apartment housing for Hermitage employees. The last part of the structure came down in 1953 and the brick was used to build the Hermitage gift shop, now part of the education building.

2.6 **OLD HICKORY** – To the east of here is The Hermitage, the last home of Andrew Jackson and his wife Rachel. Old Hickory was the nickname that Andrew Jackson received during his military service. This was their fourth home after living in Nashville, on their Poplar Grove farm, and then a 640-acre plantation on the Cumberland River called Hunter's Hill. Unfortunately, Jackson was forced to sell Hunter's Hill in order to avoid bankruptcy. On July 5,

1804, he purchased a 425-acre farm from Nathaniel Hays which became The Hermitage. Along with the new farm, Jackson also opened a river port at nearby Clover Bottom on the Stones River where he operated a general store, a tavern, and a thoroughbred horse racing track. He also served as a Superior Court judge.

His various businesses allowed Jackson to slowly expand his farm, and between 1819 and 1821, he built the first version of The Hermitage mansion, a brick Federal-style house. The house was built in a style popular in the South for decades, featuring eight rooms, four on each floor and two wide center halls. The first floor contained two parlors, a dining room and Andrew and Rachel Jackson's bedroom. The second floor featured four bedrooms for guests.

In 1831, while Jackson served as president, the house underwent a major renovation, including a major redesign by "adjoining flanking one-story wings, a two-story front portico with ten Doric columns, a small rear portico and copper gutters." The east wing housed a library and a farm office while the west wing included a large dining room and pantry. A large new kitchen and a smokehouse were added behind the mansion.

A further rebuild took place in 1834 due to a fire. This rebuild changed the entrance façade to a fashionable Greek temple look by adding six, two-story columns with modified Corinthian capitals across the front porch. Similar columns with Doric capitals supported a two-story porch on the back entrance. The most noticeable change inside the home was the addition of a cantilevered, elliptical staircase in the center hall. Jackson resided at The Hermitage after his presidency, living here from 1837 until his death on June 8, 1845.

Outside in the formal garden is the Jackson family tomb. The design of the tomb closely resembles a Greek temple found on wallpaper that Rachel had chosen for the Hermitage entrance hall. Built after Rachel's death on December 22, 1828, it is also the burial place of President

Jackson. The tomb features the inscription "General Andrew Jackson, March 15, 1767 - June 8, 1845."

After the death of Andrew Jackson, the property suffered as the family wealth was lost. In 1856, the property was sold to the State of Tennessee. In 1889, the property came under the care of the Ladies' Hermitage Association. In 2014, the preservation group became the Andrew Jackson Foundation. Today, The Hermitage is considered to be one of the best preserved presidential homes in the country.

3.8 **HOPEWELL** – There are nine communities named Hopewell in Tennessee, plus four more with Hopewell as part of the name. This Hopewell is an unincorporated community in Davidson County, located to the west of the tracks. There are actually a number of planned suburbs in this area with different names, changing the formerly rural characteristics of the community.

Hopewell was a common name across the region, not just in Tennessee. Several early political leaders had the name, and Hopewell is found in just about every eastern state. However, one Hopewell is known to have impacted early settlement in this area. The Treaty of Hopewell, dated November 28, 1785, was signed at Hopewell, South Carolina, between the new United States and the Cherokee Nation. It limited white settlement west of the Appalachians, especially in the Cumberland River valley. The treaty threatened the existing settlements in this area.

A number of records state that this Hopewell, a part of Old Hickory, was predominantly African-American. Some indicate that it was in response to the segregation of the 1800s and early 1900s, while others say that it was land set aside for sharecropping and the families of former slaves from the area. What is clearly known is that when DuPont built and operated their plant nearby, Hopewell was where the African-American domestic helpers lived, literally on the "other side of the tracks" in a community known as "black town."

A school was built here for "Nashville's colored children" in the 1920s, closing in 1966 with the desegregation of the Nashville school system. Today, the school is used as the office of Global Outreach Developments, International. The community is still a poor neighborhood surrounded by richer developments, but it is also the center of an international religious effort to assist communities in helping themselves to improve their lives.

The railroad once had several tracks at Hopewell. On March 26, 1926, a 514-foot spur was built on the west side of the tracks. Tennessee Central records show that the track was retired November 23, 1927, when a new 590-foot spur track was built nearby for Guy Debow.

5.2 **LAKEWOOD** – Look for the grade crossing with 24th Street, also known as Park Circle. Lakewood is an unincorporated community with a population of approximately 2500. The community was originally established as Dupontonia, a company town for workers at the nearby DuPont plant. The community is easy to identify by its grid of streets and look-alike houses squeezed between the railroad and the Cumberland River to the east.

Apparently during the early 1900s, DuPont established a number of company towns across the country. These included: Dupont, Washington; Louviers, Colorado; Ramsay, Montana; Old Hickory, Tennessee; Hopewell, Virginia; and Penniman, Virginia. These towns served two purposes. First, many of DuPont's plants manufactured things like dynamite and gun powder. These could not be located in existing communities, so DuPont located the plants in rural areas and thus needed housing for its workers. Next, DuPont had a strategy that providing housing created a more stable work force, increasing employee skill and reducing training costs. As a part of this effort, the company designed more than a dozen standard home designs that were used in all of their towns. At least eight to ten of these designs were used in the Old Hickory-Dupontonia communities.

Eastern Division – Old Hickory Branch

Dupontonia was finally officially incorporated in 1959, but changed its name to Lakewood, and reincorporated, in 1961. With Nashville and Davidson County having already merged, Lakewood went through two elections before deciding to unincorporate and join the consolidated government on March 15, 2011. Early maps show that Dupontonia was actually just outside the property of DuPont. According to maps of the Tennessee Central Railway, the "DuPont Rayon Property Line" was just north of 22nd Street at Dupontonia. Another name used for this land ownership north of town was the DuPont Fibersilk Company.

There were never many industries at Dupontonia that required rail service. However, the Tennessee Central documented the construction of a spur for the Tom S. Hartley Coal Company at Milepost 5.3. Tennessee Central documents show that it was placed in service on October 21, 1935.

5.6 **OLD HICKORY** – Old Hickory was once the destination of the Broadway Dinner Train, operating from downtown Nashville to this location. For many years, a simple wood frame depot stood here on the east side of the tracks, opposite the entrance to the golf course. Just north of here, there was once a track known as the Joe Puckett Spur, opened on May 22, 1935.

In January 1918, the U.S. government contracted with the E. I. DuPont deNemours Company to build the world's largest gunpowder plant, located near here on Hadley's Bend of the Cumberland River. Plans for the plant had it producing one million pounds of smokeless powder each day. In less than a year, more than 3800 buildings had been constructed, with housing for 35,000 people. In addition, the communities included a post office, theaters, churches and schools, a bank, a fire department, a sewerage system, a YMCA, and many other buildings.

Even with this housing, there were not enough local workers and many people rode daily commuter trains from

Nashville to work at the plant. One of the most popular trains was the "Powder Puff Special," a 7am departure that operated exclusively for ladies. However, less than a year after construction began, World War I ended on November 11, 1918.

With the end of the war, the plant was shut down and the jobs went away. Seeing the opportunity to develop jobs, the Nashville Industrial Corporation was created to buy the plant and company towns. Much of the powder manufacturing equipment was sold off, but DuPont bought the plant and changed it into a Rayon manufacturing plant, originally named the DuPont Fibersilk Company, but later changed to the DuPont Rayon Company. DuPont also bought the company housing and improved the towns. After World War II, DuPont began selling off the housing, with any remaining unsold buildings being torn down.

Besides DuPont, the Nashville Industrial Corporation searched for other companies to locate at Old Hickory. They set up plans to work with financially strong companies with high demand for their products, and who would buy supplies and raw materials from the region. According to the *Old Hickory News*, published on Wednesday, March 29, 1929, a second major plant was built at Old Hickory when DuPont sold 500 acres of land to Stauffer Chemical Company, which formed the Old Hickory Chemical Company to operate a plant there. The plant produced carbon bi-sulphide, a product used by the DuPont Rayon plant. The article also stated that "the Rayon Company is today one of the largest industries operating in Tennessee and the largest in Davidson County."

Old Hickory was one of these communities built to house workers for the DuPont Powder Plant, later converted into the Rayon Plant. The first structures were built as temporary construction buildings in 1918, with more permanent buildings coming about in the early 1920s. The land in this area was somewhat limited by the wandering Cumberland River, and the community of Old Hickory was squeezed into the river's Hadley's Bend. Much of Old

Hickory is part of the National Register Historic District which covers the area from 8th Street to 15th Street and from Riverside Road over to Hadley and Jones. Approximately 300 homes are included in this District.

Old Hickory was the first worker community, but as the plant expanded, more housing was needed. The Cumberland River limited expansion of Old Hickory, so Rayon City was created to the north and Dupontonia grew to the south.

6.9   **MP 6.9** – This location is just south of the grade crossing with Industrial Drive and is used to provide protection for trains working the yards and plant tracks just to the north.

8.6   **DUPONT** – The Nashville & Eastern employee timetable shows this as the end of the subdivision. The tracks in this area can only be described as intensive, and there are many fewer tracks today than at the peak of business. Today, the Nashville & Eastern has a small yard, consisting of fewer than a dozen tracks. However, this area once consisted of a yard complex with almost twice as many tracks, as well as a wye to the west.

To the north of the yard, the Tennessee Central once had a long spur track that served the contractor constructing the Old Hickory Lock and Dam on the Cumberland River. Tennessee Central records show that in August 1952, the railroad put into service three tracks for this project. The Rivers and Harbors Act of 1946 authorized the dam, and the U.S. Army Corps of Engineers designed the project. Construction started in January 1952 and the dam closed in June 1954. It was declared completed in December 1957 when the last hydroelectric unit went into service. Both the dam and the lake it created are named Old Hickory to honor President and General Andrew Jackson. It is located approximately 25 miles above Nashville at river milepost 216.2. The waters that crowd the communities of Old Hickory and Dupontonia are part of Lake Old Hickory.

The railroad serves a rail-truck transload facility at DuPont. There are also still a number of customers here whose facilities date back to the DuPont Rayon plant. One of the biggest is PGI (Polymer Group, Inc.), which produces "materials – including the unique REEMAY and TYPAR brands – that serve more than 2,000 customers globally." PGI also states that, "its Old Hickory facility is one of the largest sites in the PGI family not only in physical size but in resin consumption and weekly sales." In 2014, the plant went through a modernization and expansion project.

Nearby is a facility where normally a number of covered hoppers are spotted. In 2011, 3M agreed to buy the former DuPont advanced composite technology facility here. While a fairly new facility, production had ended earlier and 3M was able to start up production again.

Tennessee Central documents provide a number of details about what was happening here over the years. The Freight Station was once east of the yard located near the Rayon Plant, on a long spur track. Tennessee Central records state that on May 31, 1926, the railroad purchased the Old Hickory freight station, and that it measured 40'-3" x 172'. There are then some conflicts in the record as a note dated April 25, 1927, says that the freight station was retired, but then a note in May says that there were several additions built onto the freight station, including a platform measuring 8' x 96'. A statement dated June 15, 1928, notes a project that enlarged the unloading platform at the freight station by 6' x 39'.

The depot was on the east side of the yard near the south switches, where a small metal shed currently sits. Just south of the depot was once a water tank serving the steam locomotives used at the time. During the early 1930s, the railroad made a number of changes in the yard, rearranging tracks, retiring some and adding new ones. Some of the construction was very temporary. For example, in July 1927, the railroad built five tracks for Gould Construction (Contracting) Company. By July 1929, two of the tracks were retired.

Gould Construction was hired to build the new Old Hickory bridge across the Cumberland River. A lightweight bridge had been built to reach the gunpowder plant, but a heavier bridge was needed. In 1926, Davidson County passed a $1 million bond issue to build the bridge. The firm Freeland-Roberts was hired to design the bridge and supervise its construction. The bridge trusses were built by the American Bridge Company, with Gould Construction doing the actual construction under the July 1927 contract. The bridge opened on March 27, 1929, at a cost of $830,000. Obviously, the tracks were built to haul in materials for the new bridge.

At one time, between the two sets of yard tracks, the Tennessee Central had a piggyback ramp. During the 1950s and 1960s, many small communities had a ramp to load trailers onto railroad flat cars, but the expense of such operations and their inefficient nature caused them to be closed and consolidated into large regional intermodal centers. The nearest container intermodal terminal is now operated by CSX in Nashville, Tennessee.

Tennessee Central Eastern Division
Carthage Branch
Carthage Junction (TN) to South Carthage (TN)
Nashville & Eastern Railroad

The original plans for the Nashville & Knoxville had Carthage as the west end of the railroad. This was based upon a plan to use the port on the Cumberland River to reach western and northern markets. However, on May 5, 1887, a revised charter was published that moved the western end of the railroad to Lebanon. Construction of the railroad from Lebanon arrived at Carthage Junction, then known as Gordonsville, on July 3, 1888. *Poor's Manual of the Railroads of the United States* (1889) stated that the Nashville & Knoxville Railroad opened its line to Gordonsville on August 11, 1888, and then on to Carthage in December of 1888.

Today, the line has been cut back to the industrial park near South Carthage. However, the zinc mine is a significant shipper on the railroad and service is almost daily on the line. In fact, the Nashville & Eastern has a small office at Carthage Junction to support this business. While once known as the Carthage Branch, the NERR knows it as the Carthage Subdivision.

0.0 **CARTHAGE JUNCTION** – This is Milepost 60.8 on the former Tennessee Central mainline. In 1888, Gordonsville was the name used by what is now Carthage Junction. Later it became known as Hickman Creek Junction, then simply Hickman Junction. By 1902, the location was named Carthage Junction.

The 1922 *Poor's Manual of Railroads* listed this location as Carthage Junction and the branch was shown to be 7.55 miles long. A note on the records of the Tennessee Central Railway states, "retire coaling station account replaced," with a date of February 1, 1923. For many years, Carthage Junction was used to turn helper engines from Monterey that assisted eastbound trains up the grades. A small coaling facility once existed just east of the wye for these helpers.

1.1 **GORDONSVILLE** – A short spur used to be on the west side of the line here, serving a depot that was retired on February 11, 1939. There were also stock pens here, located just south of the depot. Records show that much of the railroad's land, located on the west side of the tracks on both sides of Fairview Road, was sold to Gordonsville in 1976.

Gordonsville was founded in 1801 by John Gordon III, when he and his wife Alice moved to this area in April of that year. John Gordon operated a farm and kept the first store and tavern at Gordonsville. Gordon was an important local leader. He served as the election superintendent for the vote to select the county seat, as well as Justice of the Peace, deputy sheriff, and sheriff of Smith County. He started the first school in the county in the upper room of the family log house, and served as the first postmaster of Gordonsville. He also served in both branches of the Tennessee General Assembly. Reportedly, John Gordon III remained an active leader of the community until his death on January 24, 1840.

The first charter for the Town of Gordonsville was passed by the Tennessee General Assembly in 1909. Thanks to the railroad, Gordonsville became the largest Smith County community south of the Cumberland River. Also because of the railroad, a great deal of Carthage industry moved away from the river and onto the railroad at Gordonsville and South Carthage. Today, the population of Gordonsville is approximately 1200 and one of the county's two high schools is located at Gordonsville.

1.6 **INTERSTATE 40** – The Carthage Branch passes under Interstate 40, just south of the Tennessee Industrial warehouse complex. Tennessee Industrial stores and supplies parts such as motors, gears, pulleys, lubricants, electrical parts, and many other industrial items to industry in the area. They represent dozens of major and minor industrial suppliers, basically being the parts closet for local industry. A railroad spur once served this facility.

Eastern Division – Carthage Branch

The Carthage Junction depot sat unused and for sale on March 8, 1995, just south of Interstate 40. Photo by Barton Jennings.

Interstate 40 is one of the major roadways in the United States. It stretches from Barstow, California, to Wilmington, North Carolina, reportedly 2555 miles. There are more miles of I-40 in Tennessee than in any other state – 455 miles. It also passes through the three largest cities in the state: Memphis, Nashville and Knoxville.

2.2   **WEST ZINC MINE** – This switch starts a series of sidings and yard tracks that serve a series of zinc loading facilities. The entire complex is about one mile long, and includes the main track, a long siding, as well as a long spur track for holding cars awaiting loading.

The zinc mine and processing facility is now owned by Nyrstar. Nyrstar was created in 2007 by merging the smelting operations of the Australian mining company Zinifex and the alloy manufacturing of the Belgian company Umicore. They have zinc mines in Peru, Honduras, Chile, Canada, and Tennessee. The mine here is operated by NTM – Nyrstar Tennessee Mines. According to the company, the Middle Tennessee (MTN) operations consist of "three underground zinc mines; Gordonsville, Elmwood and Cumberland and a processing plant located at the Gordonsville mine site." The Middle Tennessee mines were acquired in

2009; the mines were originally opened in 1969 and operated by Jersey Minière Zinc Company.

N&E 5323 working the zinc mine near Carthage Junction. Photo by Barton Jennings.

3.2 **EAST ZINC MINE** – This is the north switch – railroad east switch – of the zinc operation on the Carthage Subdivision. North of here, the railroad passes through an industrial park.

3.7 **MULHAREN CREEK BRIDGE** – In Tennessee Central Railroad documents dated June 30, 1918, this was Bridge #E3.69, replaced on December 20, 1928. Drawings show it to be 231 feet long, with timber spans on the south end and a 100-foot "deck truss" on the north end over the waterway. The Tennessee Central showed the spelling of the creek as Mulharen, while most modern sources show it to be Mulherrin Creek. James Mulherrin once owned much of the land along the creek, received as payment for the surveys he made along with Edwin Hickman during the 1780s and 1790s. The purpose of the surveys was to locate land for land grants to Revolutionary War veterans.

Just south of the bridge is a spur track into Graphic Packaging International. The company is a wholly owned subsidiary of Graphic Packaging Holding Company, headquartered in Atlanta, Georgia. The company makes

Eastern Division – Carthage Branch

paperboard and folding cartons for the food, beverage, household products and industrial products markets. This facility manufactures mainly consumer packaging.

4.2 **BONNELL** – This is the switch into Bonnell Aluminum. Bonnell Aluminum is a subsidiary of Tredegar Corporation, a manufacturer of plastic films and aluminum extrusions. The company has operated in North America for more than 60 years. The Carthage facility has 361,000 square feet (8.2 acres) in their building and does casting, extrusion, and a number of other manufacturing steps based upon customer orders.

The tracks beyond this location have been removed. The tracks once went three more miles to the north to South Carthage (Milepost 7.0), located on the south bank of the Cumberland River. Much of the former rail route is now a walking trail.

4.6 **BLUFF CREEK** – The railroad had a passenger shelter and freight platform here. The passenger shelter was retired on September 1, 1933. This station was on the bank of the Caney Fork River.

4.8 **BLUFF CREEK BRIDGE** – Bluff Creek forms from several small streams in pasture land about five miles to the west. Known as Bridge 4.81 by the Tennessee Central, the bridge was replaced in November 1928 with a 50-foot deck plate girder center span.

5.3 **SPUR TRACK** – A 442-foot-long spur track once existed to the east. Today, this area is the location of the former Carthage Junction depot. Built about 1888, the depot is a unique style for the Tennessee Central Railway, with several rounded edges and a short witch's hat roof over the former baggage room.

The Carthage Junction depot has been moved several times, and was being restored in 2017. Photo by Sarah Jennings.

The station was rebuilt in the mid-1960s with a number of improvements, but it soon closed with the end of the Tennessee Central. It was eventually sold and moved to Interstate 40 at the Highway 56 exit. It was used by several businesses, including the Gordonsville Motor Company. It was again abandoned and sat empty for a number of years. Preservationists from the area took interest and acquired the building, with it being donated by the developers of the Taco Bell® at the site. The station was moved three miles further north to South Carthage on October 23, 2014. It now sits across the street from the end of a rails-to-trails path. During late 2017, the station was being rebuilt with plans to use it as an "internet café, train and history museum, and local arts gallery."

The tracks north of here have been removed and converted into a walking path.

7.4 **SOUTH CARTHAGE** – At South Carthage, there were a number of tracks serving local customers such as Ayer & Lord Tie Company, Bilbrey-Welch Spoke Company, Chess Wymond Company, and Carthage Tobacco Works. There were also stock pens and a long incline track down to the Cumberland River. Records state that on December 19,

1935, the railroad replaced the Carthage depot at a new location.

Carthage, the county seat of Smith County, is located on the north bank of the Cumberland River across from where the Caney Fork flows into the Cumberland River. It was an important river port during the 1800s, with steamboats handling tobacco, hemp, and livestock. Carthage exchanged hands several times during the Civil War and was used as a supply base during most of the war for Union forces. As railroads built through the area and steamboat service ended on the Caney Fork River, much of the area business moved south to Gordonsville and South Carthage. Carthage was never directly served by the railroad.

Tennessee Central Eastern Division
Crawford Branch
Monterey (TN) to Wilder (TN)
Nashville & Eastern Railroad

This route was once the Crawford Branch, the longest branch on the Tennessee Central. It stretched more than 21 miles to the north to Wilder, Tennessee. The Nashville & Knoxville Railroad started the line in 1901, building 13 miles to Hanging Limb. The branch was extended by the Tennessee Central another 3 miles to Crawford in June, 1903. The Tennessee Central provided daily passenger service over this branch, with train #202 departing Crawford at 11:45am, arriving at Monterey at 12:45pm. The train would then return to Crawford, departing Monterey as #201 at 2:40pm, and arriving back at Crawford at 3:40pm. Both trains operated daily except Sunday.

By late 1903, the Crawford Branch had been extended to Wilder, and the name Wilder Branch began to be used in some documents. In 1910, the passenger service was based in Wilder, where it left as train #21 at 10:00am. This train arrived at Monterey at 12:01pm, in plenty of time to catch #1 to Nashville, but too late to catch #2 to Harriman and Knoxville. Train #22 headed back to Wilder at 2:50pm, after #1 arrived from Harriman. It was scheduled to arrive at Wilder at 4:10pm. These trains also operated daily except Sunday.

The branch served a number of coal mines as well as several timber companies, making Monterey a busy terminal town. Abandonment of the branch started in 1959 as the coal mines played out. All but the south end of the line was abandoned by the Tennessee Central in 1969 after the Louisville & Nashville acquired the mainline through Monterey. The L&N wanted to keep one mile of the branch so they could use the wye. The Nashville & Eastern extended the track to serve the sand plant.

0.0   CRAWFORD BRANCH SWITCH – The Tennessee Central showed trains heading northward on the branch as heading timetable east. For convenience, this document will also show the line as heading east-west.

0.2 MONTEREY PLANING MILL SWITCH – Just east (north) of the now-gone wye switch was once a spur track to the south (west) that served the Monterey Planing Mill. There is now a small shopping center in this area. East of here, the Tennessee Central had a multi-track yard, used to switch Crawford Branch trains.

0.6 EAST LOUIS AVENUE – This grade crossing marks the east end of the yard in its later years. Records from 1925 show that the yard once went further east all the way to Milepost 0.75. Records from that year indicate that a runaround track was built on the north side of the yard between Mileposts 0.50 and 0.73. Records from 1931 state that the railroad rearranged the "east end of Old Yard" about Milepost 0.75. Tracks mentioned in this part of the yard included a scale track (installed in 1919), a new crossover track from the main track to Track #5, and yard tracks #3, #4, #5, #6 and #7. Today, these tracks are all gone and only barely visible grades can be seen in the brush and trees.

0.9 J. H. SMITH LUMBER COMPANY SWITCH – To the north was once the J. H. Smith Lumber Company, a company that seemed to have moved around the region. In this area today is the Cumberland Container factory. Cumberland Container states that it began production in July 1969 in Monterey in a 6000 square foot facility on three acres with five employees. Today, the company serves the southeastern packaging market from a 300,000 square foot facility that employs 75 workers on its 25 acres of land.

This area was the end of the Crawford Branch starting in 1969. The track north of here is new construction.

1.9 LAKE HILL ROAD – Just east of this road crossing, the railroad crosses Garrison Branch. The stream is dammed both upstream and downstream, serving as the water source for the community of Monterey.

Eastern Division – Crawford Branch

2.3 WEST MONTEREY SAND SWITCH – The south track is used for sand loading using a simple conveyor system. Also to the south are the abandoned pits and current operation of Monterey Sand.

An excursion train passes Monterey Sand in 2016. Photo by Barton Jennings.

2.6 EAST MONTEREY SAND SWITCH – The main entrance to Monterey Sand is in this area. Monterey Sand opened here in 2005 as a partnership between Highway Materials Inc. and Premier Leasing LLC.

2.7 END OF TRACK – East of here, the former Crawford Branch grade is gone. It was abandoned in 1969 after the Tennessee Central was split between the Louisville & Nashville, Southern, and Illinois Central. The L&N kept the mainline and only the first mile of this branch, the rest was abandoned by the Tennessee Central.

3.1 COUNTY LINE – This is the county line between Putnam County (to the southwest) and Overton County (to the northeast). **Putnam County** has a complicated history.

It was first created on February 2, 1842, from parts of Jackson, Overton, Fentress, and White Counties. However, in 1844, an injunction charged that it violated state constitutional requirements, making some of the counties involved too small to meet legal requirements. Because of this, the Tennessee general assembly reestablished the county in 1854, but Putnam County's borders were still disputed for decades. The name Putnam comes from General Israel Putnam, a general in the American Revolutionary War who earlier was a hero in the French and Indian War. Cookeville is the county seat.

Overton County was created on September 12, 1806, from parts of Jackson County and Indian lands. The county was named for Judge John Overton, a friend of Andrew Jackson. Overton served on the Tennessee Supreme Court, and was a partner in the founding of Memphis, Tennessee. The county seat is Livingston.

The railroad was essential for the coal mines of Overton County to succeed. In 1901, Overton County reported 680 tons of coal produced. This was up to 3447 tons in 1902 as the railroad began to build into the area. In 1903, production totaled 84,930 tons.

3.9   **MINERAL SPRINGS** – The name Mineral Springs comes from nearby Mineral Springs Branch. The road that the railroad grade follows is known as Hanging Limb Highway.

5.4   **DOUBLING SPUR** – For years, an 18-car track was located here and was used by trains to double the hill into Monterey.

6.9   **OBEY CITY** – This general area was once known as Cliff Springs, and the name still exists for a small community several miles to the northeast. One of the first documented shippers at Obey City was the Holcomb-Lobb Tie Company, which leased a tie yard from the railroad in January

1905. The railroad had a water tower at Obey City, as well as a 17-car siding.

Obey City was the first station on the line where the Wilder coal seam could be accessed, and a number of small mines soon opened here. Some of the mines documented to be at Obey City include Obey City No. 1, No. 2, No. 3, No. 4; the Paul Farmer mines; East Fork Coal and Coke Company; Peacock Coal and Coke Company; and Jeffrey Coal Company. All of these mines were closed by 1960.

The records of the Tennessee Central Railway have several interesting documents about the Jeffrey Coal Company. In October 1940, the coal company bought Tennessee Central #221, originally #21. This locomotive, a 2-8-0 built by the American Locomotive Company at their Manchester facility in July 1902, was repossessed in December after the mine was sold and the new owners failed to make payments.

Topographical maps for this area show a number of strip mines on both sides of the East Fork Obey River, which is located to the east of the tracks. In 1905, the Tennessee Central Railroad built a railway bridge across the East Fork Obey River to reach a mine. Today, the community of Obey City is a collection of rural houses along the highway. A post office existed at Obey City from September 13, 1906, to January 31, 1912.

8.3 **LOVEJOY** – Today, Lovejoy is a collection of houses. However, in January 1905, the railroad was providing storage space for the Holcomb-Lobb Tie Company here. The Bill's Branch Mine opened near here in 1919. The lowest point on the Crawford Branch, at 1620 feet, is just south of here.

10.2 **BONSACK** – Bonsack was a 24-car siding. In this area, the railroad peaked at 1920 feet of elevation.

10.4 **GREEN POND** – Green Pond is a rural community south of the Wilson Elementary School on Hanging Limb Road.

Opened in 1966, Wilson Elementary replaced eight single room schoolhouses in the county.

Green Pond was never a major stop on the railroad and the only contract in the Tennessee Central records about Green Pond is a lease for lumber storage, dated January 1924, for A. P. Welch. However, reaching Green Pond was a major accomplishment for the railroad as it required a number of sharp curves and steep grades to climb over Green Pond Mountain, located to the southeast. The railroad had a short siding here capable of holding eleven cars. A post office was here 1904-1906.

12.5 HANGING LIMB – Hanging Limb received its name from a large tree that stood near a watering hole. The tree had a huge limb on which people hung saddles and saddle bags. Hanging Limb had a post office from 1888 until 1937. Of the communities in the area, Hanging Limb is still pretty large, covering several blocks. Its elevation is 1896 feet.

The railroad built a spur track for A. P. Welch in March 1921. Because there were a number of coal strip mines several miles away, the railroad also built coal loading ramps for trucks to haul coal to the railroad. These include ramps for the Stoddard & Vanhook Coal Company (May 1948) and Price Norrod (August 1949).

The railroad headed straight north out of Hanging Limb, closely following Honey Springs Road.

15.3 CRAWFORD – The Tennessee Central arrived here by June 1903. The community of Crawford was named after Leonard Crawford, one of the first settlers in the area and also a surveyor for several area mining companies. Today Crawford is an unincorporated community in Overton County with a few houses and a post office, at an elevation of 1878 feet.

Crawford was never a large town, but it was a part of the coal mining center of Overton-Fentress Counties. Known by some as the Wilder-Davidson Coal Mining complex,

Eastern Division – Crawford Branch

the area flourished from 1903 until the mid-1930s. The Crawford Coal and Iron Company started here, but the Brier Hill Collieries was operating Mine Number 1 here by 1902, and opened Mine Number 2 in 1903. The Obey River Coal Company, also known as the Peacock Coal and Coke Company, got started in the area about 1902. The mines of the Brier Hill Collieries were reported to be some of the most productive in Overton County, with coal seams of around five feet. To handle the coal, the railroad had a wye and a 30-car siding at Crawford.

The drop in coal production during the Depression led to a reduction in services. For example, in April 1939, Oates Norrod was issued a contract to raze the Crawford depot and platform. However, the railroad was still busy moving coal, even building a new coal ramp in February 1952.

Heading north from Crawford, the old railroad grade follows Tennessee Highway 164. It then turns east to follow Wilder Highway, Tennessee Highway 85. However, to avoid the steep hills to the east, the railroad built a large horseshoe curve to turn south and follow Big Laurel Creek towards Wilder in Fentress County.

15.9   **LANE** – There was a 20-car siding at Lane for a number of years. It was a handy place to hold cars outside of Crawford. Some early documents show a track named Welch near here, probably named for A. P. Welch who contracted for a number of tracks along the line.

18.3   **BAKER** – Baker was a named point on passenger schedules from the late 1910s.

20.0   **COUNTY LINE** – Overton County is to the west while Fentress County is to the east. **Fentress County** is famous as the home of Alvin York, a hero at the Meuse-Argonne Offensive during World War I. His house and farm are now part of the Sergeant Alvin C. York State Historic Park, declared a National Historic Landmark in 1977. The park is in Pall Mall, about nine miles north of the county seat of Jamestown. Alvin York established the Alvin C. York Agricultural Institute in Jamestown in 1924 to benefit other local farmers.

Fentress County was created in 1823 from land taken from Morgan, Overton and White counties. The name Fentress honors James Fentress, who served as speaker of the Tennessee state house. He also held numerous other county positions across the state. Fentress County was known by the Civil War as the site of several saltpeter mines, a main ingredient in gunpowder. Some reports state that the mines were being worked by the War of 1812.

20.5 HIGHLAND JUNCTION – In 1908, the railroad built an 0.8-mile branch north from here to Davidson (station DG) and named the switch Highland Junction. Within several years, the Davidson, Hicks and Green Company extended the line another mile to reach their coal mine. For the next few years, they operated the branch as the Highland Railway. By early 1916, the Tennessee Central had acquired the line and was operating it themselves. In August 1917, the Tennessee Central reached an agreement with the U.S. Post Office to provide mail service between Davidson and Highland Junction.

Tennessee Central records show a large number of contracts involving track construction for coal mines in the Davidson area. The C. M. Gooch Mining Company had additional tracks built in December 1919, and July 1923. The Highland Coal & Lumber Company had a track built in October 1925, and the Highland Mining Company reached an agreement on a spur track in November 1937. Finally, the Davidson Mining Company leased track and material in July 1929, but had some tracks removed in January 1930.

The railroad had a yard here capable of holding 144 cars. There was also a wye and a water tank. The Airdale Coal Company had a spur track built at Highland Junction during February 1925. Later, a coal loading ramp was built at Highland Junction in June 1951 for J. C. McDonald. This was a sign that coal was moving to trucks, and the line through Davidson was removed in 1959.

20.9 WILDER – Wilder is an unincorporated community in Fentress County, Tennessee. Coal mining began about 1900, and a post office opened December 18, 1902, a year before the railroad arrived. Wilder was a company town from the start, designed to provide housing for the employees of the Fentress Coal and Coke Company. The first survey and plans for the town took place in 1901, and the mines were open by 1902, meaning a large amount of coal was ready to move when the railroad arrived in late 1903. The town included the first school in the area, a town church, and later a high school.

The population of Wilder reached 2350 by 1924, with more than 10,000 living in the entire mining area. From 1919 to 1924, many of these workers were represented by a local labor union, and few labor-management issues resulted in strikes. During the late 1920s, the United Mine Workers began to represent the miners. As the Depression hit, a one-year contract was reached which expired on July 8, 1932. The coal company refused to keep the wages steady as sales fell, and the union called a strike. News about the strike was covered in papers nationwide, especially with the violence, property damage, and killings involved. The winter of 1932-1933 was also especially cold, and many religious and social organizations headed to Wilder to prevent starvation.

A particularly bad episode took place on April 30, 1933, when after a series of attacks on mine property, company guards Jack "Shorty" Green and Doc Thompson shot and killed local union president Barney Graham. Green was acquitted of murder charges, and eventually the mines opened up at a much smaller production rate. The mines and town never fully recovered from the violence, and the last mine, Horse Pound, closed on June 1, 1951, in spite of reports that tens of millions of tons of coal are still in the ground. By 1957, the population of Wilder had dropped to 400, and then to 249 in 2013.

Tennessee Central Eastern Division
Isoline Branch
Campbell Junction (TN) to Isoline (TN)
Abandoned

This branch was built by the Cumberland Plateau Railroad Company with plans to reach new coal mines to the north. The coal mines were under the control of Richard Orme Campbell, an early landowner in the area. By 1903, when the company was sold to the Clear Creek Coal & Lumber Company, the Campbell Coal and Coke Company, founded in 1884, was reportedly the South's largest coal company with mines in Tennessee and Kentucky. Later, Cumberland Coal Company owned and operated mines at Isoline.

Tennessee Central purchased the line on September 30, 1902, and operated it as their Isoline Branch. Business on the line was heavy for several decades, but the mixed passenger/freight train, which operated Monday-Wednesday-Friday, ended on April 1, 1933. All service ended by 1939 and the branch was removed in June of that year.

0.0   CAMPBELL JUNCTION – Located at Milepost 118.8 on the mainline, Campbell Junction was a junction with the Isoline Branch. The location of Campbell Junction is easy to find as it is at a sharp curve of Highway 24, and the old railroad reservoir is still visible to the north. The railroad grade across this small lake is also still visible. A new pump house was built on the west leg of the wye on October 20, 1936, designed to pump water from the reservoir to the railroad water tower that was located just west of the wye on the north side of the tracks.

Campbell Junction was never a major passenger station, and its passenger shelter was retired in 1924. However, during the early 1900s, Campbell Junction was a major freight station.

Heading north, the railroad followed a route that closely follows today's Plateau Road, which uses parts of the grade.

4.9 **PLATEAU** – At Plateau, the railroad turned east and followed No Business Creek to Isoline.

7.5 **ISOLINE** – Isoline was a typical company town, with employee houses, a hotel, company store, and other similar facilities. Isoline actually had two industries that employed workers. These were a coal mine and a big logging operation. A post office existed at Isoline from 1901 until 1935.

Isoline was a busy station for a number of years for the railroad. More than a dozen contracts were written to build tracks, lease facilities, or to provide special services at Isoline. Some of these include a spur track for D. H. Tanner (September 1914), multiple leases with C. B. Wheeler (April 1920 and March 1922) and Joe Youngs (May 1921 and April 1923), and spur tracks for A. E. Tabor (April 1926) and A. B. Pugh (December 1929).

Several contracts were clearly for coal companies. The Cumberland Coal Company had a contract signed in April 1927 for a spur and siding to serve a coal tipple, and in April 1931 to connect to the railroad telephone line. In July 1934, the Rocky Branch Coal Company leased part of the Isoline Branch. Finally, the Isoline Coal Company bought Tennessee Central steam locomotive #211, originally #11, in February 1936 for $1300. This locomotive was one of a number of 2-8-0 locomotives built by the Manchester plant of American Locomotive in 1902.

Today, Isoline is a collection of farms and homes located on U.S. Highway 127.

Tennessee Central Western Division
Nashville (TN) to Hopkinsville (KY)

Tennessee Central Western Division
Nashville (TN) to Hopkinsville (KY)

The Western Division of the Tennessee Central Railway included the tracks from Nashville, Tennessee, to Hopkinsville, Kentucky. Most of this Division is abandoned, however parts are still in service, operated by the Nashville & Western and the Fort Campbell Railroad.

The Western Division was some of the last track built by the Tennessee Central. Work began on the Nashville to Clarksville line in June 1902. The railroad considered several routes past Clarksville, including to Cairo, Illinois, to reach the St. Louis market. The railroad's charter was amended on August 8, 1902, to extend the line into Kentucky by way of either Gracy or Hopkinsville. The railroad was completed to Ashland City by August 1903, and grading was almost completed on to Hopkinsville. Track reached Clarksville in October of that year, and the line was completed in February 1904. This route provided interchange to the west – the Louisville & Nashville at Clarksville, and the Illinois Central at Hopkinsville.

While the Illinois Central connection at Hopkinsville did result in some overhead business, little bridge business was received from the L&N as that railroad served both Nashville and Harriman with their own routes. A six-month waybill sampling in 1965 showed no Clarksville to Emory bridge traffic, but a few Clarksville to Harriman movements. However, of the 747 bridge movements during the six months, 225 were Hopkinsville to Harriman, 215 were Hopkinsville to Emory Gap, and 106 were Hopkinsville to Nashville. This was obviously business from the Illinois Central.

Directions on this railroad will be based upon the railroad's own terminology. A train heading from Nashville to Hopkinsville is heading railroad-west, so to the left is railroad-south, and to the right is railroad-north. To make matters easier, north and south directions will generally be used for the direction from the mainline. However, in many places, the Western Division actually runs north-south, and even to the northeast when heading railroad-west.

The mileposts in the field on the Western Division have been changed and no longer reflect those used by the Tennessee Central Railway. It should also be noted that valuation maps of the Illinois Central show mileposts from the north marked as either JE or E. For example, Tennessee Central Milepost 20, shown as N-20 on valuation maps, was Illinois Central Milepost JE-195 or E-195. These mileposts were an extension of the line from Evansville, Indiana, to Hopkinsville, Kentucky, thus the "E" letter. The Tennessee Central mileposts went from Nashville to Hopkinsville, while the Illinois Central mileposts went from Evansville to Hopkinsville to Nashville. A quick way to calculate the milepost for either railroad is that they always add to 215. If you know the milepost of one railroad, simply subtract it from 215 to get the milepost of the other.

Additionally, the Nashville & Western Railroad uses new mileposts that don't include the eight miles of the abandoned Belt Line around Nashville. This means that their mileposts are approximately eight miles less than those of the original Tennessee Central. This guide will use the original Tennessee Central mileposts, but will often reference these other mileposts.

Illinois Central (1969 - 1972)
Illinois Central Gulf (1972 - 1981)

The Illinois Central (IC) was always the most important interchange partner on the Western Division. The company operated the Western Division 1905-1908, and later owned and operated the route after the failure of the Tennessee Central Railway. On March 18, 1969, the Western Division officially became the property of Illinois Central for $800,000, becoming part of the Evansville District. The payment was $600,000 for the railroad, plus another $200,000 for land along the Cumberland River in northwestern Nashville. This property was for some time the home of a number of shippers, including the W. G. Bush Brick Company (where the Lone Star Industries cement plant now sits along the river at Interstate 65), Nashville Roller Mill (Taylor and First), Jones & Hopkins Manufacturing Company (Monroe and First), Cumberland Telephone Company (Madison and First), Power Packing Company (Jefferson and First), and Progressive Coal Company (Jackson and First). Most of the tracks are now gone in this area, but in 1970, both the Tennessee Central and the Louisville & Nashville had a number of industrial lines here, with both having their own line down the middle of First Avenue North.

On August 10, 1972, the Illinois Central Railroad merged with a longtime competitor, the Gulf, Mobile & Ohio Railroad, creating the Illinois Central Gulf Railroad (ICG). This merger was fought by other railroads and some shippers, and even though it was approved by the Interstate Commerce Commission, the case was heard by the U.S. Supreme Court, which approved the merger during January 1973.

The Illinois Central Gulf, like many railroads after the Staggers Act of 1980, looked to sell or abandon their lightly used and unprofitable lines. The route from Princeton to Hopkinsville to Nashville was never a big money maker for the ICG, and the limitations of the line combined with a more direct and higher capacity CSX line led to efforts to sell the line. A report from about 1980 showed that the gross ton miles (weight of locomotives, cars and contents) on the Western Division were only 120,000 tons northbound and 140,000 tons southbound, meaning that only about 3000 cars a year, or less than ten a day, moved over the route. By the mid-1980s, the line was abandoned or sold off. The eastern part of the former Tennessee Central Western Division line is now the Nashville & Western Railroad, with the track owned by the Cheatham County Railroad Authority, while the north end is the Fort Campbell Railroad.

Tennessee Central Railway: History Through the Miles

Tennessee Central Western Division
Southern Junction (TN) to Vine Hill (TN)
Nashville & Eastern Railroad

This line, known as the Vine Hill Subdivision by the Nashville & Eastern Railroad, was once the Tennessee Central Western Division mainline. Known by many as "The Beltline," this route was built around the south side of Nashville. With land through town difficult to obtain, and the L&N unwilling to allow the Tennessee Central to share its Union Station and associated tracks, the railroad had no choice but to build their own route. This line was part of the Nashville & Clarksville Railroad, later the Tennessee Central Railroad Company, and finally the Illinois Central Gulf. The line between Southern Junction and Vine Hill still exists and is used by the Nashville & Eastern for interchange with CSX.

2.0   **SOUTHERN JUNCTION** – This is the junction with the Nashville Subdivision, located just east of the former Shops Yard. All mileposts on this line are from downtown Nashville. This location was known as Belt Line Junction until 1905, when it was renamed Southern Junction when the mainline east of here was leased to the Southern Railway.

2.2   **INTERSTATE 40** – The railroad passes under Interstate 40, which is shared with Interstate 24 at this location. Interstate 40 stretches from Barstow, California, to Wilmington, North Carolina, reportedly 2555 miles long. There are more miles of I-40 in Tennessee than in any other state – 455 miles. It also passes through the three largest cities in the state: Memphis, Nashville and Knoxville. I-24 is the major route between St. Louis and Atlanta, however the highway only stretches from south of Marion, Illinois, to Chattanooga, Tennessee, about 315 miles. It is basically a diagonal shortcut between I-75 at Chattanooga and I-57 near Marion.

2.7   **BROWNS CREEK BRIDGE** – While much of Browns Creek has been channelized around Nashville, the stream here is still where it has been for years. Just south of here, the railroad has a grade crossing with U.S. Highway 41, known as Murfreesboro Pike.

Track charts of the Tennessee Central show this to be Bridge H2.80. It was a timber trestle structure, 1103 feet long. Heading south, the grade stiffens to 1.5%

3.1 **FACTORY STREET** – Known as Factory Street to the east and Lewis Street to the west, there was once a Southern Oil facility just north of the grade crossing to the west. It was one of several local industries that the Tennessee Central served.

3.4 **CSX RAILROAD** – The Nashville & Eastern (NERR) passes under the former NC&StL line, later Louisville & Nashville and now CSX. This CSX line connects the tracks in downtown Nashville to the Radnor Cutoff and then heads on south to Chattanooga, Tennessee, and Atlanta, Georgia. The CSX uses a concrete arch to cross over the NERR. The switch to send CSX trains either to Radnor Yard or Chattanooga is on top of this arch.

At one time, the Tennessee Central served the Hester Batter Company, located on the north side of the arch on the east side of the tracks, where Perk Products & Chemicals, and Granite Masters of Nashville, have their facilities. Just south of the arch, the Tennessee Central served the Murray Chair Company, located on the west side of the tracks.

3.7 **NOLENSVILLE PIKE** – At one time, the highway bridged across the railroad, with tell tales just north and south of the bridge. Just north of here at Milepost H3.6, the Tennessee Central had a grade crossing with the Nashville Street Railway.

4.2 **NORTH YARD SWITCH** – The Tennessee Central knew this location as Five Points. A passenger platform once existed on the west side of the tracks, using the name Cumberland Park. This is the north end of a small yard. Today, there are three tracks plus a spur track into the Coca-Cola facility to the west. The Tennessee Central considered the center track to be the mainline with the west track known as Track #12 and the east track known as Track #11. There were once several more industry tracks to the east.

4.7   **SOUTH YARD SWITCH** – The timetable of the Nashville & Eastern shows this as Vine Hill siding, a track that is 2100 feet long.

4.8   **VINE HILL** – This is the junction with CSX, Milepost 189.3 of the Nashville Terminal Subdivision to Brentwood. The Nashville & Eastern uses rights over CSX to reach their sister railroad – the Nashville & Western – that is located on the west side of downtown. Until the 1970s a tower stood here to control movements through the diamond and junction. The tower was finally torn down in 1998. The telegraph code for Vine Hill was TC, later changed to simply N. A famous part of Vine Hill history was the live broadcast of the passing of the southbound *Pan-American* passenger train, operated by the Louisville & Nashville Railroad between Cincinnati, Ohio, and New Orleans, Louisiana. Each evening, the passage was broadcast by WSM-AM radio. The broadcasts began on August 15, 1933, and ended in June 1945.

   The Tennessee Central once continued on around the south side of Nashville, serving several shippers and connecting with their line on to Clarksville, Tennessee, and Hopkinsville, Kentucky. The line beyond Vine Hill was sold to the State of Tennessee for use in building the Interstate 440 bypass around the south side of Nashville. At Milepost H10.3 was Central Junction, renamed for the Illinois Central when it leased the Western Division in 1905. Before that, it was known as East Side Junction.

Tennessee Central Western Division
Vine Hill (TN) to Van Blarcom (TN)
Abandoned

The Tennessee Central once continued on around the south side of Nashville, serving several shippers and connecting with their line on to Clarksville, Tennessee, and Hopkinsville, Kentucky. In 1966, 3.85 miles of the line beyond Vine Hill was sold to the State of Tennessee for use in building the Interstate 440 bypass around the south side of Nashville.

4.8 **VINE HILL** – This is the junction with CSX, Milepost 189.3 of the Nashville Terminal Subdivision to Brentwood. The Nashville & Eastern uses rights over CSX to reach their sister railroad – the Nashville & Western – that is located on the west side of downtown.

The Tennessee Central used to go straight, crossing today's CSX and Interstate 65. Heading west, the railroad curved to the south, and the grade now is used by Interstate 440. In the 1930s, several new spur tracks were built here. In July 1935, a track was installed for the Little & Dickey Coal Company. In June 1938, a track agreement was reached with the Little Coal Company.

5.0 **NASHVILLE INTERURBAN JUNCTION** – At one time, the Tennessee Central also interchanged traffic with the Nashville-Franklin Interurban Company at Vine Hill. The connection was about 0.1 miles past the CSX tracks. The line was chartered as the Nashville Interurban Railway on January 18, 1905, and completed about 1907, stretching about 20 miles to the south to a connection with the Middle Tennessee Railroad at Franklin. Some Tennessee Central track charts show the line to be the Nashville & Columbia Interurban. The Tennessee Central reportedly encouraged this interchange by providing favorable rates versus a direct L&N interchange, and traffic was busy and lasted until the Nashville-Franklin (created by a 1933 reorganization of the company) started using buses in the early 1940s.

7.4 **PITTSFIELD** – This was an early station listed by the Tennessee Central, although no shippers are listed in various Tennessee Central documents. However, Pittsfield played an important role for trains heading to Hopkinsville. It was a 49-car siding located at the top of a steep grade from near the Five Points area, and blocks of cars were often hauled to here from the yard at Southern Junction. Later, westbound trains would stop to add them to their consist.

8.4 **RICHLAND STATION** – The Richland-West End neighborhood was created in 1905 by a group of investors around Richland Pike. They laid out the streets and sidewalks and subdivided the property into small lots. Many of the streets were built wide enough for trolley lines, which the developers paid to have built from downtown. The neighborhood is listed on the National Register of Historic Places due to ninety percent of the houses being built 1905-1925 during the peak of the development. In the 1930s, there were a number of rail shippers at Richland. These included Nashville Builders' Supply Company and Barnes & Stanfield.

The Richland Golf Club, now the Richland Country Club, was located to the south. It was established in 1901, but it wasn't until May 7, 1921, that the Richland Golf Club officially opened. Byron Nelson and Ben Hogan won the first two Nashville PGA Invitational Golf Tournaments played on the course. Because of the construction of I-440 during the early 1980s, the club decided to move, selling their land to local developers. A new course was built in the 1980s with Jack Nicklaus doing much of the new design work.

Just west of Richland Station, the railroad crossed over Harding Pike, the highest point on the Western Division of the Tennessee Central at 582 feet. Harding Pike is also known as West End Avenue, or U.S. Highway 705.

Western Division – Vine Hill to Van Blarcom

9.0 **33RD AVENUE STORAGE TRACK** – This is where the Tennessee Central bridged over the Nashville to Memphis line of the Nashville, Chattanooga & St. Louis Railway, the Dixie Line. It later became part of the Louisville & Nashville and is today part of CSX. In late 1903, an "N.C.&St.L. Connection" was listed here.

Eastbound trains coming out of Jefferson Street Yard faced a steep grade, 1.5% or more, and they often doubled their train up the hill to Pittsfield using the siding at 33rd Avenue. North of here, westbound trains curved east towards downtown Nashville, leaving the route of today's Interstate 440, before curving back to the north near Fisk University.

9.7 **VAN BLARCOM** – Located at 31st and Charlotte Avenues, some early documents show this to be Van Blarcom Place. This was an industrial area and the railroad leased land adjacent to the railroad to several companies, including Litchfield Shuttle Company and Star Block Mills. In June 1937, John Oman Jr. leased a siding in the area. During the early 1900s, Van Blarcom was a station, but in April 1934, the railroad contracted with H. L. Pack to "tear down old depot building at Van Blarcom."

The name Van Blarcom came from J. C. Van Blarcom, a St. Louis financier who invested in the railroad and was president and a director of the Tennessee Central Railroad Company in 1903. The depot at Van Blarcom was often used by passengers to connect to or from the Nashville Street Railway, which the railroad crossed at grade. There are numerous reports that passengers on eastbound trains could get to downtown Nashville hotels faster by taking the trolley here, rather than by staying on the train to the Tennessee Central station. Probably the largest transfer of passengers from the trolley line to the Tennessee Central took place in October 1927, when the body and funeral party of Governor Austin Peay loaded here for a trip to Clarksville for burial in the Greenwood Cemetery.

Tennessee Central Western Division
Van Blarcom (TN) to Gravelotte (TN)
Nashville & Western Railroad

Nashville & Western Railroad

In 2000, the Nashville & Western Railroad (NWR) was formed as a subsidiary of the Nashville & Eastern to take over the operation of the old Tennessee Central from Nashville to Ashland City. This route was originally chartered as the Nashville & Clarksville Railroad in April 1901, and built along the Cumberland River from Nashville to the northwest at Clarksville. After a reorganization and merger with other railroads, the line became part of the Tennessee Central and was extended to the Illinois Central at Hopkinsville, Kentucky.

On March 18, 1969, the line officially became the property of Illinois Central for $800,000, but was abandoned and sold off by the mid-1980s. The south part of the line is now the Nashville & Western, with the Cumberland River Bicentennial Trail using the line northwest of Ashland City. The rest of the line is abandoned, except for the Fort Campbell to Hopkinsville route, which became the property of the U.S. Department of Defense.

The former Tennessee Central route between Nashville and Ashland City was acquired by the Cheatham County Railroad Authority by 1988. As stated in their documents, "The Cheatham County Rail Authority was established in 1986 as a state governmental entity under the laws of Tennessee to acquire the unused facilities of a short-line railroad of approximately twenty-eight miles running between Nashville and Ashland City, and to encourage the continuation of railroad service to Cheatham County." (In 1988, Metropolitan Nashville and Davidson County established a railroad authority to join with the Cheatham County Rail Authority to share in the operation and ownership of the railroad.) It has been operated by several shortlines, including the Nashville & Ashland City (1983-1986); McCormick, Ashland City & Nashville (1986-1992); and Central of Tennessee Railway and Navigation Company (1992-2000). The Central of Tennessee (CTRN) was known for its fleet of freight cars leased by Southern Pacific, and later by Union Pacific.

After a decade and a half of changing operators, the Nashville & Eastern acquired the operating rights in 2000 and set up the Nashville & Western (NWR) to operate the line. The Nashville & Western shows as the Western Subdivision in employee timetables of the Nashville & Eastern. The State of Tennessee says that the line, "runs from Nashville to an industrial park near Ashland City, a total distance of 16.7 miles. This line is located in Davidson and Cheatham Counties of Tennessee." The NWR states that inbound cars carry "a wide array of commodities (plate steel, ethanol, bio-diesel, plastics, perlite, cement, etc.) to its diverse customer base. Outbound freight currently consists largely of recyclables (paper, glass, scrap metal & waste oil)."

When planning a route west out of Nashville, those creating what later became the Tennessee Central had two routes to choose from. The first was a route through several existing communities along a series of ridges. The cost of grading led to the use of the river route along the Cumberland River. Construction on the line between Nashville and Clarksville, Tennessee, and on to Hopkinsville, Kentucky, was well underway by the early 1900s, with grading accomplished over much of the route by late 1902. In January 1903, track laying began on the west side of the Cumberland River near Nashville, and headed toward Clarksville. It progressed enough that mixed train service between Nashville and Ashland City began on October 27, 1903. Train service was extended on to Clarksville by November 30, 1903.

The route chosen had its challenges – mainly the need to construct a large number of timber trestles over streams flowing into the Cumberland River. However, it did avoid the need for steep grades. The report *A Geographic Study of the Tennessee Central Railway: An East-West Transport Route Across the Cumberland Plateau of Tennessee* by Dennis E. Quillen (1969), covers the elevation change on the Western Division. Unlike the Eastern Division which had to climb over the Cumberland Plateau, this part of the Tennessee Central avoided mountains. Quillen reported that "over this route the rail line climbs from an elevation of 423 feet above sea level at Southern Junction (Nashville), in the Nashville Basin, then proceeds for 39 miles along a water-level route generally paralleling the Cumberland River, then climbs the escarpment of the Northern Highland Rim near Clarksville, and finally proceeds across the Highland Rim to Hopkinsville, which lies at an elevation of 528 feet. The total rise involved is 105 feet, or a mean average rise of about one and one-half feet per mile. The highest elevation on the division – 592 feet – is reached at two different places, a point on the Northern Highland Rim near Hopkinsville and a point on the Tennessee Central beltline in South Nashville. The lowest point in elevation along the Tennessee Central between Nashville and Hopkinsville, 389 feet, is at a point alongside the Cumberland River at Gratton."

During the time of Quillen's study, the Tennessee Central operated two trains over the Western Division, daily except Sunday. The first train left Nashville about 8:30am and ran to Clarksville or Edgoten ("Edge of Tennessee," today Fort Campbell), then returned to Nashville about 9:00pm. The second train, operating as scheduled train #71 westbound and #72 back, left Nashville about 1:30pm and ran to Hopkinsville. Besides handling the interchange with Illinois Central, it worked anything that the earlier train could not before returning to Nashville about 3:00am the next morning.

Today, the railroad is owned by Cheatham County and operated by the Nashville & Western Railroad Corporation. Trains operate most weekdays and serve the line as needed by the shippers.

MUSIC CITY STAR

Note that this route is FRA excepted track, thus no passenger trains can operate on the line at the time this was written. However, this route has been proposed as the second *Music City Star* route. The route would use the existing line between Nashville and Ashland City, and then the original Tennessee Central grade on to Clarksville. The Northwest Corridor Study, released in 2016 by Parsons Brinckerhoff and funded in part by the Regional Transit Authority, called for the project which would cost an estimated $525 million. The major advantage of this route is the lack of existing heavy rail traffic, and the ability to direct development along the more rural route. This route would also have the ability to reach the Nashville Farmers' Market and the state capitol area near downtown.

9.7 VAN BLARCOM – Located at 31st and Charlotte Avenues, some early documents show this to be Van Blarcom Place. This was an industrial area and the railroad leased land adjacent to the railroad to several companies, including Litchfield Shuttle Company and Star Block Mills. In June 1937, John Oman Jr. leased a siding in the area. During the early 1900s, Van Blarcom was a station, but in April 1934, the railroad contracted with H. L. Pack to "tear down old depot building at Van Blarcom."

The name Van Blarcom came from J. C. Van Blarcom, a St. Louis financier who invested in the railroad and was president and a director of the Tennessee Central Railroad Company in 1903.

This is the west end of the tracks of the current Nashville & Western Railroad. The tracks head to the northeast to Central Junction and then turn north. Additional tracks head on east to the shops of the railroad, as well as the new interchange track with CSX. These tracks have all received new mileposts over the years, causing some confusion. For example, the line from here towards downtown Nashville has been renumbered starting from downtown. Between Van Blarcom and Central Junction, the grade crossing data from the Federal Railroad Administration (FRA) demonstrates these changes. They include 27th Avenue (Tennessee Central Milepost 9.8, FRA 2.2) and Clifton Pike (Tennessee Central Milepost 10.1, FRA 1.8). From 26th Avenue (Tennessee Central Milepost 9.9, FRA 2.0) to Central Junction, the railroad is two tracks, ended by a crossover at Central Junction.

10.3 CENTRAL JUNCTION/CLIFTON – Look for the crossover at the north end of a 2000-foot-long siding. This is the junction with the mainline west to Ashland City, the former Beltline around the south side of Nashville, and what is known today as the North Nashville Lead which heads east to U.S. Tobacco. This area was once known as East Side Junction, but was renamed Central Junction for the Illinois Central when it leased the Western Division in 1905. The name stuck even when the Tennessee Central took back responsibility for the railroad's operations on July 1, 1908. Later, the area was Clifton Yard, which stretched from here to the southwest near 28th and Charlotte, for about one-half mile. **For information on the North Nashville Lead, see page 261.**

Heading compass-north (railroad-west) on the mainline, the railroad crosses a number of streets before reaching several customers near the old Jefferson Yard. The railroad crosses Herman and Hermosa Streets at-grade. West of Hermosa Street, the railroad begins to climb and bridges over local streets before passing under Interstate 40. These streets include Albion, Alameda, Meharry, an alley, and then Jefferson before passing under Interstate 40 less than two miles to the north of Central Junction.

The traffic on Interstate 40 is heavy at all times of day and night. I-40 stretches across Tennessee and serves the three largest cities in the state: Memphis, Nashville and Knoxville. The Interstate is 2555 miles long, starting in Wilmington, North Carolina, to the east, and ending in Barstow, California, to the west.

11.4 **JEFFERSON STREET YARD** – Jefferson Yard was once the western Nashville yard for the Tennessee Central. Several locals were once based here to serve the rail customers on the western side of the city. The yard was at the bottom of grades in both directions, with the grades the steepest (1.5%) heading south and then east around the south side of Nashville.

The yard was located between where the railroad passes under Interstate 40 and then west through Heiman Street and then on west. Today it is all located west of Heiman Street. Illinois Central property maps from 1970 show that the land on the south side of the tracks (compass-west here) just north of Heiman Street was railroad property, and that it was being used by the Sherman Concrete Pipe Company. A handwritten note on the map about an inspection dated 8-22-75 states "approx. 2 acres operating for piggyback facility."

West of here the railroad has a long siding to the south. On the north side of the mainline at the west switch is the Dicaperl Minerals Corporation facility, a rail shipper. According to the company, the plant "produces Dicaperl Perlite Microspheres, Horticultural Aersoil, and Chemsil (CS) Industrial Perlite grades." According to a May 1970 Illinois Central engineering map, this is the old Chemrock Corporation facility. On the south side of the tracks and to the east was once the Agrico Chemical Company, about where several planned apartment complexes now sit.

12.1 WOODWARD – The railroad crosses through the intersection of Buchanan Street (once Hydes Ferry Turnpike) and Ed Temple Boulevard at Milepost 4.1, Illinois Central Milepost JE-202.9. This is the north end of a small three-track yard complex, with a spur to the south into what was once Standard Oil Company. Today, the spur track is still used for unloading railroad tank cars, but now by Tri Star Energy, a Shell Oil dealership and bulk diesel/oil distributor.

12.5 BORDEAUX DRAWBRIDGE – Known by many as the Cumberland River Drawbridge, it was located at Illinois Central Milepost JE-202.5. The bridge crosses the Cumberland River on the northwest side of Nashville. The bridge is listed as being 1890 feet long. A study of the bridge states that from east to west, it includes 103 timber trestle spans, each 12 feet long, a 186-foot through truss approach span, a 300-foot pivot through truss span, and a 166-foot through truss approach span on the west end. The through truss spans have been described as being Polygonal Warren through truss spans with sub-panels.

The east timber approach has a grade of 0.2% to take trains up to the bridge. When built, the tracks south of the river were owned by Nashville Terminal Company, those north of the river by the Tennessee Central. The companies received approval from the Secretary of War to build the bridge on August 18, 1902. It opened in late 1903 as a steam-powered turn span. It was changed to electric motors in 1956.

In 1998, the United States Coast Guard declared the bridge a "Navigational Hazard." This was due to the swing span providing about 130 feet of open clearance, while many barge tows are 105 feet wide, making a tight passage through the bridge. There are plans being investigated to replace the bridge.

Bordeaux Drawbridge over the Cumberland River at Nashville. Photo by Sarah Jennings.

The name Bordeaux comes from the local community on the north bank of the Cumberland River. The community dates from the early 1800s when a number of Scots-Irish, German, and Italian families moved to the area. It later became a popular area for freed slaves. The name Bordeaux came about in 1849 when the community applied for a post office. The area was agricultural in nature until the 1920s, when many farmers moved away due to flooding and the area turned into suburbs.

To the north of the bridge on its east end is the Ted Rhodes Park and Golf Course. The course was built as the nine-hole Cumberland Golf Course in 1953. It was renamed in 1969 for Theodore "Ted" Rhodes, an early African-American golf professional who was from Nashville. The course was redesigned in 1992 and became an eighteen-hole course.

13.2 RIVERSIDE – Riverside was a short siding to the south. It was listed as a station by Illinois Central in 1971. The siding was just west of what is today County Hospital Road, once known as Asylum Avenue. Maps from the 1920s show the "County Farm" to the south.

West of here, several former timber trestles have been retired and filled in. One of note was the 784-foot-long timber trestle at Tennessee Central Milepost 14.06, or milepost 6.1 today.

14.8 WHITE CREEK BRIDGE – What the Tennessee Central called Bridge 14.76 was a large bridge. It had a 103-foot through truss span on the east end, crossing White Creek (Whites Creek on earlier maps). The west end of the bridge was timber trestle, making it 941 feet total in length.

White Creek forms to the north of Nashville and flows southward to here. Several miles further to the south, the stream flows into the Cumberland River. The area near its headwaters was a community known as Whites Creek, famous as the farm of Frank and Jesse James while they were in hiding.

15.5 JORDONIA – Look for the grade crossing with Jordonia Station Road. Located at NWR Milepost 7.4, Jordonia was once a busy railroad community. The Tennessee Central had a 300-foot siding and team track as well as several section houses at Jordonia. Contracts for industry included a spur track for River & Rail Phosphate Company (November 1946) and crosstie storage space for Potosie Tie & Lumber Company (May 1956). Reportedly, the siding was removed during the late 1940s or early 1950s. However, Jordonia was listed as a station by Illinois Central in 1971. The location was also considered as the location for a new IC yard, but it was never built.

Jordonia is at an elevation of 423 feet. Today, it is essentially a suburb of Nashville. Jordonia was once the location of the Tennessee Reformatory for Boys, opened in 1911. It was originally designed to house males aged 11-23, and was a cross between a prison and an educational facility. As stated in several sources, the facility was known as a reform school, including incarceration and chilling punishment for bad behavior. It was finally closed in 1971 after decades of investigations and bad publicity.

Just west of Jordonia, the railroad passes under Briley Parkway (NWR Milepost 7.7), a modern circle road around Nashville named for former Nashville mayor Beverly Briley. A spur track into Siskin Steel & Supply is at the same location. Just to the west are several heavy industries, none served by the railroad. The complex includes a barge port on the Cumberland River. Heading on west, the railroad crosses several timber trestle bridges, and locations where such bridges have been filled in.

18.6 SULPHUR CREEK BRIDGE – This bridge is a tall timber trestle bridge with a deck plate girder span over Old Hickory Boulevard. Known as Tennessee Central Bridge 18.60, it is 292 feet long.

Sulphur Creek drains the hills to the north and is about five miles in length. Just south of here, Sulphur Creek turns to flow west into the Cumberland River.

19.0 SCOTTSBORO – Today, Scottsboro is basically a rural community of houses on large pieces of property, serving as a home for people working in Nashville. The name comes from the Scott family that settled the area soon after Davidson County was created. It was an important community for some time as it was located on Hyde's Ferry Turnpike. The Hyde's Ferry Turnpike Company was chartered on January 25, 1848. The reason for the company was to build a turnpike from Nashville to Sycamore Mills. It never reached that length, getting to Hickman's Ferry in 1853, and reaching Marrowbone several years later. Construction stopped during the Civil War, but it reached Lyceum Mills (24 miles from Nashville) in 1878. Improvements continued until 1884.

The railroad had a siding to the south of the mainline, as well as two section houses located just west of the main grade crossing. Scottsboro was listed as a station by Illinois Central in 1971.

The hill to the south is Potato Hill, with an elevation of several hundred feet above Scottsboro. Just to its southeast is Buzzard Bluff. A series of similar hills to the south forces the Cumberland River to take a southern loop known as Bells Bend, instead of a shorter route via Scottsboro.

20.1 McHENRY – McHenry was located where the railroad, coming from the east, comes alongside the Cumberland River. A map from the official 1871 survey of Davidson County shows this area to be Chalk Landing. Topographical maps from 1929 show that Whites Bend is the name of the river bend. No map clearly shows the location to be McHenry. It was likely a short-lived spur track named for J. S. McHenry, Treasurer of the Tennessee Central in the early 1910s.

21.2 FISH CAMP – Old Tennessee Central valuation maps show a right-of-way for a spur track to the north in the area of what is today NWR Milepost 13.2. The Tennessee Central grade seems to have been moved some in the area when the adjacent roadway was expanded.

21.7 ISLAND CREEK BRIDGE – This was once Tennessee Central Bridge No. 21.66. In December 1936, the railroad filled the bridge and closed a road crossing at this location. About 1870, this area was known as Hampton's Mill.

To the south in the Cumberland River is Gower Island. Versions vary, but most sources say that the island was named for Abel Gower, Sr., who moved to Tennessee from North Carolina by 1780. Gower was reportedly killed by Indians while bringing corn to market. The island is claimed to be 16 acres and is privately owned.

22.4 BULL RUN CREEK BRIDGE – This is Bridge No. 22.40, a 195-foot-long timber trestle structure. It crosses Bull Run Creek, and on the east end, a private road to several houses on the Cumberland River. Over the years, this stream has also been known as Bullrun Creek and simply Bull Run. It drains the hills off to the north and flows into the Cumberland River near the Bull Run Recreation Area, just to the west.

22.5 BULL RUN – Located at NWR Milepost 8.5, just east of the Davidson-Cheatham County Line, was a spur track named Bull Run. The 373-foot-long spur, located on the north side of the mainline with the switch on the west end, was retired July 24, 1934.

22.6 COUNTY LINE – Just west of Bull Run at NWR milepost 14.6 is the county line between Davidson County (to the east) and Cheatham County (to the west). **Davidson County** dates back to when this area was part of North Carolina. In 1783, the legislature of North Carolina created the county. It was named for General William Lee Davidson, who was killed while trying to prevent a British crossing of the Catawba River on February 1, 1781. Nashville is its county seat. Davidson County and Nashville were the first European settlements and governments in Middle Tennessee. Much of its early law was set by the

Cumberland Compact, a document created to establish a basic rule of law and to protect the land titles of the settlers.

Cheatham County, organized on February 28, 1856, was created from parts of Davidson, Dickson, Montgomery, and Robertson counties. The name Cheatham came from Tennessee legislator Edward Saunders Cheatham. Cheatham had a career in politics, and had just ended a term in the Tennessee House of Representatives and had taken a seat in the Tennessee Senate, where he served as Speaker. In 1860-1861, Cheatham served as the first president of the Louisville & Nashville Railroad. The creation of the county called for the establishment of a new county seat, which eventually became Ashland City. In the 2010 census, the population of Cheatham County was 39,105.

Just west of the county line at Milepost 14.8 is the Bull Run Recreation Area, 50 acres of parkland that Ashland City has leased from the U.S. Army Corps of Engineers since 2004. The park includes a lake and boat ramp and is popular for fishing and dog walking. It includes the winding Bull Run Creek.

23.8 **BORROW PIT** – There was once a railroad borrow pit at this location, as was Tennessee Central Bridge No. N-23.8. This bridge was rebuilt in 1919 with pine piles, then cedar piles in 1922.

24.0 **ASHLAND INDUSTRIAL PARK** – The Nashville & Western timetable shows that the Ashland Industrial Park is at Milepost 16.0. This is also Illinois Central Milepost JE-191. The county government knows it as the Cheatham County Industrial Park. The city limits of Ashland City extend south and east along State Highway 12 to Davidson County to include the entire industrial park.

The switch into Trinity Marine Products, on the Cumberland River to the south, marks the eastern limits of the industrial park. Trinity Marine builds new river barges here and launches them into the river for pickup by their customers. A typical river barge is 200 feet long and 35 feet

Western Division – Van Blarcom to Gravelotte

wide, and they are made on a moving assembly line to build the keel, hull, and other parts. Trinity Marine Products is a leading manufacturer of inland barges and fiberglass barge covers in the United States.

24.6 **GRAVELOTTE** – Located at what was NWR Milepost 16.6, Gravelotte was a 50-car siding to north, where a siding still exists today. The east end is at the Bluegrass Drive grade crossing. The west end of the siding once had a one-mile-long spur to a large gravel pit on Little Marrowbone Creek. Records show that the gravel spur was retired on November 25, 1935.

Gravelotte once had a number of rail facilities. What were identified as a "car body" and a "waiting room" were on the south side of the tracks just west of the grade crossing. There were also stock loading facilities here. The Tennessee Central constructed a stock loading chute here on November 18, 1926, but retired it on September 22, 1937.

To the north is the large facility of Gate Precast Concrete. Gate started as Gate Petroleum, but in 1980 got into the concrete casting business. Today, they are one of the country's "largest producers of architectural precast concrete, pre-stressed hollow core slabs, transportation/infrastructure and marine components, operating eight manufacturing facilities located in North Carolina, Alabama, Kentucky, Tennessee, two in Florida and two in Texas." The company does everything from designing and manufacturing to delivering and installing architectural and structural concrete items.

The last open grade crossing on the line is Thompson Road at NWR Milepost 16.8, although the railroad often shoves as many as twenty railcars north of here. To the south is Strategic Materials and their Ashland City – Abrasives facility. Strategic Materials, which loads covered hoppers, processes recycled glass and plastic for use in a wide array of industrial and consumer products.

25.0 END OF TRACK – The track has been removed west of here, NWR Milepost 17.0.

Tennessee Central Western Division
Gravelotte (TN) to Edgoten (TN)
Abandoned

The Illinois Central applied to abandon the Nashville to Hopkinsville line in 1980. The U.S. Army quickly protested the filing to protect Fort Campbell. The abandonment filing was soon changed to Ashland City to Edgoten, and the Illinois Central ended service over this part of the line in July 1981. The tracks from Chapmansboro to Edgoten were abandoned soon after the Illinois Central ended service over the line. The line east of Chapmansboro was preserved as the Cheatham County Rail Authority, and other parties attempted to save the tracks to industry in the Ashland City area. In 1989, the tracks west of Ashland City to Chapmansboro were abandoned, leaving tracks from Nashville to the Ashland City industrial park near the historic station of Gravelotte. Parts of this line have been turned into walking trails, including north of Ashland City, in Clarksville, and north of Clarksville.

25.0   **END OF TRACK** – The track has been removed west of here, Nashville & Western Railroad (NWR) Milepost 17.0.

25.8   **PEGRAMVILLE** – On February 28, 1919, the railroad built a passenger shelter here. There was also a short spur to the north, all located at what was once NWR Milepost 17.8.

   The community of Pegram is on the CSX line heading west out of Nashville toward Memphis. However, maps from the late 1800s also show a Pegramville in this area of Cheatham County. According to the book *Some Pegrams of Middle Tennessee* by Dorothy Pegram Rowland, Pegramville was located near Marrabone Creek, where William Mastin Pegram once owned land.

27.0   **SULPHUR SPRINGS** – Sulphur Springs is one of many area springs that were noted for their sulphur content. A number of these were popular during the late 1800s and early 1900s. Located at NWR Milepost 19.1, there was once a passenger shelter here on the north side of the tracks. It was officially retired on February 14, 1931, less than a year after passenger service ended on the Western Division in 1930. At NWR Milepost 18.8 (Tennessee Central N-26.8) was once a spur track 277 feet long. It was retired on October 23, 1928.

Some maps still show a Sulphur Springs at this location, basically a cluster of woods surrounded by a few rural houses. East of here the railroad ran very close to the Cumberland River.

27.9 MARROWBONE CREEK BRIDGE – This is a big bridge for what sounds like a small creek. However, this bridge is 861 feet long with a 151-foot pin-connected Pratt through truss span. In reality, at this location, Marrowbone Creek is backed up as part of the Cumberland River's Cheatham Lake. The lake is created by the U.S. Army Corps of Engineers' Cheatham Lock and Dam, located 11 miles to the northwest, and downstream of Ashland City. What is known as Big Marrowbone Creek flows off of the hills to the east, making the stream less than twenty miles long.

The bridge was known as Bridge No. 27.89 by the Tennessee Central. The west end of the bridge was just short of Milepost N-28. An interesting note on Tennessee Central maps show that the mileposts were once renumbered from the north by the Illinois Central. This milepost had been renamed JE-187. Just northwest of the bridge at milepost 20.2 (Tennessee Central Milepost N-28.2), was once a large railroad water tower. In January 1936, the railroad replaced the "water station with 15,000-gallon tank connected to city water supply."

Just east of the bridge at Milepost 27.7 were a series of borrow pits used for fills in this area. Earlier, the black shale mines of the DuPont Paint Company of Nashville operated in this area. The black shales were hauled to Nashville where they were crushed and heated, producing about ten gallons of oils per ton of shale that were used in paints.

29.3 **ASHLAND CITY** – Until recently, this was the end of the remains of the former Tennessee Central out of Nashville, shown in older Nashville & Western Railroad employee timetables. Ashland City was once a busy station for the railroad. There was a depot, two section houses, and several tool houses on the north side of the mainline and a 55-car siding. There were a number of team and industrial tracks here, too. In 1931, the railroad's tobacco shed was retired and a tool house replaced. In 1939, the tool house had an underground gasoline tank installed. When the Tennessee Central got into the piggyback business, the depot was torn down to make way for a ramp (later operated by the Illinois Central). All of these facilities were once located northwest of Cumberland Street at what is now the ball fields at J. W. Jones Jr. Park. Ashland City was listed as a station by Illinois Central in 1971, but nothing of the Tennessee Central is left here today. The tracks northwest of here are also gone, abandoned from here to Chapmansboro in 1989. The tracks east of Ashland City remained for a number of years, with many areas paved over at grade crossings. The track was eventually abandoned between Ashland City and the industrial park to the east.

Running through town, the mainline ran down the middle of Water Street. A number of the rail facilities here were actually built by the Illinois Central during its period of control of the western half of the railroad. In 1946, the Tennessee Central finally acquired all tracks and land owned by the "ICRRCo." Historically, there have been two major shippers here. The first was Evans Transportation, a rail car manufacturer that closed in early 1986. The second manufacturer is why there is any sign of railroad still at Ashland City. A. O. Smith Water Products/State Water Heaters still operates a huge manufacturing plant here, making water heaters and other similar products. They employ about 1500 workers, making the plant the largest employer in the area.

Ashland City was created in 1856, and incorporated in 1858, as the county seat for the new county of Cheatham. The city was established on 50 acres of land owned by James Lenox. The county raised money for the building of a courthouse by selling lots in Ashland City. A temporary building went up in the late 1850s, and the current courthouse was built in 1869.

When founded, Ashland City was very rural, but several small industries already existed in the area. Montgomery Bell operated a forge, built in 1818 at the Narrows of the Harpeth, several miles to the southwest. Just north of Ashland City, Samuel Watson operated a gristmill and powder mill along Sycamore Creek, built by 1835. Ashland City has never been a major community, its 2010 population was only 4541. However, between 1990 and 2010, the population of Ashland City grew 178 percent, according to the U.S. Bureau of the Census. Even with that growth, however, it is still one of Nashville's smallest suburbs. Besides the water heater factory, the only other area business with more than 100 employees is Trinity Marine Products, builders of barges & deck fittings, with about 450 employees.

Ashland City was originally named simply Ashland. The "City" came along slowly after the community was incorporated. There is no clear explanation of the name. Some argue that is was named for the ash trees in the area. However, at least several histories say that it came from Ashland, Henry Clay's estate. Reportedly, several involved with the new county were fans of 19th-century Kentucky statesman Henry Clay, who had died just a few years earlier. They decided to name the community after his Lexington plantation.

30.0 MARKS CREEK TRAIL HEAD – Heading west, the railroad grade closely follows the Cumberland River. Because of the route's scenic nature, efforts have been made

Western Division – Gravelotte to Edgoten

for decades to turn the rail line into a hiking trail. Located just west of the Markes Creek, now Marks Creek, bridge is a grade crossing with Chapmansboro Road. West of here is the Cumberland River Bicentennial Trail. This trail had long been promoted when in 1992, a group of trail enthusiasts from the region met to develop plans for building a trail on the abandoned Tennessee Central grade. The original goal was to build a trail from Nashville to Clarksville, and then on to the Land Between the Lakes in Kentucky. The trail has been completed for a few miles west of this location, with efforts continuing to expand it.

33.2 **SYCAMORE CREEK BRIDGE** – Near here is where the first settlers claimed land in what later became Cheatham County. Sycamore Creek, named for the trees that line its banks, wanders out of the hills to the east and flows into the Cumberland River near this bridge. Upstream several miles is the community of Sycamore, once Sycamore Mills. It was the site of several gristmills, and soon after the Civil War, a powder mill. The mill was moved here from the former Confederate Powder Works at Augusta, Georgia, in the late 1860s.

With the work to make the Cumberland River navigable, the lower parts of Sycamore Creek are essentially a part of Cheatham Lake, even though there was once enough drop here to operate a gristmill. To cross Sycamore Creek, the Tennessee Central built a 550-foot-long bridge, with a 230-foot-long Parker through truss span over the main channel. The span was built by the American Bridge Company in 1901, and the entire bridge was converted into a pedestrian bridge in 1997 as part of the Cumberland River Bicentennial Trail.

33.8 **CHAPMANSBORO** – Chapmansboro was the site of a siding on the north side of the mainline, with a spur off the west end to serve the Nashville Tie Company, and later J. A. Stewart. A depot and a freight shed were to the south at the west end of the siding, and three section houses further west on the north side of the tracks. Railroad company records show that the tobacco shed at Chapmansboro was retired on July 24, 1931, and that the furniture and fixtures from the freight house were retired on June 18, 1936.

N. C. Chapman was an early investor with Colonel Baxter in building the Tennessee Central. He served as a director and as vice-president of the Tennessee Central Railway in 1900, according to *Poor's Manual of Railroads*. Chapman was later involved with Tennessee coal mining, and was president of the Fall Creek Mine at Ozone, Tennessee.

Chapmansboro is unincorporated, but a post office opened here in 1921. At the grade crossing with Chapmansboro Road is the Eagle Pass Trail Head for the Cumberland River Bicentennial Trail. Just to the west, the railroad had a 447-foot-long timber trestle over Indian Creek and a public road, with section houses just off the west end of the bridge. Heading west, the railroad grade passes the Dyson Ditch Wildlife Refuge.

36.5 FOX BLUFF – A post office opened at Fox Bluff on September 15, 1904, not long after the railroad was built through the area. In April 1907, several sidings were built at Fox Bluff for the Monarch Stone & Lime Company, and then the Nashville Tie Company in 1911 and 1922. However, by the end of the 1920s, the location was closing down as the section tool house was retired in November 1929, and then the passenger shelter and freight shed were retired in January 1935. Railroad records indicate that on November 6, 1946, the last of the Illinois Central land holdings at Fox Bluff were sold to the Tennessee Central.

During the construction of the Cheatham Lock & Dam on the Cumberland River, a siding was built to hold construction materials for the navigation project. A survey benchmark from the era states that the elevation at Fox Bluff is 406 feet above sea level. Today, this area is the Lock A Campground. The Cheatham Dam Trailhead for the Cumberland River Bicentennial Trail is here.

36.8 GOVERNMENT DIAMOND – During the 1920s, the U.S. Government had a narrow gauge railroad that crossed the Tennessee Central at this location. Maps show a railroad west from a warehouse on the north side of the Tennessee Central to a Lock "A" on the Cumberland River. Work on the Cumberland River was first funded by the Federal government in 1832, and by the 1840s steamboats could travel up from the Ohio River as far as Nashville. In 1924, the last of 15 locks and dams was completed on the Cumberland River. On August 24, 1923, the railroad placed a new 80# diamond for the government narrow gauge track, part of the construction of the Cumberland River locks.

On July 30, 1954, Lock "A" was blown up with 10,000 pounds of explosives as part of the work on a new Cheatham Lock & Dam. Reportedly, more than 2000 people watched the event in 100-degree heat, and those in boats were able to gather more than 600 pounds of fish that were stunned or killed by the explosion.

38.4 FALL CREEK BRIDGE – This 165-foot bridge crossed a small stream which flows about ten miles off of the hillsides to the east.

39.6 DODDSVILLE – Doddsville was located on the west end of the 440-foot bridge over Mill Hollow. The railroad had a 16-car siding to the north, with a depot on it. To the south there was a long spur that served stock yards. Hagewood's Ferry operated on the Cumberland River in this area until 1958.

41.4 HALF PONE CREEK BRIDGE – This stream creates a deep and curving valley as it flows off the hillsides to the east. Half Pone Creek was an early landmark for settlers. To provide for their safety from Indians, a blockhouse was built at the fork of Half Pone and Raccoon Creeks, several miles to the east.

The railroad had a 248-foot bridge over Half Pone Creek, with a single 60-foot deck plate girder span directly over the stream.

41.5 **HINTON** – Hinton was known locally as Hinton Crossing for the ferry that once crossed the Cumberland River. E. H. Hinton was the Traffic Manager for the Tennessee Central when the Western Division was built. In the 1920s, the road that passed the railroad's tobacco platform and shed was known as Moseley's Ferry Road. This tobacco shed was retired in January 1939, long after the Hinton spur track was removed.

Heading west, the railroad crossed a number of small streams, each requiring a series of timber spans. Railroad records show an almost continuous effort to replace piles and stringers to keep the bridges safe.

42.3 **COUNTY LINE** – Heading west, the railroad passes from Cheatham County into Montgomery County. **Cheatham County**, organized on February 28, 1856, was created from parts of Davidson, Dickson, Montgomery, and Robertson counties. The name Cheatham came from Tennessee legislator Edward Saunders Cheatham. Cheatham had a career in politics, and had just ended a term in the Tennessee House of Representatives and had taken a seat in the Tennessee Senate, where he served as Speaker. In 1860-1861, Cheatham served as the first president of the Louisville & Nashville Railroad. The creation of the county called for the establishment of a new county seat, which eventually became Ashland City.

Montgomery County was created when Tennessee became the 16th state in 1796. At that time, Tennessee County was split into Montgomery and Robertson counties, and Clarksville became the county seat of Montgomery County. The name Montgomery came from John Montgomery, the founder of Clarksville. Montgomery had earlier fought in the American Revolutionary War, and soon after moved to land along the Cumberland River, land that became Clarksville.

According to various *Annual Reports of the Railroad Commissioners for the State of Tennessee*, there were 26.44 miles of Tennessee Central track in Montgomery County.

42.6 MIREY BRANCH BRIDGE – A 170-foot-long ballast deck trestle crossed this small stream that forms several miles to the northeast and flows west into the Cumberland River.

43.6 SHELTON – Shelton was a small station just west of Little Brush Creek. By the time that the Illinois Central acquired the Western Division, there were no facilities at Shelton.

44.6 BIG BRUSH CREEK BRIDGE – The railroad crossed this stream using an 85-foot deck plate girder span as part of a 146-foot-long bridge. The creek flows into the Cumberland River immediately to the south.

45.9 HICKORY POINT – Trains heading west arrived at Hickory Point by crossing Midnight Hollow on a 515-foot trestle. A post office opened at Hickory Point in 1900 and closed during 1955. The location was never very busy, but did include a short siding, a spur track, three section houses, and a depot. In June 1909, J. W. McCormac contracted to do work on the freight house and waiting room, and then leased the space. The spur track was built in 1912 for the Mansfield Engineering Company. Today, the area is becoming a collection of large rural homes, commuters from nearby Clarksville.

Documents of the Tennessee Central Railway showed that much of the land in this area was owned by "Gholson & Lyle."

47.1 GHOLSON – The name Gholson is pretty common in this area, with a number of members of the family living here in the 1800s. The family is so common that there is a

Gholson Cemetery in Clarksville. Among the Gholsons in the area was Richard Dickerson Gholson, who served as the 3rd Territorial Governor of Washington. Richard Gholson was a supporter of President James Buchanan and helped him win the Kentucky vote. He served as the governor of Washington from 1859 until 1861, when he returned to Kentucky. He then moved his family into this area of Tennessee to protect them from the Civil War.

Another famous Gholson in the area was Colonel Milton G. Gholson, who moved to Montgomery County from Kentucky as a young man. During the Civil War, he served as a lieutenant colonel with the 14th Tennessee Regiment. He rose through the ranks during the war and was commissioned as a Brigadier-General.

The location of Gholson Station, as it was known initially, was on the farm of Judge Alexander R. Gholson, located on Cumberland River near Hickory Point. When the railroad built through the area, a small depot with a team track was built to the north of the mainline at Gholson. The station was used by a few locals to make trips to and from Clarksville, but the freight business never materialized and the team track was removed during the 1930s. There was a post office here 1904-1913.

49.6 SPALDING – Spalding is located where the railroad came back briefly to the Cumberland River. A benchmark indicates that the elevation is 401 feet as the railroad continued its slow descent down the Cumberland River. For a number of years, a water tower and short siding existed here. Today, the area is a thick patch of woods east of McAdoo Creek.

Early maps show that the area once featured a number of Indian mounds.

50.2 BIG McADOO CREEK BRIDGE – This was the second longest bridge on the Western Division of the Tennessee Central Railway. It was 1141 feet long and included a 100-foot through truss span on the east end. Heading railroad-west, a train was actually heading north and starting a three-mile 1% upward grade to climb out of the Cumberland River Valley and up into Clarksville, Tennessee.

Big McAdoo Creek is created by a number of small streams that drain the hills to the east. Like many streams that flow into the Cumberland River, Big McAdoo Creek is backed up by the navigation waters of the larger river.

50.4 **GRATTON** – A post office was at Gratton 1904-1911. Early documents show the station was originally named Gratton Station. To the east are several blocks of houses, suburbs for Clarksville.

51.5 **COKE CREEK BRIDGE** – What was known as Tennessee Central Bridge No. 51.46 was 1060 feet long, spanning the hollow created by Coke Creek. While many may think the name of the creek is related to the coal industry, the Coke family lived in this area during the 1800s.

51.8 **NORTH FORK COKE CREEK BRIDGE** – This was Tennessee Central Bridge No. 51.83. The wooden trestle bridge was 458 feet long. The two forks of Coke Creek merge just downstream, and then quickly flow into the Cumberland River.

54.0 **SUMMIT YARD** – Summit Yard was named because it was at the top of the grade coming into Clarksville, at an elevation of 425 feet. In 1971, the Illinois Central showed a wye to the south and two tracks to the north at Summit Yard. However, when the railroad was being operated by the Tennessee Central, it was a busy complex that could handle more than 100 railcars. The Tennessee Central used Summit Yard as a base for local switching, and the railroad had plenty of facilities here for both local and through trains. These facilities included a coaling tower, apparently the only coal fueling facility between Nashville and Hopkinsville. There was also a water tower, a sand tower and ash pit, a crew office, and a boarding house for train crews.

The wye track was used to turn steam locomotives. A February 1942 contract went to J. F. Anderson of Clarksville for grading on the wye tracks at Summit Yard. Later maps show that the wye was used to serve Acme Boot Company. There was also a spur track to the railroad-north to serve a TOFC (Trailer-on-Flat-Car) ramp.

Today, Summit Yard and the mainline in the area is gone and has been replaced by Crossland Avenue. The east switch of the yard was near Kelly Lane; the wye was located near where Boillin Lane now exists. The west end of the yard was near Pageant Lane, where the railroad bridged over the street. There are few signs of the railroad in this area.

Heading west of Pageant Lane, the railroad grade was a short distance south of the new Crossland Avenue. Just west of Greenwood Avenue, the railroad made a curve to the left, passing around today's Norman Smith Elementary School. Just west of Cumberland Drive, the westbound railroad turned right more than 120 degrees, taking the railroad from heading southwest to due north.

55.5 **HIGH STREET** – High Street was a common reference point for the railroad, and was often used to protect operations at the railroad station and freight house just to the north.

55.7 **BRIDGE 55.68** – This bridge spans the valley used by the Memphis Line of the Louisville & Nashville. The bridge was 757 feet long, with a 183-foot Parker through truss on the railroad-west end. Today, it is used as part of Clarksville's greenway trail system, the Upland Trail. The Upland Trail connects the downtown Riverwalk to the bridge, which is used as an overlook at the north end of Valleybrook Park.

The Tennessee Central, and later the Illinois Central, had a motor car house and several tool houses just railroad-west of this bridge.

Western Division – Gravelotte to Edgoten

This bridge crosses the former L&N line in Clarksville, and is today used by the Upland Trail. Photo by Barton Jennings.

56.2 CLARKSVILLE – Welcome to The Queen City, Queen of the Cumberland, The Gateway to the New South, and most recently, Tennessee's Top Spot! Clarksville has doubled in population over the past decade, and is now the fifth-largest city in Tennessee behind Nashville, Memphis, Knoxville, and Chattanooga. The population is estimated to be more than 150,000. Clarksville was incorporated in 1785, making it the first incorporated city in the state.

The Clarksville area was first surveyed by Thomas Hutchins in 1768. The next exploration of the area occurred in the early 1770s when John Montgomery and Kasper Mansker visited the area several times while hunting. However, the area was still owned by the Cherokee tribe, and it took a number of years for James Robertson to negotiate an agreement for settlement. After the Revolutionary War, the land in the Clarksville area was set aside to be given to soldiers of the Continental Army in lieu of pay.

On January 16, 1784, John Armstrong registered the town of Clarksville with the Legislature of North Carolina, and his partners John Montgomery and Robert Weakley laid out the town and began selling lots. Weakley and Montgomery built the first cabins, and soon the town began to grow due to its location on the Cumberland River.

The name Clarksville was chosen to honor Revolutionary War hero General George Rogers Clark, brother of William Clark of the Lewis and Clark Expedition.

One of the first major products of local farms was tobacco. This led to Clarksville becoming an official inspection point for tobacco in 1789. This local production of tobacco explains the many tobacco sheds built along the Tennessee Central Railway that lasted until the mid-1900s. Clarksville is also the home of Tennessee's oldest newspaper, *The Leaf-Chronicle*, established in 1808.

In 1942, Camp Campbell, now known as Fort Campbell, was built near Clarksville to house and train as many as 23,000 troops, and today is the home of the 101st Airborne Division. Clarksville is also the home of Austin Peay State University. Clarksville is also reported to be the subject of the song *Last Train to Clarksville*, a #1 song by The Monkees. Many locals claim the song was about soldiers leaving for war from Fort Campbell, but the writers claim the Clarksville name just fit the music. Either way, the band filmed parts of the song's music video in Clarksville.

Partly because of the military base, a number of famous people have been born in or passed through Clarksville. These include Austin Peay, governor of Tennessee; musicians Roy Acuff and Jimi Hendrix; Clarence Saunders, founder of Piggly Wiggly; Frank Sutton, the actor who played Sergeant Vince Carter in Gomer Pyle, USMC; and athletes Wilma Rudolph (first female athlete to win three gold medals in a single Olympic Games) and Pat Summitt (University of Tennessee at Knoxville women's basketball coach).

Western Division – Gravelotte to Edgoten

Much of the right-of-way through Clarksville is now the Upland Trail, a community walking path. Photo by Barton Jennings.

Railroads at Clarksville

The first railroad reached Clarksville more than forty years before the Tennessee Central arrived. The railroad, the Memphis, Clarksville & Louisville (MC&L), was designed to connect the three cities in the railroad's name. The first Cumberland River bridge was built in 1859, but it was too low for boats to pass under and it had to be rebuilt before service could start. Clarksville was a major backer of the project, and the railroad's first locomotive received the name *The Clarksville*. The locomotive was delivered to Clarksville via steamboat, and construction of the railroad also began here.

The MC&L was a project of the Louisville & Nashville, and when the route opened in 1860, it quickly became known as the L&N Memphis Line. Regular passenger service through Clarksville, running between Bowling Green, Kentucky, and Memphis, Tennessee, began on April 14,

1861, just in time for much of the railroad to be destroyed during the Civil War.

The first MC&L/L&N station, freight house and railroad hotel were located near today's Cumberland Drive. A new station was built in late 1881, and the building still stands. As the market changed, the L&N station was renovated in 1901, 1916 (when the 320-foot-long butterfly shed was added), 1924, 1948 and 1960. For many years, the railroad station saw three sets of passenger trains, with the Memphis section of the *Pan American* (#198/#199) being the premier daytime train. There was also a local daytime train (#102/#103) and an overnight *Fast Mail* (#101/#104). The daytime local train was discontinued in 1955 and the *Pan American* began to handle that business. However, it was discontinued on November 15, 1965, and trains #101/#104 made their last runs on February 28, 1968.

The L&N station was rebuilt as a Tennessee Bicentennial project in 1996, and it now houses the Montgomery County Historical Society. A small railroad museum is displayed inside the building. The shed built to protect railroad passengers now protects vendors and customers of Clarksville's Farmers' Market. A GP30 locomotive and a caboose are on display at the station. The locomotive is R. J. Corman #3501, originally built for Southern Railway in October 1963, with serial number 28596. The caboose is a former Illinois Central car built for their Iowa Division. Reportedly, it was used at Fort Campbell before being moved to this location.

Heading towards Memphis, the L&N crossed the Cumberland River using a bridge that included a turn span. The L&N freighthouse was located at the east end of the bridge at Adams and Riverside. Today, this line is part of the R. J. Corman Memphis Line. This railroad operates the line from Bowling Green, Kentucky, west to Cumberland City, Tennessee.

Western Division – Gravelotte to Edgoten

The L&N depot is a noted lankmark in Clarksville, Tennessee. Photo by Barton Jennings.

The Tennessee Central at Clarksville

Clarksville was the original goal of the Nashville & Clarksville Railroad. From there, the railroad considered several routes to reach a western interchange partner. One plan was to extend the line from Clarksville to Cairo to obtain St. Louis business. After the Nashville & Clarksville was reorganized as the Tennessee Central, construction on the Nashville to Clarksville Western Division began in June 1902. The charter was amended on August 8, 1902, authorizing the company to extend the railroad into Kentucky by way of either Gracy or Hopkinsville. The track reached Clarksville on October 1, 1903, and train service began on November 28, 1903.

For years, Clarksville was the second largest city served by the Tennessee Central. The railroad's records are full of agreements with shippers at Clarksville. These shippers included W. A. Chambers (April 1908), C. K. Smith (May 1912), Tennessee Products Company (December 1919), Manning-Orgain Supply Company (June 1922), Summit Coal & Fertilizer Company (June 1926), Merritt Stave & Lumber Company (December 1936), White Bluff Quarry (February 1943), Taylor Limestone Company (February

1945), Clarksville Burley Pack Houses (March 1949), and Simpson Stone Company (May 1949).

The Tennessee Central had a depot and freight house on the river side of the mainline between Franklin and Main Streets. An interesting set of contracts dealt with leased space in the passenger depot. There were a number of these, including several that allowed local Boy Scouts of America groups to use rooms at the station. These brick buildings were sold to the City of Clarksville on January 28, 1982, and have been modernized and are used today as city offices. The railroad grade was also sold to the city and has been rebuilt as Spring Street.

The former Tennessee Central Railway's freighthouse has been restored and is used by the City of Clarksville as city offices. Photo by Barton Jennings.

There were a number of shippers surrounding the depot. These included the Manning-Orgain Supply Company immediately to the south of the depot, W. A. Chambers on a spur track across the tracks from the depot, and the Clarksville Tobacco Board of Trade to the northeast where the Riverview Inn now stands.

56.3 JEFFERSON STREET BRIDGE – Heading railroad-west from the station, the railroad crossed a series of trestles. This first trestle was 1188 feet long and included a deck plate girder span over Jefferson Street. The National Register of Historic Places explained the many trestles on the

Western Division – Gravelotte to Edgoten

Tennessee Central by saying that the route closely followed the Cumberland River and crossed a number of streams and hollows. Specifically, the report commented that, "The fact that the bank slopes down steeply toward the river necessitated the construction of an elaborate and intricate timber trestle when the line was built around the turn of the century."

Just to the north was another timber trestle, this one 1040 feet long, that curved along the riverfront. The railroad then curved around Riverview Cemetery to the northeast.

57.4 FURNACE SPUR SWITCH – During the early 1900s when the Illinois Central operated the Tennessee Central, it built this 1.27-mile-long spur that curved back to the southeast to serve several shippers in downtown Clarksville. The Furnace Spur, also known as the Beltline, also served as an interchange track with the Louisville & Nashville, and connected to that line several blocks east of the L&N station.

Some of the major industries on this line included the Red River Furnace and Dunlop Milling Company. The furnace company started as the Clarksville Foundry & Machine Shop in 1847. It operated under a number of names. In 1906, The Red River Furnace Company incorporated the Clarksville Foundry & Machine Company to operate a machine shop and nearby blast furnace. The firm was known for its plows, iron stoves, and corn shellers. Today the firm makes all sorts of specialty castings. In 1987, the Clarksville Foundry was added to the National Register of Historic Places. The Dunlop Milling Company is a complex of industrial buildings and structures constructed between 1892 and 1913 for milling wheat and corn. It is also listed on the National Register of Historic Places.

57.7 RED RIVER BRIDGE – This was Tennessee Central Bridge No. 57.66. The bridge was once 1645 feet long and included a 254-foot steel through truss span over the river.

A 1971 Illinois Central document showed that the bridge had been shortened to 805 feet by filling in much of the timber trestles on the approaches to the steel truss.

The name Red River comes from the natural color of the river. The river contains a great deal of clay and silt with large amounts of iron oxides. The Red River is approximately 100 miles long, starting in Sumner County northeast of Nashville, Tennessee. The river flows westward, closely following the Tennessee-Kentucky state line. Just upstream from here, the West Fork of the Red River enters the Red River. The Red River used to pass under the Tennessee Central here, and it flows into the Cumberland River just a mile downstream. During the 1700s and 1800s, the river was used by small commercial boats.

58.2 **ADAIRVILLE** – There was a 1700-foot siding to the railroad-north of the mainline, compass-east at this location. From here, the Tennessee Central Railway's track headed generally north-northwest to Hopkinsville. For the next mile, the railroad grade closely followed the West Fork of the Red River. Because of this, and the risk of flooding and track damage, there was a track watchman's house at Milepost 59.0. There are also several borrow pits in the area that were used to rebuild the railroad grade when it was damaged.

The next 4.6 miles of the railroad have been turned into a part of the Clarksville Greenway,

61.1 **BRIDGE 61.08** – This bridge passes over a valley. For the railroad, it was a 514-foot trestle. Today, the bridge has been replaced by the Raymond C. Hand Trestle, a modern stone and steel structure.

62.9 **KENWOOD** – Kenwood is at the top of a ridge, with grades of 0.8% from each direction for several miles. Because of this, there was a long siding at Kenwood, often used for doubling trains. The station and siding were located at the grade crossing with Peachers Mill Road, where the

Western Division – Gravelotte to Edgoten

Kenwood Elementary School now stands. The old depot from Kenwood was leased to W. C. Phillips in June 1930 as the railroad streamlined its passenger service. Even after passenger service ended, the railroad kept several section and tool houses at Kenwood. In June 1945, J. B. Michael & Company contracted with the Tennessee Central for an unloading conveyor at Kenwood.

Nearby was the community of New Providence, and the station sometimes also used that name. In several publications, New Providence was described as a small railroad town. Today, it has been annexed by the City of Clarksville.

At Milepost 64.0, the railroad turned to the northeast using a five-degree curve that turned the track 120 degrees. This curve looped around a housing subdivision. Just to the north a spur track served a blending and storage facility. The grade then crossed what is today Tennessee Highway 374, the 101st Airborne Division Parkway.

65.3 LITTLE WEST FORK BRIDGE – This is the Little West Fork of the Red River, a stream that flows to the southeast before entering the West Fork of the Red River. This bridge was at the bottom of grades from each direction, with a 1% uphill grade heading north. The bridge was 1297 feet long, with a 150-foot Warren through truss with all verticals over the water.

66.1 RINGGOLD – Development in this area started in 1810 when Thomas Rivers built a gristmill on the bank of the Little West Fork Creek. The mill went through a number of owners, until M. D. Davie added a dam and more modern machinery in 1853. The mill was destroyed in 1863 by the Union Army, but was rebuilt after the Civil War. It burned from a lightning strike in 1885, but was immediately rebuilt and further modernized. The mill became known as the Ringgold Mill in 1907, and it operated until 1974. The mill was placed on the National Register of Historic Places on July 8, 1980.

Ringgold first received a post office in 1847, and it closed in 1906. Ringgold was once the location of a stagecoach stop. The stop still exists and is known as the Old Post House. It was listed on the National Register of Historic Places on March 8, 1978. In December 1909, the Forbes Manufacturing Company contracted for a spur track at Ringgold. In August 1928, Moore & Boyd contracted for a temporary spur track.

The Ringgold station was at the Tobacco Road grade crossing, which according to a survey benchmark was at an elevation of 488 feet. Not far west of Ringgold, the railroad turns back to the north, passing around the end of the Clarksville Regional Airport, once known as Outlaw Field.

66.8 END OF TRACK – The track south of here was abandoned after the Illinois Central ended service and sold the tracks on to Hopkinsville to the U.S. Army.

Tennessee Central Western Division
Edgoten (TN) to Tulane (KY)
Fort Campbell Railroad

The Illinois Central applied to abandon the Nashville to Hopkinsville line in 1980. The U.S. Army quickly protested the filing to protect Fort Campbell. The Illinois Central abandoned the line east of Edgoten, and in 1981, the U.S. Army agreed to buy the line from Fort Campbell to Hopkinsville, Kentucky. Before buying the railroad, the army trucked equipment to and from Hopkinsville, taking days to do what the railroad could do in hours. However, the railroad had to be rebuilt, and in 1990-1991, Fort Campbell spent $11 million to rebuild the line and make it safe.

With the abandonment of the Illinois Central line into Hopkinsville, the Fort Campbell Railroad was later forced to rebuild the Hopkinsville Belt and add a yard and tracks to connect to CSX, the former Louisville & Nashville. Interchange between the Tennessee Central and L&N seldom occurred, so this is a new routing for railroad freight cars.

Records of the Federal Railroad Administration show that the Fort Campbell Railroad – Department of Defense – Army (DODA) uses the Illinois Central mileposts. While the Tennessee Central mileposts will still be used, the Illinois Central mileposts will also be quoted.

66.8 **END OF TRACK** – The track east of here was abandoned after the Illinois Central ended service and sold the tracks on to Hopkinsville to the U.S. Army. The DODA milepost is 148.2.

67.4 **EAST YARD EDGOTEN** – The name Edgoten is unique. It is actually is an abbreviation for the phrase "Edge of Tennessee" as the station is near the Tennessee-Kentucky state line. In 1941, this facility developed to support the new Camp Campbell, today's Fort Campbell. The military built their own railroad into the facility, so an interchange yard was needed at this location. The yard featured a water tower, wye, and agent's office.

Today, the wye still exists as well as a siding. A line heads west into Fort Campbell that branches to serve most of the base. One important branch heads due west to serve a major military intermodal terminal on Market Garden Road, named for a World War II parachute drop in which the 101st Airborne Division participated. Much of this facility was built in 2001, noted as a $20 million project to build 4.3 miles of tracks to allow faster mobilization by rail of troops and their equipment.

68.7 STATE LINE – To the south is Montgomery County, Tennessee, while to the north is Christian County, Kentucky. Look for the grade crossing with State Line Road at DODA Milepost 146.3. The Commonwealth of **Kentucky** became the 15th state on June 1, 1792. It is the 37th largest state and has the 26th largest population. Frankfort is the state capital. Kentucky is the *Bluegrass State* and is famous for horse racing, bourbon distilleries, moonshine, coal, and being the home of Kentucky Fried Chicken.

Christian County was created in 1797 and was named for Colonel William Christian, a veteran of the Revolutionary War. Christian had worked in the law office of Patrick Henry, and he later married Patrick Henry's sister, Anne. Christian and his wife moved from Virginia to the Louisville area in 1785, and established Fort William as a defensive point against Indian attacks. He was killed the following year by Wabash Indians while scouting southern Indiana. Christian was famous enough to have counties named after him in Kentucky, Illinois and Missouri. The City of Christiansburg, Virginia, was also named after him. Hopkinsville is the county seat of Christian County, Kentucky.

Tennessee became the 16th state on June 1, 1796. It is the 36th largest and the 16th most populous of the 50 United States. Nashville is the state capital. Tennessee is known as *The Volunteer State*, a nickname based upon the number of volunteer soldiers from the state who reported for the War of 1812. This was not the only example, as Tennessee furnished more soldiers for the Confederate Army than any other state besides Virginia, and more soldiers for the Union Army than the rest of the Confederacy combined.

Montgomery County was created when Tennessee became the 16th state in 1796. At that time, Tennessee County was split into Montgomery and Robertson counties, and Clarksville became the county seat of Montgomery County. The name Montgomery came from John Montgomery, the founder of Clarksville. Montgomery had earlier fought in the American Revolutionary War, and soon after moved to land along the Cumberland River, land that became Clarksville.

Heading on to Hopkinsville, the railroad has climbed out of the Cumberland River valley and crosses the Northern Highland Rim, an undulating terrain that is a mix of farms, pasture and woods. This area is also known as the Pennyroyal Region, named for a common branched annual plant in the mint family that grows to 18 inches in height.

68.8 EDGOTEN – This area was once known as McKenzie, and had a depot and section houses. In May 1941, as Camp Campbell was being built, the United States of America contracted to use a track here to unload cars of gasoline.

70.2 LOUISVILLE & NASHVILLE CROSSING – The L&N had a branch northward from Princeton Junction on the Memphis Line, through here, and on north to a junction with the Illinois Central at Gracey, Kentucky. The line started as the Indiana, Alabama & Texas Railroad (IA&T), a narrow gauge line between Clarksville and Newstead, Kentucky. The Louisville & Nashville bought the IA&T in 1887, extended the line to Gracey and Princeton, and standard gauged the line. The L&N leased the line north of Gracey to the Ohio Valley Railroad (later the Illinois Central) on June 26, 1892. With other connections to the IC, the IA&T route was abandoned in 1934 and this crossing became history. The DODA milepost is 144.8.

71.1 THOMPSONVILLE – Thompsonville was originally located at this milepost, at the grade crossing with Thompsonville Lane, but later was shown to be at Milepost 70.4. In 1907, the Oak Grove post office burned when the Samuel Gordon general store burned, and the store and post office were moved to Thompsonville on the railroad. Based upon Tennessee Central records, the name Thompsonville continued to be used for the station. In October 1939, W. D. Hudson opened a bulk oil station on the railroad here.

72.9 INTERSTATE 24 – I-24 is approximately 315 miles long, with its north end at I-57 south of Marion, Illinois. Its south end is at I-75 at Chattanooga, Tennessee. The highway is designed to connect Atlanta, Georgia, and the Southeast, with St. Louis and the Midwest.

The name Naomi was used for a simple passenger shelter in this area during the early days of the Tennessee Central. The name Naomi came from the daughter of a prosperous landowner in the area whose land was crossed by the railroad. The milepost for the Fort Campbell Railroad (DODA) is 142.1.

75.1 FIDELIO – Look for the grade crossing with Fidelio Road. In the January 1904 *Official Guide of Railways*, this station was named Chester. The name was apparently changed before 1908, probably by the Illinois Central.

Many local documents spell this station Fidelio, claiming that it was named for local land attorney Fidelio Sharp. The name apparently appeared in 1903 when the railroad was built, and disappeared during the 1930s. The railroad had a siding, tobacco shed, and depot here. In January 1910, Theodore R. Troendle of nearby Hopkinsville signed a contract to use the Fidelia depot as a store and blacksmith shop. Most Tennessee Central documents used the spelling of Fidelia.

The highest elevation on the Western Division is 592 feet, and it is reached just south of here and on the Belt Line around Nashville, Tennessee.

Western Division – Edgoten to Tulane

77.9 **MASONVILLE** – Established by the railroad in 1903 as Pierceton, Masonville was renamed by 1908 for the Mason family who had a large amount of property in the area. With a depot and several section houses, this former station was located north of where U.S. Alternate Highway 41 passes under the railroad, at the Masonville Road grade crossing. The railroad uses a pair of deck plate girder spans to cross the U.S. Highway. The DODA milepost is 137.1.

80.1 **ROCK BRIDGE BRANCH BRIDGE** – This 34-span timber trestle is located at DODA Milepost 134.9. This stream forms several miles to the east and flows west before entering the South Fork of the Little River less than a mile to the west. To the east is the Kentucky Veterans Cemetery West, opened in 2004 and located on 80 acres.

When the U.S. Army proposed their changes in the Hopkinsville area, the first plans had a siding built to the west here to hold trains during interchange with CSX. Later, the siding was moved to a location closer to CSX.

80.9 **TULANE** – Tulane, called Renshaw before 1908, was never more than a flag stop passenger shelter. It was located where the railroad begins to turn to the northeast for the new connection to CSX. This new connector was opened in 2001 and was designed to speed up the interchange of trains between the Fort Campbell Railroad and CSX. As the military stated, "the new spur is designed to move up to 275 rail cars a day. It replaces one that was limited to 95 cars a day." When the new track was opened in October of 2001, the Army abandoned the original Tennessee Central line on into Hopkinsville.

Previously, the Fort Campbell Railroad used the Hopkinsville Belt Line to interchange trains with CSX. An issue with this was that the L&N, Illinois Central, and Tennessee Central interchanged only a few cars at Hopkinsville, therefore the interchange tracks could hold only a few cars. According to the *Final Environmental Impact Statement* –

Ft. Campbell, Kentucky Rail Connector, the following was the interchange process before this new track was built.

"Currently, a train deploying from Fort Campbell travels north on the Branch Line into Hopkinsville, past the Hopkinsville Belt Line. The train then reverses direction to access the Hopkinsville Belt Line and travels northeast to the Hopkinsville Interchange. At the Interchange, rail cars are backed up five cars at a time onto the existing switching rail. These five cars are disconnected from the Ft. Campbell train and switched to the CSX mainline track and connected with a CSX southbound train. The switching is repeated five cars at a time until all cars have been transferred to the CSX mainline and connected. During these switching operations traffic on Walnut Street is blocked by the CSX train for the duration of the switching operation. For long trains, Walnut Street can be blocked for up to one hour. Interruption of switching to allow traffic to pass is at the discretion of CSX."

To replace this interchange system with a direct connection that could handle unit trains of military equipment, a line almost three miles long was built to the east, located south of the Hopkinsville Bypass, U.S. Bypass Highway 68. The new line curves east just south of the interchange between Interstate 169 and the Hopkinsville Bypass. The line includes a new two-span bridge over U.S. Alternate Highway 41. Just east of the highway, the railroad has a two-track yard to the south of the new mainline, used to store and switch trains during interchange operations. The east end of the yard is near a new through plate girder bridge over Bradshaw Road. Just east of the bridge is a full wye that connects to CSX at their Milepost 235.8, known as the Ft. Campbell wye on the Henderson Subdivision of the Nashville Division. The Casky Siding and new yard complex is just south of the Ft. Campbell wye and is used to serve a number of shippers in the Hopkinsville Industrial Park to the east.

Tennessee Central Western Division
Tulane (KY) to Hopkinsville (KY)
Abandoned

The Illinois Central facilities used by the Tennessee Central were abandoned in 1988, after the tracks south of here were turned over to Fort Campbell. This left the Hopkinsville Belt Line as the interchange route with the Louisville & Nashville/CSX. The Tennessee Central tracks north of Tulane were abandoned after 2001 when the military built a new route to CSX.

80.9 **TULANE** – The tracks north (railroad-west) of here were abandoned in late 2001 when the U.S. Army opened its new interchange track with CSX. Just north of here is the new interchange between Interstate 169 and Lovers Lane.

82.2 **SOUTH FORK LITTLE RIVER BRIDGE** – The headwaters of the South Fork Little River are in the rolling hills about ten miles to the east of Hopkinsville, Kentucky. The river flows to the southwest to Hopkinsville, where it has a reputation of causing sudden flooding. The river turns to the south and is joined by the South Fork Little River Tributary and Rock Bridge Branch. The river joins the North Fork Little River to create the Little River several miles downstream of where the Rock Bridge Branch flows into the river.

Just north of the bridge is the new Hopkinsville Bypass, U.S. Alternate Highway 68.

83.1 **VIRGINIA STREET** – The street is named Lafayette Road to the southwest and Virginia Street to the northeast. Just a short distance to the north, the railroad crossed Country Club Lane. This road serves the Hopkinsville Country Club which is to the east. The DODA milepost was 131.9.

83.4 **PARDUE ROAD** – To the west is Pardue Park, the south access point to the Hopkinsville Rail Trail, also known as the Pennyrile Rail Trail. This trail is 3.1 miles long, with

1.8 miles of the trail using the former Tennessee Central Railway grade. Plans for the trail have it being more than seven miles long, using more of the former Tennessee Central grade as well as other railroad grades in the area. The trail's first phase opened in September 2014 and extends from here north to North Drive, where the trail heads east on former Illinois Central grades.

84.0 HOPKINSVILLE BELT LINE – The switch, located at Illinois Central Milepost 131.0, connected with a 1.1-mile-long line to the east. The Hopkinsville Belt Line was built in 1906 by the Illinois Central to reach several downtown warehouses when the company operated the Tennessee Central. This explains the direction of the switch, as IC trains came down the Tennessee Central from the north. The Illinois Central maintained ownership of the Belt Line even after the railroad was returned to the owners of the Tennessee Central. The two railroads signed an agreement in January 1911 allowing joint use of the Belt Line. Until 1917, the IC operated over a few miles of the Tennessee Central to reach this line before selling it to the Tennessee Central. When the Tennessee Central acquired the line, the railroad extended it and added an interchange track with the Louisville & Nashville near the Hopkinsville Milling facility at 18th Street. As described in the Fort Campbell Railroad section, the interchange was via a 5-car switchback.

84.1 COX MILL ROAD – The railroad used to cross this street using a wooden trestle. The bridge was removed when the grade became city property because the bridge was lower than the required sixteen feet for truck traffic. A new and taller bridge has been installed for the trail.

84.9 15TH STREET – Located at Illinois Central Milepost 130.1, there was a wye at this location to connect to the Illinois Central. When the Ohio Valley Railroad, later the Illinois Central, arrived at Hopkinsville in 1892, they built a two-stall roundhouse and turntable here. The Western Division of the Tennessee Central was finally completed to Hopkinsville in February, 1904. The wye was installed by the Tennessee Central when it arrived, with the engine house and turntable inside the wye. The turntable was removed in 1907, and the engine house was gone by late 1909. When the Tennessee Central planned their line to Hopkinsville, there were plans for an extensive shop and yard facility here. It was to be located on the north side of the Little River, across from the IC facilities. However, the railroad had no money available to build the facility, so it initially agreed to use the existing IC facilities.

The Tennessee Central jointly used many Illinois Central facilities in Hopkinsville. Trains heading to the passenger station and freight house would head east to the facilities on 9th Street. To the west was the Illinois Central yard, filling the space between here and the first of three bridge crossings of the North Fork Little River. When the Tennessee Central arrived at Hopkinsville in February 1904, an agreement was reached to use the IC yard and facilities. A new agreement was reached in July 1908 after the Illinois Central stopped operating the Tennessee Central. The agreement had the Tennessee Central pay a monthly fee to use the IC depot, freight house, yard, water tank, stock pens, and other facilities. The agreement also had the Tennessee Central pay to have the IC fuel, clean and turn Tennessee Central locomotives.

The Tennessee Central had a series of such agreements over the years. In March 1922, the two railroads reached a new agreement involving interchange and the inspection of equipment, and in 1966, again there was a new agreement between the Tennessee Central and IC that clarified the sharing of Illinois Central facilities at Hopkinsville.

The Illinois Central facilities were sold to the C&J Railroad as part of the sale of track from here to Gracey, Kentucky, in 1986. The shortline filed for bankruptcy in March 1987 and ran its last train on November 12, 1987.

Nothing is left in this area except for the North Drive access to the walking trail.

85.4 HOPKINSVILLE – Hopkinsville, with a population of more than 30,000, is the county seat of Christian County, Kentucky. 1200 acres of land around Hopkinsville became the property of Bartholomew Wood in 1796, land that he claimed in return for his service in the American Revolution. When Christian County was created, Wood offered to donate five acres of land and half-interest in his Old Rock Spring if the county seat was located on his land. A log courthouse and jail, along with other facilities, were built by 1798. In 1799, the town of Christian Court House was laid out by John Campbell and Samuel Means. However, locals renamed the town Elizabeth after Bartholomew Wood's oldest daughter. This name was rejected by the state as it was already being used by a town in Hardin County.

In 1804, the county seat of Christian County was officially organized. Having rejected other names, the Kentucky Assembly was able to name the new town after one of its members, Samuel Hopkins. Hopkins had previously served in the Revolutionary War, working on General Washington's staff for several years. He served in both state and federal legislatures before being given the rank of Major General and being appointed Commander in Chief of the western frontier (Illinois and Indiana Territory) in 1812. Hopkins County, Kentucky, was also named for Samuel Hopkins.

A unique part of Hopkinsville is that 60 percent of the world's bowling balls are manufactured here. They are manufactured by Ebonite International, one of the oldest and largest bowling ball manufacturers.

Night Riders

A major part of the history of Hopkinsville deals with tobacco and the Night Riders. The Night Riders were a part of what was known as The Dark Fired Tobacco District Planters Protective Association of Kentucky and Tennessee, better known as "The Association." This was a large organization of tobacco growers in the 35-county region of Western Kentucky and Tennessee known as the "Black Patch" where dark-fired tobacco was grown. Members of The Association wanted higher prices and more control over the production of tobacco products.

The almost decade-long series of battles involved three parties – James B. Duke's American Tobacco Trust, tobacco growers loyal to Duke, and The Association. The war started after several bad crops and the importation of English tobacco, keeping the prices low. On September 24, 1904, The Association was formed and the split between growers began, with acts involving destroying the crops and properties of non-members, beating workers and whipping farmers, and burning tobacco warehouses becoming common. Members of The Association typically wore black hoods and wore white sashes across their chests during their raids. These bands became known as "Possum Hunters," "Night Riders" and "The Silent Brigade."

The Hopkinsville Raid started pre-dawn on December 7, 1907, at the Illinois Central station, where six bands of men went after various targets in town with the goal of destroying tobacco; capturing the telephone, police, fire and railroad offices; and attacking managers of the tobacco firms. After a series of attacks, three tobacco warehouses were burned, a number of homes and businesses were damaged, a railroad employee trying to save freight cars was shot in the back and a number of other citizens were hurt, and one Night Rider had been killed.

Burned in the raid was Latham's People's Tobacco Warehouse, the warehouse of Tandy & Fairleigh, and the Association Warehouse. The violence was so bad that troops were assigned to the area. By the summer of 1910, the raids had come to an end and The Association ended its violence.

Illinois Central

The Illinois Central wooden railroad station, with a separate freighthouse to the north, both built in 1892 by the Ohio Valley Railroad, once stood on the east bank where 9th Street crossed the North Fork Little River. The railroad had a small four-track yard here. There was also a track down the center of 10th Street in the late 1890s to serve the Ragsdale, Cooper and Company tobacco warehouse. The station complex was torn down in November 1942, and today the land is used as the parking lot for the Hopkinsville Public Library.

The Illinois Central at Hopkinsville is due in great part to General John Echols, a Confederate General and earlier a member of the Virginia House of Delegates. After the war, he built up a fortune and became President of the Staunton National Valley Bank. Looking for investments, he became the receiver and general manager of the bankrupt Chesapeake, Ohio & Southwestern Railroad. Echols rebuilt the railroad, and leased the Indiana, Alabama & Texas Railroad Company (IA&T) in January 1892. The IA&T had already built a line from Princeton to Gracey, Kentucky, and Echols had it extended to Hopkinsville later that year.

The properties changed hands a few more times before failing again in 1894. Edward H. Harriman acquired the system on August 1, 1897, and he assigned operations to the Illinois Central. During June 1898, Harriman officially sold the line to the Illinois Central, which opened Hopkinsville to the markets of Chicago, St. Louis and New Orleans. In 1910, the IC operated three pairs of passenger trains to and from Hopkinsville. One pair, #5/#8, were Chicago trains, while #321/#322 were to and from Evansville, Indiana. The true locals were #340/#341 which were to and from Princeton, just thirty miles away. In 1925, passenger schedules were very similar, but trains #333/#334 to and from Evansville showed a connection with Tennessee Central service to Nashville.

By 1949, Tennessee Central service to Hopkinsville had ended, and the *Official Guide* showed the stations of the IC and L&N still being 1/4 mile apart. Passenger service had almost ended on the Illinois Central as the only trains serving Hopkinsville were mixed trains #243/#244 from Princeton. These trains came down to Hopkinsville in the late morning and went back north in the early afternoon. This really left Hopkinsville at the end of a branchline, and as the system grew, the line became less important. As the railroad looked to sell off lightly used lines in the 1980s, the line from Gracey to Hopkinsville was sold to the C&J Railroad in 1986. This line failed in 1987 and was abandoned.

Louisville & Nashville

In downtown Hopkinsville at 425 E. 9th Street is the Louisville & Nashville depot, listed on the National Register of Historic Places on August 1, 1975. CSX still passes by the station on a railroad originally built by the Evansville, Henderson, & Nashville Railroad right after the Civil War. The railroad became part of the Louisville & Nashville in 1879, and this station was built in 1892 as passenger business in Hopkinsville increased. The station was remodeled in 1909 when the stucco exterior was added, as well as the two-block-long train shed. The station served its last passengers in 1971, and the train shed was removed in 1982. The station is now used by the Pennyrile Arts Council.

The single-story station is noted for its round rooms and unique roof line. It was built with a Ladies Waiting room, a General Waiting Room, a Colored Waiting Room, a ticket office, and a baggage room. The Hopkinsville depot was a favorite short stop for rail travelers as it was the only town between Evansville, Indiana, and Nashville, Tennessee, where it was legal to drink alcohol. Many passengers took advantage of "Hop Town" by jumping off the train, grabbing a drink, and then getting back on before the train departed.

Tennessee Central Railway: History Through the Miles

The L&N depot at Hopkinsville is listed on the National Register of Historic Places and is the center of the downtown historic area. Photo by Barton Jennings.

The area around the L&N station was once full of warehouses, many of them related to the tobacco trade. Across the tracks is the former L&N brick freighthouse. This building features a two-story office wing and a one-story freight building, built in 1905. Across the street is Peace Park. A historical marker explains the significance of the location. "Bequest to city of Hopkinsville with funds for beautification and maintenance by John C. Latham of New York, a native of Hopkinsville. A generous and forgiving gift, Mr. Latham was owner of a large tobacco warehouse on this site that was destroyed, when burned by Night Riders, disgruntled tobacco growers, Dec. 8, 1907. The next year death came to Mr. Latham."

Of all of the railroads that served Hopkinsville, the former Louisville & Nashville, now CSX, is the only one that still exists.

Tennessee Central Western Division
North Nashville Lead
U.S. Tobacco to Central Junction
Nashville & Western Railroad

The North Nashville Lead is the former Tennessee Central branch from Central Junction to the many industries around the Nashville Union Stock-Yards on the northwest side of downtown. Today, it is used to serve a few shippers and to interchange with CSX Transportation, the former Louisville & Nashville, earlier the Nashville, Chattanooga & St. Louis Railway. Federal Railroad Administration records show that the line is called the North Nashville Lead. The mileposts on the FRA grade crossing database and those used by the Nashville & Western (NWR) do not agree. Those presented here are based upon those shown in the FRA records.

0.4　**U.S. TOBACCO** – U.S. Tobacco is listed as the first station on the Nashville & Eastern Railroad (NERR) Western Subdivision, technically the Nashville & Western. U.S. Smokeless Tobacco Company, an Altria Company, is located several blocks northwest of the Tennessee state capitol at 800 Harrison Street in Nashville. U.S. Smokeless Tobacco is the leading producer of moist smokeless tobacco, using 100 percent American-grown tobacco and processing it at their Hopkinsville, Kentucky, plant. To make their products, the company blends and stores that tobacco in hogshead barrels for aging for three to five years. Once aged, it is moved to this plant, or one in Franklin Park, Illinois, for manufacturing, packaging, and distribution. The railroad serves the plant with several tracks on the north side in Herman Street, also known as Tredco Drive.

　　　The rail line once passed through the area and extended to the northeast to serve The Nashville Union Stock-Yards, which closed in 1974, the W. G. Bush Brick Company, and a number of other industries in the area along the Cumberland River. Today, this is the end of the line, located at 9th Avenue North at the east side of the U.S. Smokeless Tobacco packaging facility.

Just to the south of the tobacco company is the CSX 8th Avenue Wye. This wye connects the north-south Nashville Terminal line between the Mainline Subdivision (Louisville Division) and Radnor Yard (the same line that the NERR Vine Hill line passes under), and the Bruceton line west toward Memphis, Tennessee. Nashville Union Station is just a few blocks south of here.

0.6   WESTERN SHOP – Heading west from U.S. Tobacco, the railroad runs down the middle of Herman Street to 11th Avenue North, where the Nashville & Western locomotive storage area is located. This area once included a depot building, a tool house, and a freight shed. Illinois Central maps as late as June 1971 still showed an IC Depot here.

In 2012, the Nashville & Western shop area included former Conrail and Santa Fe locomotives. Photo by Barton Jennings.

Just west of here, the railroad passes under Interstate 40/65. Illinois Central maps show the Interstate and note that 140 feet of overhead rights were "sold to the State of Tenn for Hwy purpose."

West of the Interstate and to the north is a large facility that was once the Phillips & Buttorff Manufacturing Company. In 1881 the Phillips & Buttorff Manufacturing Company was incorporated, and succeeded the Phillips, Buttorff & Company which had a history dating back to 1858 as the first stove and tinware business in the city of Nashville.

Western Division – North Nashville Lead

The firm acquired most of its competitors and soon became one of the nation's largest in the field. During the late 1800s, Henry W. Buttorff, one of the partners, was considered to be connected with more important businesses in Tennessee than anyone else. Phillips & Buttorff closed in the mid-1950s. The building is now the Nashville Tent & Awning Company.

0.9 CSX CONNECTION – Located between 14th and 16th Avenues, the Nashville & Western has a track that curves south to a connection with CSX. The actual connection is just west of Interstate 40/65 at the west end of the CSX wye at a location known as 11th Avenue, CSX Milepost OON-0.7. This area became the only junction with the Louisville & Nashville after the Belt Line around Nashville was abandoned in 1985.

An interesting structure just south of the Nashville & Western junction with CSX is the former Marathon Automobile car factory, which now houses Antique Archaeology – Nashville, a store supported by the *American Pickers Show* on the History Channel. The Marathon Motor Works started as the Southern Engine and Boiler Works, founded in 1889 to manufacture industrial engines and boilers. The Marathon automobile was manufactured from 1907 until 1914. The factory complex is now a village of stores, bars and restaurants.

This area was once a center of heavy manufacturing and business for the Tennessee Central Railway. A few of these companies included the Andrews Coal Yard, a Marathon Motor Works factory (in a building that originally housed the Nashville Carbon Oil Company), Cassity Oil Company, and the Tennessee Burley Tobacco Company. Today, the main route of the Nashville & Western North Nashville Lead wanders southwestwardly through a light industrial area to near Clifton Avenue, where a switchback leads to the mainline which curves to the north. A siding exists there to allow trains to reverse direction.

The former Marathon Motor Works facility still stands just south of the railroad. Photo by Barton Jennings.

The former Marathon complex today includes a number of stores and clubs. Photo by Barton Jennings.

1.2 WESTROCK RECYCLING SPUR – Once known as Rock-Tenn, WestRock is a packaging materials company. Their recycling division processes materials that can go back into their packaging products. WestRock is a regular shipper on the railroad.

1.7 **CENTRAL JUNCTION** – This is the junction between the North Nashville Lead and the former Tennessee Central mainline west to Hopkinsville, Kentucky.

About the Author

For almost three decades, Barton Jennings has been organizing charter passenger trains and writing the route descriptions, both for planning purposes and for the enjoyment of the passengers. These trips have been from coast to coast, often covering operations that haven't seen a passenger train in decades. In addition, he has written a number of articles about various railroads for rail hobby magazines. His basement has several rooms full of books, timetables and other documents about this and other railroads – important research items from a time long before today's internet. Today, Bart Jennings, after years working in the railroad industry, is a professor of supply chain management and teaches transportation operations. He also still teaches regulatory issues for the railroad industry, a way to stay in touch with the industry he loves.

Author Barton Jennings, somewhere along the route of the Tennessee Central Railway. Photo by Sarah Jennings.

www.ingramcontent.com/pod-product-compliance
Lightning Source LLC
Chambersburg PA
CBHW050628300426
44112CB00012B/1701